# A Country Fiddler

# A Country Fiddler

Keep a tune in your heart!

Joe Dobbs

Joe Dobbs

Mid-Atlantic Highlands

Mid-Atlantic Highlands
Huntington, West Virginia



Cover and interior design by Rachel Hoeft

10 9 8 7 6 5 4 3 2 1

Printed in the United States of America

ISBN-13: 978-0-9833947-6-1

Mid-Atlantic Highlands
An imprint of Publishers Place, Inc.
821 Fourth Avenue – Suite 201
Huntington, West Virginia 25701

www.publishersplace.org

# A Country Fiddler

# INTRODUCTION

I've always had a desire to write about my experiences growing up in the swamps of Louisiana. At the time, of course, I did not think my life in the swamps was unique, but now, I do, and I wanted to leave some of these experiences for my six children.

My family and I lived much as families did during the mid 1800s, not the mid 1900s. There was no electricity or running water. Roads were almost non-existent. Everyone traveled by wagon or horseback. Livestock ran wild, so all the farmers had their fields behind fences.

In 1985, I purchased a computer to use in my business. After learning how to use the word processor, I thought it would be easy to write my memoirs. I just couldn't figure out how to begin.

Several years later, Dave Peyton introduced me to Dr. Patrick Grace. After taking one of his Life Writing classes, I was inspired.

I have many people to thank. Dr. Grace, Charlie Bowen, Pamela Bowen and several members of my family who encouraged my efforts.

My sister, Lucille Davis, did much of the family research. Without her, I could not have written the book. I dedicate this book to her memory and regret she did not live to read the final draft.

The editor of the first drafts of this book, Pamela Bowen, I cannot thank enough.

A very special thanks to Dr. Patrick Grace and editor Candis Stout.

I am most grateful to fiddlers and musicians around the world who have shared tunes with me.

# MUSIC FINDS ME

When I was five years old, I got a metal ukulele for Christmas, but I never had any idea how to play it. I thought it was just a toy. I don't remember seeing anyone play an instrument before I was eight years old, except the piano at some funeral.

During World War II, we would listen to a battery- powered radio. It had a dry cell battery about the size of a cereal box that was connected to the radio by two wires. When the power was used up, the battery was discarded, since it was not rechargeable. You could get a new battery at the hardware store in Oak Grove or you could mail order one from Sears & Roebuck. We didn't always have the money to purchase a new battery, so sometimes we would go as much as two months without one.

That radio was our only communication with the world outside the Louisiana swamps. We never got a newspaper.

When the radio had power, we would listen to WSM Grand Ole Opry from Nashville, Tennessee. I can remember Dad saying he hoped the man who played the mandolin so fast would be on the show. That was Bill Monroe. I'm sure that's the first music I heard outside of church.

When I was about eight years old, I went to singing school at the

Church of Christ where we sometimes attended. Musical instruments weren't permitted in that church. The preacher came from somewhere in Arkansas and taught "shape note singing." You learned the pitch of the note by the shape of it. I was very interested, but I didn't learn much about theory or reading music. Most of the time was spent singing hymns we already knew.

The thought of playing a musical instrument never crossed my mind and I never considered it until I was nine years old. I was in the fourth grade and there was a girl who brought her guitar to school and accompanied her singing. She sang several cowboy songs, one of them was "Jack and Joe."

Though I always sang in the fields where we worked and I always sang while walking to and from the school bus, I still did not think about playing an instrument until I spent a weekend with Frank Staggs.

The Staggs family attended the same church we did. Frank was their only child. I liked Frank but I didn't think he was very smart. I was surprised to learn that he played a variety of tunes on the harmonica. I knew if Frank could play the harmonica, I could. He taught me to play a couple of tunes that week-end and gave me an old harp that he no longer played.

Learning to play those tunes on the harmonica gave me the boost I needed to realize that I could play an instrument. For about a year, I carried a harp in my pocket until I traded two bicycle petals for an old Stella guitar. The strings were so high off the neck that I learned to play only a few chords. Dad let me trade two hogs for a Gibson ES 125 guitar that was cracked but that I repaired. It was electric and I hooked it up to the radio. I don't think that radio ever worked again.

I was unable to learn much on the guitar since I didn't have a chord book or any instruction. So I borrowed a violin that I later bought from a neighbor boy, Keith Fowler. It cost me $10 and I worked in our neighbor's cotton fields to earn the money. Keith didn't know much about the fiddle. He could tune it and that was about it. I was on my own. I think that the first tune I learned to play on the fiddle was "Goodnight Irene," a Huddie Ledbetter song.

Mr. Edwin Cox was the song leader in our church. Though no instruments were allowed in the church services, I heard him play and sing at home. Edwin was a sharecropper from southern Missouri who farmed near our farm. He had a resonator guitar made by National in the 1930s. Carved into the headstock was "WOWO," the call letters of a 50,000 watt radio station in Fort Wayne, Indiana. At one time, he had been a ballad singer on that station.

In the 1940s, radio stations carried numerous programs of live music. I listened to Bradley Kinkaid, a ballad singer on WWL in New Orleans, and Harmie Smith, a ballad singer who had a show on KWKH in Shreveport, Louisiana. His show was sponsored by Sunway Vitamins.

Edwin didn't play the fiddle, but he knew several fiddle tunes and "Soldier's Joy" was one of the tunes he taught me. His brother Hugh played the fiddle, but he lived in the state of Washington.

Hank Williams, Sr. records were very popular at the time and I wanted to learn the fiddle parts of his songs. Tunie Mullins was the only fiddler who lived in West Carroll Parish. (Louisiana has parishes, not counties.) And he was very good at playing hillbilly songs. I'd only been playing a short time when I got some help from Tunie. Mom didn't want me going down to his house, because he was bad to drink and played for dances and in bars. But she never knew.

When I was in high school, one of the fiddle players that I liked to listen to on the radio was Jerry Rivers. He and Hank Williams, Sr. had a very early morning live show on KWKH in Shreveport. It was on the air even before the school bus ran. I wasn't that interested in Hank Williams, but Jerry played the old fiddle tune "Sally Goodin" each morning as their theme song.

About that same time, there was an excellent fiddler on the Louisiana Hayride with Johnny and Jack, by the name of Paul Warren. Kitty Wells was married to Johnnie Wright, so she was also on the show. I thought Paul was such a smooth fiddler. He later became one of the "Foggy Mountain Boys" with Flatt and Scruggs.

Bastrop, Louisiana, was about twenty-five miles from our farm and on Saturday mornings, their radio station KTRY had a show with Jody

Anders, an accomplished fiddler. Jody told me once that Eck Robinson beat him in a fiddle contest in Fort Worth, Texas, in 1941. First prize was a 24-pound sack of flour. He was not only a great influence on me but also a fine gentleman.

There was a lot of music in that family. The weekly radio performance was performed by Jody and his two sons, Keith on bass fiddle and J. W. playing guitar and singing. Jody's father had been a fiddler and his nephew, Tony Joe White, wrote "Poke Salad Annie" and "Rainy Night in Georgia." I went to school with Tony Joe's sister, Sadie Mae, who played the guitar and sang. Tony Joe was only six or seven years old when I moved away.

When I was attending Louisiana Tech in Ruston, we would go to the next town of Monroe, Louisiana, to see live music performed by local musicians. One of our favorite haunts was this cowboy bar on Highway 80, I don't remember the name, where a very good country fiddler was playing.

This one night the place was full and there was no air conditioning, so I stood just outside the open door. Behind me was a very large man that I recognized. He was Bryan Ritter, the guitarist in the staff band on the Louisiana Hayride in Shreveport.

I was small and looked much younger than my age and he asked me why was I there. I explained that I was an aspiring fiddler and I liked the style the guy in the bar was playing. Bryan Ritter said something to me that has stuck with me all these years. He recommended that I learn to play as many different types and styles of music as I could.

He looked down at me and said that it would make me a better player. "Don't make the mistake of just playing the music you like," was his advice. Through the years I never forgot his suggestion. He was from over near Henderson, Texas, and could have been related to the famous Tex Ritter, who was from that area. I remember he played a Super 400 Gibson guitar, the largest electric jazz guitar made at that time.

In 1968, Amy and I moved our family to West Virginia and I quit playing. Times were hard and I was trying to support a large family. I was tired of playing country and western music, so I sold my two fiddles. For about five years, I did not own an instrument.

During this time, we did a lot of things as a family, like camping and fishing all during the summer. I never regretted the time I did not play, for it was a special time with all the kids.

I think it was about 1973 when my oldest son, Dale, and I were at a flea market in Huntington. He found a fiddle for $20 and said he thought I should go back to playing. The fiddle needed some repair so I got it in playing condition and began playing again.

Also about this time someone gave me a Kenny Baker album. Kenny was a coal miner from Jenkins, Kentucky, and played fiddle for Bill Monroe. I was mesmerized with the melodious style of his playing.

Had it not been for my meeting Kenny, I doubt very seriously if I would have ever gone back to music. I was helping a teenager at the time, Ron Eldridge, with his fiddle playing. During one of our sessions, I told him about hearing a Kenny Baker recording and he asked if I would like to meet Kenny.

It happened that when Bill Monroe and his Bluegrass band came through our area, Kenny would stay at Ron's house. I couldn't believe that this musician who had influenced me so much was a friend of a friend!

During one of the times Kenny was visiting, Ron introduced us. Kenny and I became very good friends. He died at the age of 85 in 2011. I still think of him every day. After meeting Kenny, I continued to play and traveled to many countries, playing the fiddle. Hearing him play enriched my life.

And really that is where all my music began.

# MY PARENTS

Cotton had been King in the Mississippi River Delta since long before the Civil war. After the War came Reconstruction, then World War I, the 1927 Flood and the Great Depression. The cotton plantations survived all these difficult times.

Freed slaves and their descendants provided most of the labor necessary to grow and harvest the cotton crops. But many poor white families also worked on these plantations. Most of these families were from Scotch-Irish immigrants who had settled in the hill country of Kentucky, Tennessee, Alabama and eastern Mississippi. The possibility of sharing the wealth of the flourishing cotton-growing industry lured them out of their homes in the piney wood hills to the Delta.

There were three types of farmers: landowners, renters and sharecroppers. A farmer who rented had all the tools he needed for farming and horses or mules for plowing. He received three-fourths of the harvest of the crops and the landowner received the other fourth.

A sharecropper did not furnish anything except his furniture and other household items and he received one-half of the harvest. The landowner furnished the farming tools and livestock and received the other half.

Each cotton plantation had a cotton gin and a company store. Invented by Eli Whitney, the cotton gin was a machine that separated the fiber or lint from the seed. Prior to the gin, the lint was separated from the seed by hand, requiring long hours of labor. By the late 1800s the gins were steam or combustion-engine-powered.

As a small boy it was a treat to go with my dad when he took a bale of cotton to the gin. On arriving, there would be a long line of farmers waiting turns at the gin. Each farmer would be driving a wagon pulled by a team of horses or mules. As their turn came, each wagon would pull up under the flexible suction pipe, which was about ten inches in diameter. It took about an hour for the workers to suck all the cotton out of the wagon and produce a bound 500-pound bale of cotton lint. The separated seed was shipped away for processing. It could be used for a variety of products. Cottonseed oil was used in food products, and cottonseed meal and cottonseed cakes for cow feed.

The cotton gin and country store created a community much like the coal mining companies in Appalachia. Most families who lived and worked on the plantation had credit at the company store. Many could never leave because of debts owed to the store.

Both of my parents were from large families with a Scotch-Irish heritage. Each family had moved from the Mississippi hills to the Delta in hopes of having a more prosperous life working the cotton fields. They were sharecroppers.

Walter Dobbs, my dad, was from a family of eleven children, eight boys and three girls. His father, Joe Thomas Dobbs (1888-1954) and mother, Ruth Agnes Blassingame Dobbs (1889-1977), had eleven children, Walter (1908-1975), Jesse, Lydia, Roland, Marvin, Elsie Mae, Buck, Rasse, Alice, Elmer and Charlie.

My mother, Lillie Berry, was from a family of fourteen children, seven boys and seven girls. Her father, Rube Berry (1887-1968) and mother, Lizzie Bailey Berry (1892-1968), had fourteen children, Lillie (1910-1985), Lillian, Arthur, Leon, Lloyd, Nathan, T. S., Juanita, Laura, Gladys, Vera, Vivian, Charles and Dewey.

The Berry family moved to the W.O. Pepper farm near the Delta town of Ruleville in 1917. In 1928 the Dobbs family became their neighbors on the W.O. Pepper farm. This farm was across the Quiver River from Ruleville.

Both of these families had things in common. They had their beginnings in the hills along the Natchez Trace, they were sharecroppers, and they attended the Quiver River Christian Church north of Ruleville.

Sometime in 1928, Lillie Berry and Walter Dobbs met. Dad was twenty and Mom was eighteen years old.

In 1932, Lillie's father, Rube Berry, moved his family to Washington County and the Halliburton Plantation near Greenville, Mississippi. Most of the houses occupied by the sharecropper families had four large rooms with a porch on the front and back. Mom's family was so large they lived in two of these houses. The parents and the girls lived in one house, where the meals were served. Across the gravel road, the boys lived in another.

Walter, my dad, and two of his brothers, Jesse and Roland, worked some with the Berrys and they roomed with the Berry boys in the house across the road.

Walter and Lillie were married in 1933. I was born in 1934, the year the farmers could not sell their crops. The Great Depression had hit. There was no need to harvest -- there was no market. Some cotton crops were left in the fields. The Dobbs family had lost everything and my grandfather, Joe Thomas Dobbs, moved his family back to the red clay hills of Mississippi in the fall of 1934. He never returned to the Delta cotton fields.

In parts of rural America, the people living in the country endured the Great Depression better than people in the cities. Farmers almost always had food. There was an abundance of wild game and everybody grew vegetables in their gardens. Most families had a milk cow. My dad once told me how they would butcher a cow and take the meat into town to be sold to families living in the residential areas of the city. Since there was no market for their crops, this was one way the farmer could raise money to buy goods he could not grow himself.

It was during this time that my dad began to look outside the Delta cotton plantations for opportunities. There was no optimism for opportunity for a sharecropper cotton farmer. And both of my parents' education was limited since they had only finished the eighth grade.

Across the river in Louisiana, land was advertised for sale and Dad was convinced that communities of small family-owned farms provided a better environment to raise a family.

Only the choice virgin timber had been harvested off this land. Large stands of hardwood timber remained that could be made into lumber to build houses and barns. There was more than enough oak timber for making fence posts and the much-needed firewood that was used to cook and heat the home. And most attractive of all was the price. It was possible for a poor sharecropper to come up with enough money to buy forty acres. With his knowledge of farming and hard work, Dad believed there was enough Delta-rich soil on the west side of the river to support a family.

*Walter Dobbs and Lillie Berry Dobbs were married for forty-two years. They had four children, Joe (1934), Lucille (1939), Dwayne (1945-1981) and Dennis (1950). Mom went to work in the sweet potato cannery in Oak Grove in 1961. Dad sold the farm in 1963 and went to work as the custodian at Goodwill Grade School. He retired in 1971 at the age of sixty-three. Dad died in 1975. Mom lived another ten years.*

# BARNSTORMING

My dad, Walter Dobbs, was born in 1908, the oldest of eleven children. When he was a teen-ager, his family lived on a farm in Choctaw County, Mississippi. The rolling red clay hills were covered with pine and hardwood trees, but some of the valleys or bottoms were cleared of trees and vegetation where they grew a variety of crops. Most families had livestock such as cows, hogs and goats. Every farmer had a team of horses or mules that were used for working the farm and for transportation. Poor farmers could not afford a car or truck.

It was a warm June morning. The day promised to be very hot and humid and my dad planned to go fishing but, his mother insisted that he help with the canning. When the fruits and vegetables were ready, they had to be canned so the family would have food in the winter. There was no electricity to provide any refrigeration. With many fruits and vegetables, there was a very short time between being ripe and ready to can and spoiling. During this time the entire family worked to take advantage of their harvest of food.

"Walter, we need several things from the store so you will have to take the wagon," his mother said. My grandma Dobbs was a petite woman who spoke with a slow drawl. She had long black hair, a round face and dark eyes because of her Choctaw Indian heritage.

"We need a 100-pound bag of wheat shorts." Wheat shorts was a type of ground wheat that was used to feed the hogs. "And I need two boxes of canning jars," she said. "Hurry back because we have tomatoes and cucumbers to pick. I'd like to put up a few quarts of that corn that's ready in the field out back of the barn," she added. "Oh, I almost forgot. Get a forty-eight pound bag of flour. I'm just about out."

Dad hated to have to spend a good fishing day in a hot kitchen. All the canning was done on an old wood fired cook stove that produced a lot of unwanted heat during the summer. It would be so cool under the trees down on the creek bank. But he knew the importance of canning, so he put his plans aside.

The morning sun was shining in his eyes as he and the mules topped the hill at the McCoy place. Pulling on the lines and stopping the wagon, he could not believe his eyes. In Mr. McCoy's pasture about 200 yards down from the barn was a yellow double-winged single-engine airplane. He had seen airplanes flying overhead but never one up close. The plane appeared so much larger when it was on the ground.

The previous day, Mr. Crawford had stopped at the house and asked, "Have any of you seen that feller that is taking folks for airplane rides? He's charging one dollar each to take them up in his flying machine."

My grandfather asked if Mr. Crawford was going to spend a dollar to fly in that airplane. His reply was, "I don't want to go any higher than pulling corn or any lower than diggin' taters."

Already there were several neighbors in the pasture. Some were there to take their first ride in an airplane and others just came to watch. A dollar was a lot of money in 1924.

The plane could carry the pilot and one passenger in the separate open seats. A woman was in the passenger's seat and the pilot, a tall man, was getting into the cockpit. My dad watched as a man on the ground pulled on the propeller and the engine roared to life. It was so loud that the mules nervously stamped and swished their tails. Holding the lines taut on the mules, Walter sat on the wagon seat and watched the plane taxi down through Mr. McCoy's pasture. Then it lifted up over the shade trees down by the big pond. The plane circled around the farm and then went south almost to the horizon. After making several circles over the Brooks farm, it returned and landed back in the pasture.

The small gathering cheered as the woman climbed down from the airplane. "That is the most exciting thing I have ever done," she exclaimed. "It was even better than the Ferris wheel at the County Fair in Ackerman."

Since his mom was expecting him home soon, my dad reluctantly clucked to the mules and they moved on down the road. He would have liked to watch the plane take off and land several more times.

The wagon had gone only a few yards when someone shouted, "Hey, young man! Wait a minute!" Turning, Dad saw the slender but muscular young pilot with a pleasant smile and a yellow scarf around his neck. "I noticed from the air there's a store with a gasoline pump about a mile down the road."

My dad explained that he was headed to Clark's General Store.

"I was just wondering if I could get you to do me a big favor," said the pilot. "I need gasoline and can't land this plane at the store so I need someone to bring me some fuel."

Dad was very excited to be of assistance to the only person he had ever met who could fly an airplane. The pilot put two five-gallon gas cans on the wagon bed and handed him some money. "This is a very important thing you are doing for me," the pilot said"

It was almost an hour before Dad came back down the road by the McCoy pasture. The crowd was larger and the plane was in the sky over the neighbor's farm giving someone a ride. As soon as the plane rolled to a stop, the pilot and his helper walked to the road where Dad was sitting in the wagon. He got down and placed the two cans filled with gasoline next to the two-strand barbed wire pasture fence.

As he lifted the two cans over the fence, the pilot asked, "Young man, have you ever been up in an airplane?"

"No sir, this is the first time I've ever seen an airplane on the ground. It looks like it would be a lot of fun," my dad answered, wondering how big Mr. McCoy's cows would look from up there in a plane. You probably couldn't even see the chickens.

The pilot interrupted his daydreaming. "Since you have been so kind to help me, I want to take you on a free plane ride."

Dad was excited. This was his lucky day and he was glad he hadn't gone fishing. He drove the mules up to the fence by the McCoy barn and tied them, thinking that canning tomatoes would just have to wait. Then he walked out to the pasture where the man was pouring gasoline into the plane. He would have no trouble explaining to his mom why it took him so long to go to the store and back.

Approaching the airplane, he realized it was even larger than he had thought. There was a man helping the pilot. He seemed experienced at what he was doing, so Dad thought he must have flown in with the pilot.

"Just climb up there in the back seat," instructed the pilot. Dad did as he was told and sat down in the small seat.

"Buckle that belt across your body. I don't want you to fall out when we're upside down," joked the pilot as he climbed into the front cockpit. In front of Dad was a small wooden stick about the size of a small axe handle that extended up from the floor between his legs. There was a wooden pedal board in the floor near his feet.

Looking back, the pilot said, "Now don't grab the stick and be careful not to push on the pedal board with your feet. Those are the controls that I use to fly the plane." Dad took off his cap and stuffed it into his pocket.

"Ok, Frank, we're ready," said the pilot to his helper who was standing in front of the plane. Frank stepped up and gave a pull on the propeller. After he pulled the second time, someone said "Contact." He pulled the prop again and stepped back as the engine roared to life.

As the plane began to move, Dad was thinking that his younger brother Jesse would never believe he had ridden in an airplane. He looked out and saw the small crowd of people on his left and Mr. McCoy's cows on his right as they taxied down through the pasture. He realized he had never gone this fast before.

Just as Dad worried the plane would hit the trees at the fence line, he saw the stick between his legs move straight back and the plane lifted up and climbed toward the sky. Looking down, the trees were getting smaller. They were floating along and seemed to be moving so slowly. The stick moved again. The plane tilted and turned to the right.

Looking back, the pilot shouted, "How're you doing?"

"I'm fine, sir!" Far off to the right, Walter could see the Rayburn farm. The house and barn looked like toys. There were clothes on the line.

After about twenty minutes, they landed back in the pasture. Stepping back on the ground, Dad noticed that his legs were shaking from the excitement. "Thank you, sir," he said to the pilot. "I'll never forget this plane ride."

"Well, I certainly appreciate you getting that gasoline for us. That's enough fuel to last all day. If you see anyone who wants to take a ride, tell them we'll be here all day tomorrow," said the pilot.

Then the assistant, Frank, said, "Charles, here is a woman who wants to take a ride."

My folks are not going to believe this, thought Dad as he untied the mules and drove down the gravel road toward home.

Three years later, in 1927, Dad saw a picture in a newspaper about Charles A. Lindberg's transatlantic flight. He then recognized the pilot who had taken him for a plane ride in Mr. McCoy's pasture as none other than Charles A. Lindberg.

*The Lindberg plane that Dad rode in was a Curtiss Jenny, a surplus airplane from World War I. The Jenny was a two-seater with dual controls. It was powered by a 90 hp Curtiss in-line engine with a top speed of 75 mph. After the war, many of these planes were sold to the public.*

*During the 1920s, aviation was new to the masses and barnstorming was popular entertainment. Stunt pilots and aerialists would fly over a small rural town and drop leaflets. Then, they would make arrangements with a local farmer to use his pasture for a runway and at a specified time, would put on an air show. The main source of income was giving plane rides to the public who came to see the show.*

# GO WEST, YOUNG MAN

The year was 1936. There were several factors that influenced my dad to move his young family across the Mississippi River to Louisiana to live like a homesteader. He always told me that it was because he did not approve of the Delta plantation owners' treatment of the blacks. There were no black folks in West Carroll Parish, Louisiana, so I often wondered if it could have been his racial bigotry. Then, one should consider the effects of the Great Depression that left southern sharecroppers even poorer. This was his dream of a new life and having his own piece of land.

"Shorty, when do you plan on moving to our new place?" Dad asked his brother-in-law. Arthur Berry was my mother's brother. His wife was my Aunt Kate and they had a new baby boy, Sidney. Arthur was of average height, stocky, with slightly stooped shoulders. The physical exercise of working on the Delta farm had made him lean. He had black hair, dark eyes, a square jaw and a captivating smile. My dad and all of Arthur's brothers called him "Shorty." He was not that short so I never knew where the nickname originated.

"Walter, I don't think I can persuade Kate to move over to those swamps until we get our houses built," Arthur said.

Dad and Arthur had each purchased forty acres of swampy land in Louisiana from the Bruce Lumber Company for $2.75 per acre. Bruce Lumber was almost finished with the removal of all the virgin timber in that area. The company cut only the prime, big trees so there was a lot of good hardwood, mostly oak, ash and elm left on the property.

"While I was over there last month, I went and talked with the sawmill superintendent. He assured me that if we can cut our logs and get them to the mill, they will saw the lumber we need for our houses and there will be no charge. That goes with the purchase of the land," Dad said.

"I'm trying to get Lillie to agree to take the baby and move to the lumber camp, so we can get started on these houses. If Mr. Berry helps us with the building, we just might get moved in before winter," he added. Mr. Berry was my grandfather, my mom's dad. He was a very good carpenter.

Lillie, my mother, was the oldest of fourteen children. There were seven boys and seven girls. At that time I was two years old and she was twenty-six. She was a very pretty woman with brown eyes and brown hair that fell below her waist, but which she wore in a bun on the back of her head. During her young years, working on the Mississippi Delta farm had made her strong.

Even though my grandfather, Rube Berry, was a good carpenter, he was also a sharecropper. He played the fiddle and the banjo. He had grown up in the eastern Mississippi hill country where as a young man he and his brothers had a string band that played for local country dances. He was short, bald-headed, with some brownish-red hair left on the sides. He was a kind man, but spoke with a gruff voice that frightened me when I was a child.

"There's no need for me to talk anymore to Kate about moving over to that lumber camp and living in a tent. She's just not going to move until we get the houses built," said Arthur. Aunt Kate had a lot of spunk and was not keen on moving to Louisiana. "I've talked to Papa about helping us with the houses and he has agreed. Walter, you and I can build most of the house but we have to have Papa cut the rafters," he added.

My dad, Walter, was two years older than my mother. He was a small wiry man who never weighed over 135 pounds until he was past forty. Despite being small, he was very strong in his upper body from plowing middle busters, turning plows, sawing timber with a cross-cut saw and putting up hay. Before he was twenty-one, his black hair began to recede. He was turning gray and bald by the time he was thirty-five.

Basically, Dad was a very kind and patient man with gray eyes and I never heard him swear or use profane language. I did hear him say "shit" once. That was when one of the draft horses accidentally stepped on his foot as he was buckling the collar, which held the harness for plowing, around the horse's neck.

This was during the Great Depression and everyone was poor. It took some planning to get their meager belongings tied on that old Model T Ford truck. There was the wooden trunk that was packed full of the items that my mom deemed valuable. Another wooden box held my dad's tools. It was a big assortment of hand tools one must have around the farm and for any type of basic carpentry work. A borrowed canvas tent was packed to provide shelter until the house was built.

In the swamps, there was a lot of wild game and Dad had a hammer-type double-barreled 12-guage shotgun and a Stephens Crackshot, which was a small single-shot .22 caliber rifle. Three plows were tied on the very top. They were a gee whiz, a Georgia stock and a double shovel. These were plows that you could use with only one mule.

In between the trunk and box of tools lay an ax, a hoe, two shovels, a froe, a sledgehammer, crosscut saw, post-hole-digger and a kaiser blade, used for clearing brush. The froe was used for splitting cypress-wood shingles to cover the roof.

"Walter, do you really think that old truck will get us to Louisiana?" Mom asked. "It is always broke down." My mother was very close to her family and actually did not want to leave Mississippi. It saddened her to think that she would be unable to visit her family, even once a year, because of the distance and the lack of money.

But she loved Dad. He was so excited about having his own farm, and it was a wife's duty to go with her husband. It might be a better life, she thought, but it was so far away from her family.

"Shorty and I have worked on that truck and I have no doubt that it will get us to our new place," he said. He was afraid to tell her that there were practically no roads in the part of the West Carroll Parish where they were going. The roads there were only wagon ruts and since there was no gravel, impassable except on horseback when the rains were heavy.

He knew he would have to sell the old Model T truck after they were moved. The truck would be of no use without roads. He would use the money to tide them over until he could get enough land cleared of small trees, brush, and vines to plant a crop. A newly cleared field was called the "newground." Dad decided to wait until they were in Louisiana before he would try to help her understand his plans.

With the Model T truck loaded, they pulled out of the yard of that sharecroppers' shotgun house where they had been living for the past year near Hollandale, Mississippi. It was goodbye to this Delta forever. They were moving to Louisiana to start a new life.

The Ferry across the Mississippi was located at Greenville. The ferry landing on the western shore was in Arkansas near the town of Lake Village. They would have to travel some thirty odd miles across the corner of the state of Arkansas to get to their Louisiana farm.

"I never thought Mama and Papa would ever move back to the hills," said Dad. "They have lost everything there in Ruleville. Papa is so down and out. Mama thought with this one good crop they might be able to buy a place. No one knew that the banks were going to close." A large dog ran out from under a farmhouse that was close to the gravel road. He barked viciously and ran along the side of the truck as it passed.

"Walter, did you ever think about us moving to the hills?" asked Mom. "We both have a lot of relatives around the Maben area. It might be better than moving to Louisiana."

"That red clay is so poor that you can't grow a decent crop. The cotton ain't much more than knee high. I'd never want to move to the Mississippi hills. Growing up there was enough for me."

"Once we take the ferry over to Lake Village, it'll be an easy trip across the corner of Arkansas and down to our property in Louisiana," Dad said, changing the subject.

"I am really afraid of riding the ferry," said Mom. "I don't know how to swim. That river is so big and we've got the baby with us. What if the ferry sinks?" she asked, expressing her fear.

As a child, she had lived near Ruleville and Drew in Sunflower County, Mississippi. In 1932, her family moved to the Haliburton Plantation just south of Greenville. There were a few rare trips to Maben, which was up in the hill country in the eastern part of the state and was the home of both her parents. When she was only one year old, her parents moved to Altus, Oklahoma, but returned four years and three kids later. Mom had no memory of that experience and could not remember ever being on a ferry.

"Lillie, people cross that ferry every day and there is no reason for you to be afraid. Nothing is going to happen," he said, trying to calm her.

"Well, I can thank God that I don't have to cross on that ferry every day," she answered.

We were driving down the dusty road toward Greenville where we would catch the ferry. It was just after daylight but already on each side of the road there were black men walking behind the plows pulled by two mules. We could smell the freshly plowed earth. They were making rows in the rich black Delta soil that would soon be green with growing cotton plants. Most of the rows were a half mile long, which was the distance across a half section of land.

Due to the thousands of years of the river flooding, the topsoil was more than six feet deep and flat enough to plant rice. Occasionally there would be a shotgun house near the road with a garden and a few chickens and black children playing in the yard. While sitting on the seat of that old Model T truck beside her husband with her two-year-old son in her arms, Mom wondered what her new home would be like.

Her thoughts were interrupted when the old Model T made a strange noise and began losing speed. "Walter, I told you this old truck would never get us to Louisiana. We're not even to Greenville and it sounds like it's going to die," she said.

Dad let the truck coast over to the side of the road. He knew what was wrong.

"Lillie, please don't worry. I'll have it going in no time," was his effort to comfort her. Those old Model T engines had an ignition system that ran off four coils mounted on the firewall, one for each cylinder and a magneto. This made it possible to run the vehicle without a battery. He knew that if he filed the points on the top of that number two coil, it would stop missing.

The truck had stopped just below the Haliburton Plantation Mansion, which was about seven miles south of Greenville. It was surrounded by cotton fields and unlike most old plantation homes, this was not an attractive structure. There were no big majestic trees that usually stood on the grounds of the old mansions, just a couple of small shade trees out back.

The house itself was a very large, white, two-story structure with a huge red bungalow roof that looked like a flattened pyramid. Up on the very top where the roof gables came to a peak, there was a flat spot that from the ground appeared to be a sun deck. It had a white banister around the edge. Dad said it was once used to look out over the fields to observe the black field hands, but architecturally, it was known as a "widow's walk."

Another feature that made the house unattractive was the way it was built upon brick columns instead of regular house blocks. This raised the house up high enough that an automobile could be driven underneath the floor, making the house as tall as a three-story building. Being only about five miles from the Mississippi River, it was constructed so that the floods did not get up inside the mansion. But it still was not high enough to escape the 1927 Flood, which got up in the first floor.

"I think the truck is fixed. Would you retard the spark a little, Lillie, and I'll start the motor," Dad said, taking hold of the crank.

"I smell gas," said Mom as she moved me over to her right arm. She then reached over and pushed up on the spark-advance lever on the left side of the steering column.

"No, that's the wrong way. Pull the lever down. This thing will kick like a mule," he said.

She reached over again and pulled the lever down, retarding the spark, and mumbled, "I think we're stuck right here on the side of this road with everything we own on this old truck."

With one hand on the radiator cap to brace himself, Dad gave a quick tug on the crank and the old Model T engine roared to life, hitting on all four cylinders. He flashed a big grin at Mom and slid into the seat. "On to Greenville!"

Sometime after the devastating 1927 Flood, the government had raised the levees to a new height. The old, loaded truck struggled to reach the top of the levee. At the top, you could look down at the river landing and see the ferry that would take us across the river to Arkansas.

"My God, Walter, it's a long way down this hill to that ferry. I'm scared," said Mom. "If this old truck goes into the river, we'll all be killed."

Dad kept thinking it was probably good that she did not know just how inadequate those mechanical brakes were on the Model T. He wished he had increased his speed a little before starting up the levee. The truck barely had enough power to reach the top. He hoped that the deck hands on the ferry would throw some wooden blocks under the wheels if he had trouble stopping his loaded truck.

"I'm not riding this truck down that hill," Mom warned, getting out of the truck while it was stopped on the very top. With me in her arms, she proceeded to walk down the side of the levee to the ferry landing.

Though he believed he could accomplish the feat, Dad was glad that his wife and son were walking down instead of riding in the truck. He had to get the loaded truck to stop before reaching the far end of the ferry or it would be in the river.

With a strong grip on the hand brake with his left hand, just in case, and white-knuckling the large wood steering wheel with his right hand, Dad pushed in the clutch with his left foot, which was low gear. Holding down on the brake pedal with his right foot, he let the truck creep slowly down the steep levee. The truck stopped just after rolling onto the ferry.

"Boy, I'm glad that's over," he said to one of the deckhands who had a piece of wood poised to throw under a tire if needed.

"We's a-watching out fur ya, Mista," said the deckhand with a wooden skid in his hand. The concerned worker was smiling and had a front tooth missing.

He was a black man, tall and muscular, standing barefooted and bareheaded. The denim overalls he was wearing were very worn, with a big hole in one knee. You could tell that was the only stitch of clothing he had on and the overalls were held up by one strap. "We's seed 'em ol' trucks git plum away from a feller, sir, we ain't gwine let dat happen to you," he promised, flashing that big, one-tooth-missing smile.

Down the hill came a new, 1936 Ford sedan with a family inside that was directed to the parking space on the very front of the boat. My dad was admiring the blue four-door sedan when the deckhand spoke to him again.

"Mista, dat climb up to da top of da levee on the otha' side is a lot woise than dis'en. So we's a gwine to let you be da lase one on. Dat way, you'se a gwine ta have da whole boat fur a runnin' start," he explained. "So, Mista, we needs you to back yoe truck off da boat so's we can put you on lase."

Dad carefully pushed the hand brake forward to the neutral position, pushed the middle pedal with his left foot, and the Model T began to move backwards off the ferry.

"Why did you back off the boat?" asked Mom. "Are we going back home?" she said, somewhat hopefully. She'd walked up to the truck where he was sitting and as she spoke, let me stand on the ground in order to rest her weary arms. She had not heard what the deckhand had said about the steep hill on the other side of the river.

"Everything is all right, Lillie. They're gonna put us on last," he said.

Two more wagons and a '29 Model A Ford car moved onto the ferry. A matching pair of gray horses pulled the wagon loaded with rolls of barbed wire for fencing. The horses were frightened and refused to load. But the driver got off the wagon and walking in front, led the team to the designated spot, talking to the horses to calm them.

"I'd trade this old truck for that team of pretty horses," said Dad. He loved horses and always insisted that they were smarter than mules.

One of the deckhands motioned to Dad and he drove the loaded truck onto the designated spot, which was at the very back of the boat. After setting the brake, he shut the engine off and stepped out on the deck. The deckhands put a wooden block under each one of the tires.

"I sure didn't realize that the river was this wide," said Mom, clutching me. "I'm scared and I'll be so glad when this is over."

"Let's go up and stand in the very front by the railing so we can see better while we are crossing the river," suggested Dad.

"Walter, you know that I can't swim. Me and this baby are not going near the edge of the boat. There's a lot of stuff on here; do you think it could sink?"

"I told you this ferry crosses the river several times each day and it has never sunk. Everything is going to be OK," Dad said, reassuringly, as he put his arm around her waist.

It was a warm day and Mom wore a bonnet that she had made to ward off the Mississippi sunshine. She had also made the faded print dress that reached halfway to her ankles. Firmly, she gripped my hand as I stood on the deck by her side. Dad had on denim overalls, a well-worn blue chambray shirt and an old straw hat. They stood arm in arm, not near the edge, as the ferry chugged across to the Arkansas side.

On the west side of the river, the ferry gently bumped into the piling of the landing. The engine chugged until the two deckhands had secured the lines to pilings by the wharf.

The first vehicle to load onto the boat was the first to leave. It took awhile to unload. When it came your turn to drive up the steep bank, you had to wait until the vehicle in front of you was safely over the top and there was no danger of it rolling back.

As the wagon with the load of wire, which was the last vehicle except for ours, went up the bank, the concerned deckhand asked, "Sir, you knows dat we's could tote some of yo stuff up da hill to lighten dat truck. Hit sho' would hep it git up to da top of dat ol' levee."

"Thanks so much for offering to help," said Dad, "but this old Model T will easily top that hill."

Mom was seated in the cab of the truck with me on her lap. "Walter, I think I'll take the baby and walk up that hill. I'm afraid to ride in this truck to the top of that levee."

"Now, Lillie, we have the whole length of this boat to get a good running start. There's absolutely no need for you to be scared. The ferry won't leave until we get over the top. Everything is gonna be all right. So just calm yourself and we'll soon be in Arkansas," he said, trying to comfort her.

He did get a running start, but about ten yards from the top of the Arkansas side of the river bank, the clutch band began slipping, causing the motor to race. The truck came to a dead stop. As it began to roll backwards, Mom, petrified, began screaming and crying. Dad had never seen her this way.

Dad let the loaded truck roll back toward the waiting ferry. He pulled on the hand brake and rode the brake pedal with all his weight so as not to lose control.

"We're all going to be killed!" Mom screamed. She was really crying now. I was so frightened, I began to cry very loudly, knowing that something was wrong.

Dad was so busy trying to control the truck that he could not console her. It was a most frightening, death-threatening experience for her. He managed to stop the truck at about the center of the ferry deck. Folks up on the bank and everyone on the boat were watching and hoping Dad could control the truck rolling backwards down the levee.

As soon as the truck stopped, Mom, clutching me to her breast, jumped out on the deck. She was hysterical. She and I both were still crying.

The captain stepped out of the pilothouse, which was located on the side. He had an old ladder-back, hide-bottomed chair for her to sit in and recover from the frightening experience. Dad came over and put an arm around his wife, saying, "Lillie, just sit down, calm yourself, and take care of the baby. Everything's gonna be all right."

"Do you think we should take some of the load off so you could pull the hill?" asked the captain, turning toward my dad.

"I don't think that'll be necessary. I just have to tighten the low gear band," answered Dad. He took a screwdriver and removed the four screws and lifted the wooden floorboard panel that exposed the cover on the transmission. After removing the four bolts holding the inspection plate, he could see all three band-adjustment screws. Using a wrench, he tightened the one for low gear. He replaced the cover and floorboard, then walked over to the chair where Mom and I were sitting.

"Lillie, I thought Arthur had adjusted all those bands but it's ready now and it'll go right up that hill," he said with confidence.

"There is no way that me or this baby is getting back in that truck before you get it over the Arkansas levee," proclaimed Mom. "We're walking!"

Removing his gloves and flashing a smile, the deckhand asked, "Ma'am, why don't ya lets me tote that baby up dat hill fer ya, cause ya done had a big skeer?"

Mom handed me to the deckhand as they waited for my dad to get the truck to the top of the levee. When they started up the riverbank, she told him, "I wanna thank you for toting the baby for me 'cause my legs are still weak. I thought we were all gonna die."

Up on the Arkansas bank were several groves of big cottonwood trees providing shade and relief from the southern sun. Their heavy leaves made a clapping sound in the hot mid-day breeze. Several folks waited to get on the ferry to go to the Mississippi side. The fragrance of coffee boiling on a campfire filled the air.

Dad took an empty gallon vinegar jug out of the truck. It was wrapped with a gunnysack, or burlap bag, that was held in place with heavy fishing twine. He walked across the road to a pitcher pump with the spout hanging over a large wooden trough that was used for watering horses and mules. When it flowed with cool water he held the jug under the water, wetting the gunnysack covering. This was to help keep the water cool for a while.

As he filled the jug, the ferry began to blow its whistle, signaling everyone that they were ready for all to get on board for the return trip. Walking back to the truck, Dad offered Mom a cool drink of fresh water, saying, “Well, Lillie, we’re in Arkansas.”

# OUR NEW HOME

The cool shade of the cottonwoods on the Arkansas riverbank was a welcome change and Dad did not want to leave. They had eaten a lunch of biscuits, fried salty ham and baked sweet potatoes. Mom had prepared all the food before they left. She had even baked a plain cake for the trip.

There weren't any places to eat outside of the small towns. If you had money, it was possible to stop at a country store and purchase cheese and crackers. Some type of canned meat was available. But most of the country stores had no electricity for refrigeration.

"Lillie, we still have a long way to go before we get to Louisiana," said Dad. "We need to get started. It's still about twelve miles to Lake Village."

"Let me finish feeding the baby and putting the food away and I'll be ready," she replied.

After checking the water in the radiator, he discovered it was a little low, possibly caused by the hard pull up the riverbank from the ferry. Dad walked across the road to the pump and filled a small bucket to refill the radiator. A middle-aged man was at the pump, soaking his red bandana in the cool water. Everyone else had left and gone down the levee to board the ferry.

"Howdy," said the man, washing the dust from his face. "It's a hot one, ain't it?" He looked as though he had been traveling for some time. His clothes were dirty and wrinkled and it had been several days since he had last shaved. On his head he wore a cap.

The traveler was of average height and walked with a limp, favoring his left leg. He took out a bag of Bull Durham tobacco and proceeded to roll a cigarette. After pulling the drawstring to close the sack, he licked the cigarette paper, exposing his tobacco-stained teeth.

"Where you headed?" asked Dad, removing his straw hat and rubbing his face with his wet hands.

"Been riding the freights, but there ain't no train that runs across the river to Lake Village. My sister wrote me and my maw's very sick. She lives just a couple of miles outside of Lake Village," he said, putting his sweat-stained cap on his head.

"I'm Walter Dobbs," Dad said, extending his hand. "I think we could make room on the back of the truck, if you don't mind the dust."

"Zeke Johnson here and I'd be much obliged for the ride. I've come all the way from Mobile." He exhaled smoke from his cigarette.

Mom had finished feeding me and had packed everything ready to continue. She looked across the road. There came her husband with a strange man who walked with a limp. Under the man's arm was a faded denim overall jacket. In his hand was an old, worn suitcase held together with a small rope tied around the middle. A half-smoked, roll-your-own cigarette dangled from the corner of his mouth.

"Lillie, this is Zeke, and he's going to ride on the back of our truck. He's going to Lake Village," explained Dad, pouring the water into the radiator.

Looking at the loaded Model T, Zeke said, "Looks like you folks are a' moving."

The ferry blew its whistle, signaling it was leaving for the Mississippi side. Dad said proudly, "Yes, we're moving to our new place down below Oak Grove, Louisiana."

Zeke tossed his old suitcase onto the bed of the truck.

"Howdy, ma'am," said Zeke, looking at Mom. "I'm kinda dirty. I've been on the road several days. I'm much obliged to ride with y'all to Lake Village." He lifted himself up and sat on the back of the truck bed.

As they pulled out onto the rough graveled road, Dad called out, "It's gonna be real dusty back there." Mom thought to herself, he could sure use a bath.

Dad stopped the truck on Main Street in Lake Village and wished Zeke 'good luck.'

"You folks are very kind to give me a ride. I could never have walked that far with this bum leg. I thank you," said Zeke.

Beyond Lake Village, it was about thirty miles to Eudora, Arkansas. A large stretch of the road was called a concrete road, with a slab of pavement down the middle and deep gravel on each side. Traveling was smooth until you met another vehicle. Then it was necessary for each to move one wheel over into the deep gravel for the two cars to pass.

Looking at the countryside they were passing, Mom asked, "Is this what it looks like in Louisiana? That dirt is all red clay. It reminds me of the poor farms in the Mississippi hills."

"No, no, not at all. When we get past Eudora, it's less than ten miles to the Louisiana state line. There the land is flat and the soil is black as the Delta," Dad replied. As he drove the chugging Ford south, he told her about how they were going to start their new life in West Carroll Parish.

"Lillie, there's a whole community of folks living at the lumber camp. That's just a little ways south of Sharp's Store. All of the men work at the saw mill or in the timber. They live with their wives in the shacks built by Bruce Lumber Company. The company boss told me we could set up our tent there as long as we needed to," Dad explained.

"I just know that we'll find a lot of new friends. These timber folks are friendly hard-working people just like us farmers," he continued. "It's less than a half a mile from our land. After we get the tent set up and moved in, I can walk down to our place every day. I can't wait to start clearing. We'll need a place cleared off that is big enough for the house, lot, barn and a garden. That'll get us started."

"What's that up ahead?" she interrupted. "Looks like a big town. I could see a water tower when we were back down the road."

"Oh, that's Eudora," he answered. "We're gonna stop long enough for me to check the oil and water. I'll have to buy some gas."

Eudora was like so many small county seats in the southern and western states. The streets were covered with gravel and wide enough to park a wagon with a team of horses on each side. Along Main Street was a bank, hardware store, drug store, bakery and butcher shop and down at the end was a big general store. In front of the store was a tall gas pump. Across the street were the blacksmith shop and the gristmill.

Some of the buildings were brick. At the edge of the sidewalk there was a wooden rail about three feet high held up by posts that were driven into the ground. It was called the hitching post. This rail was used for securing the draft animals and riding horses while you went about your errands.

Dad stopped the truck beside the gas pump in front of a building with a big sign with letters two-foot tall on it, "Green's General Store."

"Lillie, we can't stay here long. We still have a good ways to go. The road is a little rough once we pass Oak Grove," he said.

That was an understatement. The road from Oak Grove to their new place was impassable during extreme wet weather. You could get through only by riding a horse. Even in dry weather, the wagon ruts were deep. It was going to be a challenge for him to drive the loaded truck to the site of the lumber camp.

"Why don't you take the baby in the store? You can stretch your legs and look around while I get the gas," he suggested. "We still have a long ride ahead of us."

Dad pumped the glass cylinder on top of the gasoline pump up to the eight-gallon mark. The original gas pumps did not require any power. The long pump handle on the side was hand operated and connected to a manual pump. The desired gallons were pumped up into the glass tank. Then you removed the nozzle, put the end into the truck tank, and gravity let the gas flow out of the glass storage compartment into your vehicle.

Dad paid for the gas and two coconut cookies that Mom wanted. She had taken them out of the big glass cookie jar on the counter. "Mrs.

Curtis Cookies" was painted on the front. She said, "I'll save these for the baby."

As the loaded Model T Ford moved down the street out of Eudora, Mom asked, "Did you notice there were several saddled horses tied up along the street in Eudora? I saw one man who looked like a Texas cowboy come out and get on his horse."

"Starting here in Eudora and on west for several miles, there are a lot of cattle, hogs and some goats that run wild in the woods," said Dad. "These woods here and on down this side of the Mississippi River are thick with several different types of vines, briars and brush. It's the same down in Louisiana."

"What you saw was leather chaps." Dad continued. "The rider has to have some kind of protection while chasing livestock through the thickets. That roll tied on the back of the saddle was a slicker for riding in the rain. They always have a rifle in the scabbard on the saddle. You never know when you may run into a vicious wild boar or an angry mama bear that could injure your horse," he explained.

"What's that long building with all the sheds by the cotton gin?" asked Mom. They were driving past the gin on the left side of the road at the very edge of town.

"That's a livestock barn," Dad said. "It's one of the largest in the area. People come up here from way down in Louisiana to buy horses and mules. There's a lot of small auction barns that sell cows, goats and hogs. Well, this sale barn specializes in riding horses, draft horses and mules," he explained as they drove out of Eudora. "See all those wood fences? Those are holding pens for the animals that are to be auctioned. Those tall things are loading chutes," he added. The barnyard odors floated up along the road.

They continued on and crossed the Louisiana state line at Kilbourne. After a few miles, the loaded truck pulled up beside Pippin's Café in Oak Grove. Mom was not at all impressed. "This looks like the frontier that I've read about," she said. "There are only about six stores and the courthouse."

"Well, it's not exactly the frontier. Oak Grove started in 1860. Three years after, the Yankees came over from Lake Providence and attacked the community. In 1864, the Federal Army burned the entire town except one store. The only building the Yankees left standing," explained Dad.

"Folks say that the Quantrill Gang helped protect settlers in this area from the Yankee raiders," Dad said. "The James brothers and the Younger brothers rode with Quantrill and they came over here from Missouri. Cole Younger had a daughter who lived close to here. She and her husband lived near the Bayou Macon Church, not far down the road. Jesse James had a sister who lived near Delhi, just south of here."

"It's getting late and we have to be on our way. We don't have far to go," he said, hoping the local history would interest her.

The remaining sixteen miles to the lumber camp were the toughest. The wagon road was so marked with deep ruts that Dad could hardly manage the loaded truck. The road grew worse once they passed the community of Red Wing. Three times different items fell off the truck. They had to be reloaded and securely tied down with plow lines (ropes).

In some areas, the road was just some deep ruts winding among big oak and sweet gum trees. Dad said nothing, but certainly realized they were fortunate the road was dry or they could not have driven to the lumber camp.

By the time they pulled up under the big hickory tree at the edge of the lumber camp, everyone was exhausted, including me. It was so late, they decided to eat some of the food that Mom had packed, rather than start a fire and cook. Tomorrow, they would pitch the tent.

After seeing the area where they were to live, Mom tried to hide her disappointment. She said nothing, but thought about the terrible road back to Oak Grove. When would she get to go back to the Mississippi Delta and visit with her mother and sisters? They seemed to be so far away. She turned her back so that Dad could not see her crying.

It was the mules that occupied Dad's thoughts. In a couple of weeks, Arthur and Mr. Berry, Lillie's dad, were due to arrive. They were planning to bring two mules, the wagon, and tools needed to work in the log woods. They would cross on the ferry at Brown's Crossing, near Glen Allen,

Mississippi. This crossing was directly across from Kilbourne on the Louisiana side of the river. Kilbourne was located just eight miles north of Oak Grove near the Louisiana-Arkansas border.

The Louisiana side of Brown's Crossing was so muddy and swampy that cars or trucks could not get through. That was the reason Dad had driven the truck through Arkansas, though it was over fifty miles farther. If the mules came through Arkansas, state law required a three-day quarantine and they had to be dipped

Dipping required the animals to walk through a vat containing a solution that came up over their backs and killed all the ticks and other parasites. It was called a dipping vat. Horses, mules, cows, sheep and goats coming into the state had to be dipped, according to the law.

In Louisiana, there was no quarantine, but the mules had to be dipped.

"That's like going through a foreign country," said Arthur. They did not want the inconvenience of waiting three days in Arkansas.

"It smells so damp here. Are we close to a slough?" asked Mom. After they had passed Red Wing, she noticed a lot of green moss and gray Spanish moss on the trees.

"We're only about a half mile from Beouf River. There are a lot of sloughs and swamps around here that are filled with cypress trees," he explained. "Our place is not that low. It has a lot of oak timber."

Dad thought, "I just cannot believe that we made the whole trip in that old truck without having one flat tire."

The quality of tires in the '20s and '30s was poor and the roads were so rough that it was difficult to go any distance without suffering a flat.

# BUILDING A HOUSE

Dad wondered if he had made a mistake in moving Mom and two-year-old me from the Mississippi Delta to the sparsely inhabited wooded swampland of Louisiana. One night, while lying under the thin cotton netting of the mosquito bar, Dad heard Mom crying. He guessed that she missed her family, having never before been separated from them.

At breakfast the next morning, as he poured sorghum syrup over his buttered biscuits, Dad said, "Mr. Berry and Arthur should be here any day now. It must be raining across the river or they would have been here last week." He was anxious to have the team of mules so he could load the logs he had cut. And he thought that having her father and brother here would be of some comfort to his wife.

"The sooner they get here and get the house built, the sooner we can move out of this awful tent," Mom said. "It's damp in here, even if it is on a ridge. I'm afraid Joe is going to get sick from us living on a dirt floor."

Every day, Dad left before daylight and returned after dark, exhausted from clearing the new land. He worked so hard that she could not find it in her heart to complain. She wouldn't add to his burden by telling him how homesick she was to see her family. And how much she detested living in a tent.

"I talked to the mill boss today," said Dad as we were eating supper by kerosene lantern light. "I told him about working at the sawmill in Mississippi. How I could scale logs and set dogs on the carriage." He sopped up stew gravy with a biscuit. "The boss said that he could use me at the mill a of couple days a week."

"Why would you want to work at the mill?" asked Mom. "It will just be that much longer before we move into our new house." She was interrupted by the sound of a wagon and team pulling up beside the tent.

It was Arthur's voice that said, "Whoa." The wagon stopped and he called out, "Walter, Lillie, we're finally here!"

Mom recognized her brother's voice and ran out of the tent to hug him and her dad. Though we had only been in Louisiana a little over three weeks, it seemed like a year. She was so excited about seeing some of her family that she was crying.

"Walter, put a couple of sticks of wood in the cook stove and I'll cook for them. You both must be starved," sobbed Mom, overjoyed to have them arrive.

Mr. Berry said, "Walter, I believe we brought everything that we're going to need. We have a fine pair of mules that have pulled this wagon all the way from Glen Allen, Mississippi." He continued, "In the wagon are log chains, a cant hook, snaking tongs, two more axes and iron wedges." These were tools they would need to get the logs to the sawmill.

They also had plans to build a house for Arthur and his wife, Kate, who owned land that bordered our place. Not only would they be building two houses, there were a lot of posts that had to be split to build the fences.

"We can use the double-tree off the wagon to snake the logs out of the swampy places," said Arthur. "I'm anxious to get started."

With the help of my Grandpa Berry, they built their houses that year. To work the fields of the new ground, they only needed one animal. So once they began farming, they separated the mules. Dad kept the one named Bob and Arthur kept Jim, the other mule.

Clearing all that land without power tools was difficult for a small man of only 135 pounds. Dad had to cut down all the trees and remove most of the stumps. The trees and brush had to be burned so he could plant corn or cotton. It was possible to leave some trees in the pastures where the farm animals grazed. I remember taking him a jug of fresh water to where he was clearing the land.

Contributing to the difficulty, this work was done in the summer when the weather was hot. When he had to cut down trees, Dad would trade work with Uncle Arthur or a neighbor. This was done with a crosscut saw, which required two people.

Besides the stumps that remained, there were also holes from where tree stumps had been removed. The row crops were worked with the Georgia stock, double shovel and gee whiz. These were plows that were designed to be pulled by one mule. When there was a need to use a team, they simply put the mules back together.

The Bruce Lumber Company had begun to move all of its timber equipment out of the swamps. When a big lumber company like Bruce moved into an area to remove the virgin timber, they would set up a large saw mill in a central location. Leading to the mill would be a network of narrow gauge railroad tracks for the steam locomotives.

In the swamps, the heavy virgin timber was moved to the rail lines by multiple yokes of oxen. To get the logs onto the wagons, poles were laid against the side of the wagon. A team of mules or oxen were used to pull the logs up onto the wagons using pulleys.

To keep the big wagons' wooden wheels from sinking into the damp ground, they were six inches wide and had an iron band around the outside. Two of these abandoned iron wheel bands were in our yard for years. My mom used them as flower planters.

Teams of mules did not have enough strength to pull the logs out of the swamps, so the company had laid narrow gauge railroad tracks called "dummy lines." Steam locomotives pulled the logs to the mill.

Only the big virgin timber was harvested; the forests were not 'clear cut' like they are today. When the operation was finished, the locomotives were driven up the tracks to the main line and the tracks were removed to be taken to the next location. Years later while hoeing in the cotton field, one would occasionally uncover a rusty iron railroad spike.

One night when I was four, I was awakened by a crash -- my mom had knocked over a chair while searching for the kerosene lamp. Striking a match and lighting the lamp, she said, "It's Bob. That mule is out again. Walter, why don't you get rid of that mule? He's never gonna stay in the lot."

Pulling on his overalls, Dad said, "I just put another row of planks around top of that fence. If he can get his chin over the top, he knows he can jump out. If it wasn't for Arthur, I'd trade him for a horse."

Just across the Beouf River from us was more than 11,000 acres of wooded swamps. There was an "open stock law" in that area which meant that the farmers let the majority of their stock run wild in the swamps. Each farmer had a designated brand that was used on cattle and horses. Hogs, goats and sheep had a system of different sized notches cut in their ears. The identifying notches and brands were registered at the courthouse.

These animals were permitted to run wild and forage for themselves in the abundant forest. Their owners had roundups a couple of times each year to mark the newborn. To keep the wild livestock from eating crops, farmers had to fence in their fields. We also had to keep our farm animals behind a fence or they would go out into the swamp with the wild livestock.

Stomping in the back door and pulling off his rubber gumboots, Dad said, "Well, Bob is back in the lot. I would just love to trade him off for a good horse." He crawled back into bed. "I've never liked mules."

In 1938, Uncle Arthur moved his family, Aunt Kate, and their son, Sidney, over from Mississippi into their new house. Now I had a cousin for a playmate and Mom had a sister-in-law nearby. Though this was much easier, Mom still became very homesick for her mother and sisters back in the Delta.

Aunt Kate was a small, thin woman with short, dark brown hair. I remember her having some gold in one of her front teeth -- a fashion at that time -- that you could see when she smiled. She was always loud and vocal but very loving to all us kids.

Sometime in the winter after my fourth birthday, I awoke because it was so cold in the house. I could hear Mom in the kitchen cooking. After sliding into my overalls, I went into the kitchen where it was warm and cozy. There was the smell of pancakes cooking on the wood stove.

"You're up early, young man. How many pancakes can you eat this morning? I'm cooking a big batch because your dad has to plow in that new ground all day," she said.

"I'm so hungry," I replied. There on the kitchen wall opposite the stove was a dark fiddle hanging from a nail. When no one was in the house, I had tried to reach it by standing on a chair pushed against the wall.

"Mom, I'd like to look at that fiddle up close. Would you take it down off the wall?" I asked. I thought that was one of the most beautiful things I had ever seen. The artistic curves and general shape appealed to me even as a child.

"That is not a toy, it is a violin. It's not for little boys to play with. You might accidentally break it," Mom said. "Your dad got it in a trade and he's going to give it to your grandpa." I was standing close to the back of the stove to stay warm as she continued to cook pancakes. In another skillet she was frying eggs.

"Would you, please, take it down and lay it on the eating table so I could get a closer look? I promise I won't touch it," I begged. I had never seen anyone play the fiddle but had heard one on the radio. We listened to the Grand Ole Opry almost every Saturday night on a battery radio.

"I'm not taking that fiddle down off the wall. Now wash your hands. I hear your dad coming from the barn. It's time to eat," she said. She never let me look at the fiddle up close. Not too long after that, my grandpa came over for a visit. I never saw the fiddle again.

Some thirty years later, I was visiting with my dad and he told me those years in the swamps were the best years of his life. He knew that it had been very difficult for my mother, but he had so enjoyed living off the land. One year, he only spent about $25 cash.

We raised everything we used except salt, baking powder, black pepper, baking soda and coffee. Dad didn't use any form of tobacco. Some of the items he bartered for at the country store with eggs and butter that our farm had produced.

I remember taking corn to the grist mill that was near Sharp's Store. It's the community called Goodwill today. Wild game such as ducks, geese, rabbits, fish, bullfrogs and deer were plentiful so we always had meat.

Because of the physical labor required to live on a farm, it was most uncommon for someone to be overweight. There was no overindulgence in sugar, namely because other than sorghum molasses or ribbon cane syrup, we had no sweets except occasionally a fruit pie or a cake at Sunday dinner.

Sugar we got from the cane syrup we produced on the farm. Ribbon cane was the most popular but my dad preferred sorghum. He always had a small patch of sorghum and would cook a few gallons of the syrup every fall.

You could tell the man was very tall even though he was riding a horse. "Howdy, Mr. Dobbs," greeted Preston Crews, getting off his horse. The horse, a buckskin with a black mane and tail, looked like he had been ridden hard and you could smell the sweat. "How's your family?"

"We're doing just fine," answered my dad. I was standing beside him admiring the horse that was switching his tail to ward off horse flies. By the mud on his legs and hooves, you could tell that he'd been ridden in the swamps. "We sure could use some rain. It's about time for the corn to tassel and I noticed that some of the stalks look a little burnt on the bottom. I hope it rains soon."

"Mr. Dobbs, I sure am surprised at the work y'all have done on this farm the last two years," said Mr. Crews. "When you and your wife moved in, I thought you would last maybe a year. Life is hard out here in these woods."

"Would you like a fresh drink of water?" asked Dad, as he began priming the pitcher pump.

"Don't mind if I do," answered Mr. Crews. "Now, Mr. Dobbs, you know my brand. If your family ever needs meat, feel free to go in the woods and help yourself to any of my livestock. There's no need for you and your family to go hungry." He took off his hat and cupping his hands, got a drink of fresh cool water from the pump. He had a three-day beard and the sun made his red hair glisten.

"We certainly appreciate your kindness, Mr. Crews," said Dad. Mr. Crews, wearing leather chaps and a well-used felt hat, led his horse over to the water trough by the pump. The horse lowered his head and drank.

In the scabbard on the saddle, there was a Winchester rifle. The leather of the saddle creaked as Mr. Crews mounted his horse and said, "Good to see y'all. I gotta be going. I'm checking on some calves down near the river. I've lost I don't know how many head to the wolves this year."

"There's a pack of timber wolves in them swamps, for we can hear 'em howling at night," Dad said.

Looking down at me, Mr. Crews said, "That's a mighty fine looking boy you got there." Turning the buckskin,, he rode out of the yard past Mom's flower beds full of blooming petunias. He rode past the two big white oak trees and turned south on the wagon road toward the Fields' family farm. Looking back, he waved, then disappeared into the woods.

"Son, now that's a pretty horse," Dad said, as we walked back toward the house.

Sometime in 1938 the law was changed repealing the open stock law. Farmers no longer had to fence in their fields, but just across Beouf River, there would be an open stock law for another twelve years.

When I had just turned four years old, my dad promised that he, Mom and I were going to take a trip in the wagon. This only happened about three times a year, so it was a very unusual event.

"I know it's early but we have to get started so we can get home before dark," said Dad as he hitched the mules to the single trees of the wagon. "If there aren't a lot of folks ahead of us at the grist mill, we'll have plenty of time."

We had just finished eating breakfast and were going to Sharp's Country Store at Goodwill. It was over three miles through wooded swamps with one large slough to cross.

"Walter, do you think that the water is high in that slough?" asked Mom. "It's been raining off and on for over a week." She climbed up into the wagon and sat beside him on the seat. The heavy oak wagon bed was not anchored to the wagon -- it just lay in a frame held on by its heavy weight. On the floor of the wagon bed, I sat on an old quilt beside the bag of shelled corn that we were going to have ground into cornmeal.

It was just light enough to see the barn and so early that the fog had not yet lifted above the treetops as we drove out of the yard and onto the wagon road into the woods. The early morning air was damp and cool and the mule's breath was like a fog coming out of its nostrils. Spanish moss hanging from the big oak trees dripped with moisture. Dad whistled an Irish fiddle tune as Mom thought about what she would purchase from the store.

As we approached Mr. Keys' farm, we could smell the honeysuckle. His yard was filled with beds of blooming flowers and there were three stands of bees under the apple trees next to the grapevines. The water well was in the shade of a big fig tree.

Mr. Keys was a stoop-shouldered soft-spoken man with red hair turning gray. He possessed a great love for plants, always grafting fruit trees and crossing species of many plants. In the summer, he grew a couple of tobacco plants at the edge of his garden that he used for his own chewing pleasure. I never saw tobacco anywhere else in Louisiana or Mississippi.

The community genuinely respected his horticultural expertise as he kept an enormous collection of seeds of all kinds. These were seeds that he harvested from the vegetables and flowers he grew.

As we drove by the farm, Mr. Keys' old long-haired yellow dog announced our passing.

"Next week, I'm going to visit Mrs. Keys and get those flower cuttings she said I could have," said Mom as we drove past the orchard down toward the cypress trees. "She always has the prettiest flowers."

"There's more water here than I thought," said Dad. "I didn't realize it had rained so much. Look, those cypress knees are almost covered with water. They're usually up on dry land." The wagon ruts were over six inches deep and the mules were walking in mud that was the same depth.

To the left of the road was an old abandoned three-room wooden house. Weeds were up to the windows and the porch roof was falling in.

"Look at that burned corner next to the road," said Dad. "That's where a man got killed." He pointed to a burned area on the very outside corner near the floor of the old house. "I don't remember his name, but it was years ago. He was a worker for the Bruce Lumber Company. While walking through here to Sharp's Country Store he was caught in a thunderstorm and ran inside this old house. He sat down in that corner to get out of the rain. Lightning struck the exact spot where he was sitting. It was several days before anyone found him."

"Look how high the water is in that slough," said Mom, pointing up ahead. The road disappeared under the water. Trees on each side were in a line, signifying where the road lay underneath the surface.

"Lillie, the water's not that deep. I can tell that by the tree trunks," Dad said, as the mules waded into the flooded area up to their knees. As they continued, the water rose up over the axles of the wagon.

"Walter, this water is too deep," Mom warned as it reached near the bellies of the mules.

"Just be calm, Lillie -- everything will be OK," said Dad as he reached back and placed the bag of shelled corn upon the seat beside him and handed her the quilt.

Mom immediately took my hand and said, "Sit up here on the seat with us." She had her arm around my waist, holding me close.

Dad wished he had waited another day until the water had receded some. The mud and water were so deep that the mules could not back up the way we had come. Since the road was only as wide as the wagon ruts, there was no way he could turn the wagon and team around. We had to go forward.

If the water got so deep the mules had to swim, then the bed could possibly float off the wagon. That was not a pleasant prospect. Anchoring the wagon bed to the wagon with some rope would have been safer. But, it was too late for that.

"Oh, my God, water is coming up in the wagon," screamed Mom while immediately moving me up on her lap. She thought about what would happen if the wagon bed floated off out into the slough. It had cracks in the bottom and would soon sink. Walter could swim but she and her son would surely drown and then she would never see her mother and sisters again.

Before Dad could reply, the mules reached higher ground and the wagon rose up out of the water. Mom was crying. Seeing my mom upset frightened me and I began to cry.

"The high water will be down before we return this evening," said Dad, trying to comfort her.

When we arrived at the store, Mom visited with her friend Mrs. Sharp while Dad and I took the shelled corn to the grist mill. She looked through a variety of print fabrics and soon forgot about the high water.

I was fascinated by the grist mill. It was powered by a Model A Ford pickup truck. Mr. Simms had removed the tire from one of the back wheels. The rear of the truck was jacked up so that the wheel could turn a pulley for a large belt that also went around the pulley on the grist mill. When the belt was in place, he started the truck and put it in low gear. The pulley then turned the mill stones and ground the shelled corn into cornmeal. Once the cornmeal was bagged, Mr. Simms used a can to take a small portion out of it. Most farmers had very little cash and that was payment for the grinding.

A little later, we interrupted Mom talking to Mrs. Sharp about hatching chicks with a kerosene incubator.

"Lillie, we need to get going if we are going to get home before dark," Dad warned.

"I'm ready, Walter," she said, as she took me by the hand. We did not have any kind of lantern. No one traveled at night unless they were out coon hunting. Then you used a carbide lamp that attached to your cap.

We left Goodwill, which consisted of two stores, a planer mill, a cotton gin and a grist mill. In the wagon, we had our freshly ground meal and some groceries that Mom had purchased.

As we traveled, Dad told Mom of what he'd learned at the mill. "While we were waiting for our meal, I talked with Mr. Sharp. He mentioned something about the Farm Security Administration. It's a program President Roosevelt started to help poor farmers. There's a section of land about three miles north of Goodwill where the FSA is building homes on sixty-acre blocks of land. The land has already been cleared and it's ready to plow. The farm is then sold to families with nothing down and very low annual payments. The government lets the farmer take thirty years to pay back the loan."

"Walter, our farm is paid for and you've worked so hard clearing enough to plant a couple of fields. Why would you want to move after doing all that work?" Mom asked him.

"These farms will have a new three-bedroom home, a large barn with a hay loft, a smoke house and a chicken house," he said.

Mention of the new three-bedroom home convinced her. "Maybe you should make a trip to Oak Grove and see if we qualify," she said. Taking note of our surroundings, she said, "I wonder if the water in the slough went down?"

The water was just below the knees of the mules when we crossed on our way home. It was good to arrive before dark. Dad and Mom were still talking about the FSA when I crawled into bed under the mosquito bar.

# THE FAMILY GROWS

It was May 1939 and I'd made my second trip back to the Mississippi Delta. The first was in 1938 to attend my Uncle Dewey's funeral. The second trip was much more pleasant.

Charles, my uncle who was only six years old, and I played cars in the dirt by the ditch bank. We had roads in the dirt in several places. For our cars, we used Levi Garrett Snuff bottles. The bottles were about three inches square and four inches long with rounded corners. I must have pushed one of those brown snuff bottles a hundred miles. Because of occasional high water, all of the houses were two feet or more above ground level and when it rained, we would play under the house.

"Here's something for you boys," said the doctor, holding out his hand and giving each of us a candy sucker. He was short, fat and bald-headed with a great smile. In his other hand, he held a small black bag. As the doctor walked toward his '38 Ford Coupe, he looked at me and said, "Son, you have a new baby sister."

I never knew if it was because we lived so far from a doctor, there was no midwife, or my mother just wanted to be near her family at such special time. But my sister, Lucille, was born in my grandparents' home at Swift Water, Mississippi, in May of 1939.

Lucille was the flower in our family. She was a delightful, beautiful little girl in whom my mom took much pride. Mom was an accomplished seamstress and loved to make dresses for her daughter. But, just like everyone else, Lucille worked on the farm. Even as a small girl, she helped with all the kitchen chores and cooking meals. She spent hours shelling peas and butter beans.

In August of that same year, I turned five. For the past year, Mom had been teaching me how to read and write. Though busy with the new baby, she still took time to continue with my lessons.

When September came, she said, "Joe, you're ready to go to school. All you have to do is walk on down past Mr. Boss Daniels' house to the big gravel road. The school bus stops there and takes the kids to school."

"But Dad said that I had to be six years old to go to school," I said.

"I know that, but when you get there, you show the teacher that you can count to a hundred and write your name. See if there is a book that you can read for her," she said. "Once she understands how much you've learned at home, I'm sure she will let you stay."

Mom got me up early and dressed me in my new clothes, a pair of bib overalls and shoes she had ordered from the Sears & Roebuck catalog. It was just turning daylight when she kissed me bye. In my hand she placed a brown paper bag that contained two biscuits with bacon. "This is your lunch," she said. "There will be big kids at the bus stop and they'll help you. Mrs. Daniels' daughters will show you where to go after you get off the bus."

Walking through the woods, I felt very confident. I was big enough to go to school. There was a heavy dew on the grass and bushes. It was too early for the insects and birds to be out, so the woods were quiet. Our dog, Preacher, followed me. He was a small white dog with large black spots on his back. I scolded him and he went back down the trail toward our house.

When I arrived at the big gravel road, I saw several students waiting for the bus. I knew three of them. Donald Pollard lived on the river past our farm. (He later became a medical doctor.) He was in high school and

I liked him. The two teenage Daniels girls were there and I thought they were both pretty.

"Here comes the bus," someone called out. I looked down the road and I could see the yellow front of the bus followed by a cloud of dust. Because the land was flat, we could see it a half mile away. The closer the bus got, the more frightened I became. But I never said a word.

Tires crunched the gravel as the bus came to a stop and the driver opened the door. I'd never seen anything like it. I certainly had never seen that many kids in one group. My legs shook with fear as I approached the door. But I couldn't get on that bus.

Clutching my lunch bag, I turned and ran around the front of the bus. I heard the driver say, "Someone catch that little boy. It's his first day."

I ran as fast as I could up the road toward home. Footsteps gained on me, but I did not look back. I tried to run faster. I was not getting on that bus. Forget the new clothes.

I felt hands under my armpits. It was Leon Fields.

The Fields family farm was just south of our farm. A wagon road through the swampy forest led to their house. Mr. and Mrs. Fields had come from somewhere in Arkansas and purchased land. There were four children -- Leon, Lafon, Ott and Joanne. Joanne was my age. Before we were old enough to attend school, she and I would play while our mothers visited. The oldest, Leon, would join the Navy. After WWII, he returned home, bought our old farm and became a successful farmer.

Leon literally carried me onto the bus and held me in the seat beside him. He was a tall, skinny high school student with red hair and a freckled friendly face.

In a soft, comforting voice Leon said, "Joe, it's OK. You have to go to school. It's OK. You can sit with me." Since he was someone I knew, I felt safe.

When I looked around, it seemed that all the students were looking at me. I felt so embarrassed. They must have understood how frightened I was because I could see the sympathy in their faces. The bus driver closed the door and continued driving toward Goodwill Grade School. I began to calm down.

The older Daniels girl held my hand as I got off the bus. “Your teacher’s name is Miss Benton and you’re going to like her.” She then led me into Miss Benton’s first grade classroom and told the teacher who I was.

Miss Benton was a kind woman about twenty-five years old, neatly dressed and who walked with a limp. On her left leg, she wore a metal brace, due to polio. “Joe, why don’t you sit down here with me and tell me all about yourself?” she said, smiling. She pointed to the smallest chair I had ever seen. It was just my size.

When she found out that I was only five years old, she took me to the principal’s office. Sitting behind a big desk was a man who said, “And who do we have here?”

“Mr. Barron, this is Joe Dobbs. He is all dressed up in his new overalls for his very first day at school. But he’s five years old,” she said.

Mr. Barron was a short, chubby man wearing a brown suit. As he greeted me, he did not get up but rolled his office chair around the end of the desk.

“Joe, we’re glad you came to our school today,” he said. I liked him. “But you’re going to have to save those new bib overalls for next year. You have to be six years old to start school,” Mr. Barron said.

“Miss Benton told me that you could write your name and count to one hundred. That’s very good, but you still have to wait until next year.” Mr. Baron was smiling as he turned and whispered something to Miss Benton.

I spent the remainder of the day in Miss Benton’s room. My fear was gone and I rode the school bus back to the bus stop that afternoon with no problem.

Mom came running out of the house to meet me. She was wearing her apron and had flour dough on her hands. “How did you do?” she asked.

“The man told me I had to be six years old. And I’ll have to save my new overalls until next year,” I said. She looked disappointed.

I was too embarrassed to tell my parents about running from the bus. Mom never mentioned the incident until much later. I think that Leon Fields told her or maybe Mrs. Daniels. I don’t remember anyone ever teasing me about trying to escape that day.

Sixty-six years later while writing about this episode, I resolved my embarrassment concerning my behavior that first day of school. I had never ridden a school bus. I'm not sure I had ever seen a school bus before. I had never been to church or any place where there was a crowd of people. The nearest church at the time was miles away and we had only mules and a wagon for transportation. Only five years old at the time, I think I can be excused for running away from that bus.

# ONE-ROOM SCHOOL

In September of 1940, I was enrolled at Goodwill Grade School and my teacher was Miss Benton, whom I had met the year before. But I wouldn't be going there long. Through the FSA, we had purchased a new farm. Dad had sold our place and we were moving to a new farm at Round Hill, about three miles north of Goodwill. Having the opportunity of moving to a new house was very exciting for my parents.

We moved in January of 1941, but the house was still under construction. Down near Mr. James Strong's farm there was an old house where we lived temporarily until our house was finished. It was very small and down near Shelby Slough. I remember cracks in the floor and my mom complaining about it being too cold for the baby.

Dad had to go over a quarter of a mile to get to the fields he was plowing for the spring planting. We were in that old house about two months.

Our new house was white and about forty yards away from the gravel road. There were three bedrooms, a living room and a dining room. A handy food pantry adjoined the kitchen. The entire home was wired for electricity but the Rural Electric Administration would not run power lines until after the end of World War II. Our bathroom was used for storage because we had no indoor plumbing.

The barn, smokehouse and chicken house were all constructed from rough oak lumber and stained green. The outhouse was a two-holer. I would never understand two- and three-hole outhouses. It must have been a status symbol. I could not recall a time when more than one person would be in the outside toilet at the same time.

I remember the families that lived close. The James Strong family was the closest neighbor. Clarence Brakefield and his wife were friends with Mom and Dad. They were all good neighbors.

The roads were bad and there were very few automobiles. Mr. Brakefield had an old pickup truck but most everyone rode horses. My first day of attending Round Hill School, I rode behind Mr. Strong on his horse.

Winter mornings were always brisk and cool. The leaves had fallen off the oak, hackberry and sweetgum trees. There was always the faint smell of wood smoke in the air because every family heated and cooked with wood. From a neighbor's barn I heard a cow calling her calf.

In the distance, you could hear Mr. Fowler's jackass braying. He was the only jack in the entire community. Mr. Fowler kept him to breed to mares to raise mules, which were used as draft animals in the fields. On a clear morning his braying could be heard for almost a mile.

I was headed to Round Hill School, about a quarter mile from our farm. It was a one-room school with three grades dating back to before the Civil War. Every morning, I waited for fellow students who lived on farms farther down the road to come along so we could walk to school together.

The Turner family were sharecroppers on the Benton Farm. They lived down where the road ended at the Beouf River. Their house was on the bank of the river just up the hill from the community swimming hole. Paul's brother, Bill, was in my class. We were both seven years old and in the second grade.

Mrs. Turner was a nice lady and loved children. Regardless of how dirty we were, she would invite us in to have cake or cookies. Every family was poor but she always managed to have some kind of sweets ready for us. I thought she was a very pretty lady with her black curly hair and average size. She had a beautiful voice and you could hear her singing when she was in her kitchen.

"Joe, your dad and I do not approve of you playing with the Turner boys," Mom said. I could not believe what she was saying. My first thought was that possibly she had heard some of the cuss words the boys used when they thought there were no grownups near. They were teaching me words that I had never heard. "That family is just strange," she added.

"Mom, Mrs. Turner is such a nice woman. She feeds us cakes and pies and invites me to spend the night at their house," I said in Mrs. Turner's defense. "You should visit her, for she always asks how you are doing. I wish you could hear her sing. Why don't you want me playing with Paul and Bill?" I inquired. "I think that they're a very nice family."

"I just don't," she said, not wanting to give me any explanation.

"Mom, Paul and Bill are my best friends. I know Mr. and Mrs. Turner like me," I said, "I just don't see why you and dad don't want me visiting the Turners. They are good neighbors."

"Well, if you must know, they believe in reincarnation and that is evil," she explained.

"What is reincarnation?" I asked. That was a word that I had not heard before. Maybe it was an ugly word that seven-year-olds were not supposed to use.

"Never mind, you just stay away from the Turners," she said. Mom never attempted to explain reincarnation to me. I would be an adult before reincarnation explained so many of the mysteries of life -- some that had concerned me even as a child.

"I'm so glad we're finally through picking cotton," said Paul Turner, who was eight years old. "I thought we would never get done," he said, throwing a rock in the water of the road ditch as we walked to school. "My dad is taking the last wagon load to the cotton gin today."

"We got all ours picked, too. No more going to the cotton field after school," I said, as we walked along the road.

"We still have some corn in the fields," I said, as we approached the schoolhouse. Miss Clara, who was standing at the top of the tall steps ringing a hand bell, interrupted me.

"You boys hurry, it's time to start. I will not put up with you being late," she scolded. Miss Clara Gilbert was an old maid schoolteacher. We always addressed her as "Miss Clara" instead of Miss Gilbert. I never heard anyone -- including grownups -- refer to her as "Miss Gilbert."

She was born in 1895, a very tall woman who walked with long strides like she was plowing in the field, which I am sure she had done. Her long print dresses came down to her ankles and her graying red hair was rolled into a bun on the back of her head. When she was outside, she covered her head with a bonnet. Her freckled face was wrinkled and her piercing dark eyes gave you a feeling of stern gentleness.

Not owning any means of transportation, she could often be seen walking to the country store. Regardless of the weather, almost every weekend she would walk through the wooded swamps to her home in Red Wing, several miles distant. If she were going any distance, she would walk with a long stick or walking staff, which she could use to protect herself from an aggressive dog.

Miss Clara conducted a disciplined school that today would be considered child abusive. She was known to slap a child with an open hand and in one corner of the room she kept long, braided willow switches. These were frequently used on the older unruly boys. I don't remember her ever using a switch on any of the girls. Whatever discipline problems occurred in her classes, she resolved very quickly.

Round Hill School was a wooden structure built upon brick columns that were high enough for a seven-year-old to walk under. The high foundation was to protect the schoolhouse from flooding, though I'm sure that the 1927 Flood of the Mississippi River got up in or near it. When it was raining, we would play under the floor.

The schoolhouse was a big three-room structure. All of the rooms were very large, with rows of big windows. In the 1920s, before the construction of Goodwill Grade School, all of the rooms were used for classes. During the years I attended, we used only one classroom. One room was used for storage and Miss Clara lived in the third.

When school was in session, the students ran up the long wooden steps and into the room and immediately went to our respective desks. The smell of wood burning in the big cast iron heater mixing with the odor of the oil-treated hardwood floors was a reminder that it was back to the books.

Our desks were arranged in three locations for the first, second and third grade classes. I realized later that being exposed to the third grade lessons when you were a first-grader was an advantage.

But one thing was a mystery. The reading books told about how much fun it was for Dick and Jane to visit their grandmother on the farm. We all worked on family farms and failed to get excited about someone's visit to the grandparents' farm.

We had a mid-morning recess and everyone went outside to play if weather permitted. Playground equipment was non-existent, but we had a good time. The boys generally played "tag" or shot marbles. The girls jumped rope and played hop-scotch.

One December morning, immediately after we returned to the classroom following recess, there came a knock at the classroom door. Every child looked up. It was rare that anyone would visit the school. All of our parents were busy working in the fields.

"Just continue your reading," said Miss Clara, as she went to open the big wooden door.

It was Mr. Coody, whose farm adjoined the school property. He and Mrs. Coody were in their later years and didn't have any children attending the school, which made his visit more noteworthy.

"Miss Clara, the Japanese bombed Pearl Harbor yesterday. Many of our service men were killed." There were three women with Mr. Coody. They were all crying. As the crying grew louder, all the students were wondering just what this was all about.

"Oh, my God!" exclaimed Miss Clara. "That is just terrible."

"I heard it on the radio," explained Mr. Coody. "Folks everywhere are very upset. President Roosevelt is going to make a statement on the radio."

There was a tap on my shoulder and I turned around. Jimmy Strong, who sat at the desk behind me, whispered, "Where is Pearl Harbor?"

"I don't know," I replied, "but I think it's in Arkansas.

In 1941, there was no electricity or running water in any of the homes in our region. If your family happened to have a radio, it was a battery type. The batteries were as large as a modern automobile battery but were dry cell which meant they were not rechargeable. The life of the battery depended on how large the radio was and the amount of power it consumed.

Sometimes the battery ran down or lost all of its power. It could be several months before the family had enough money to purchase a new one. Most people acquired new batteries by mail order from the Sears & Roebuck catalog. All members of the family were warned to use the radio sparingly.

The radio was the main source of entertainment. Families who didn't own a radio often gathered at someone's home on Saturday night to listen to the Grand Ole Opry. Every evening, there were dramas and live music programs broadcast on the three radio networks -- ABC, CBS and NBC. Occasionally there were live broadcasts of prizefights from Madison Square Garden in New York City.

At that time in Northeast Louisiana, the radio was the only source of news from the outside world. Newspapers were not that available. A month or more might pass before a farmer would travel the twelve miles into Oak Grove where a newspaper could be purchased. Most people were busy working their farms, striving to exist, and news from the outside world was not a top priority. I remember that an occasional family would subscribe to the weekly Grit newspaper, which would be delivered by mail.

It would be many years before I understood what a contribution Miss Clara Gilbert made to our lives. She was not only a very capable teacher, but genuinely interested in the education of poor rural farm children. It was a sacrifice to leave her comfortable home and farm at Red Wing and live in one of the classrooms in the old Round Hill Schoolhouse.

She was seventy-two years old when the school closed and she retired. Miss Clara Gilbert died in 1980 at the age of eighty-five. I will never forget her.

It is somewhat ironic that my mother lived all of her adult life in the lowlands of the Mississippi River and never learned to swim or to tolerate snakes.

Early one brisk October morning after I had turned nine years old, I was helping my dad with the barn chores. He had just taught me how to milk a cow.

"Joe, you milk that young muley cow and I will milk Pansy because the young cow does not give as much milk," explained my dad. (A muley cow does not have horns.) We were milking two cows at that time, which provided our family with milk and butter. There was enough milk produced that Mom could churn and mold a pound or two of butter each week to be used for bartering at the country store.

The cows were fed in barn stalls and milking was done by hand as they ate from the feed trough. Across the aisle was the corncrib.

"Hey, Dad, come here! I just saw this big black snake crawl under the floor of the corncrib. He had some small yellow spots all over his back," I exclaimed. I had the milk bucket in my hand as I was going into the stall to milk the muley cow. "That snake is really big. He must be as long as I am tall!"

"That's a king snake, son," explained Dad. "He's lived in this barn ever since we moved here." Dad never stopped milking because I could hear the streams of milk striking the bottom of the milk pail. "They're harmless. They eat other snakes but their main food is mice. He lives off the mice and rats that come to feed off our corn in the crib."

"As much time as I've spent shelling corn and picking off peanuts and I haven't seen him til today!" I exclaimed. "Boy, he is big!" I sat down on the stool and began milking the muley.

"Son, you gotta promise me one thing. You must never tell your mom about that king snake living here. If she knew it lived under the corncrib she would never come in here to get chicken feed," said Dad. "And that means you'd have to feed the chickens." I could hear the milk streaming into his bucket. "If she saw it, she'd probably chop its head off with a hoe."

"Why don't you just tell her that it is harmless?" I asked.

"She's so afraid of snakes that it would make no difference," he answered as my cow switched her tail to ward off flies, striking me in the back of the head.

"We don't want to lose that snake and I just think it's much better not to tell her," said Dad. "I'm finished, so hurry with your milking. We need to get that corn out of the field and in the crib today before the rains set in." Thank goodness, Mom never found out that a snake lived under the floor of our corncrib.

It was September of 1944 and we had started picking cotton. The cotton plants were higher than my head and covered with green leaves that would not fall off until the first frost. Every plant was loaded with open cotton bolls that looked like snow.

"I believe we'll harvest two bales to the acre this year," said Dad, who was picking two rows beside me. "This has to be the best crop we've ever raised," he added, shaking the cotton down the nine-foot sack he was pulling with the wide strap over his shoulder.

"Walter, if we do that good, maybe you can buy a used farm tractor so you won't have to make another crop with them horses," said Mom. She was picking the two rows on the other side of me. They were both pulling long cotton sacks that could hold as much as sixty-five pounds before you had to go to the scales. Being smaller, I used a seven-foot cotton sack. At the scales, the sacks were weighed and emptied into the wagon, then we started filling them again. My sister, Lucille, was five years old. She was playing with her dolls in the shade of the partially loaded wagon.

"It would be so much easier and then we would not have to raise all that corn and hay to feed the horses," he agreed. There was the sudden loud barking of our dogs about forty yards deeper into the cotton field. Dad kept two Walker foxhounds and we had another pet dog, Spot, that I used for rabbit hunting.

"Why are the dogs barking?" I asked. "Maybe they've jumped a rabbit." Cottontail rabbits were everywhere before the extensive use of pesticides and herbicides.

"It's not a rabbit -- they are bayed (staying in the same spot). If it was a rabbit, the dogs would be running and my hounds are trained not to run rabbits," said Dad. He always boasted that his foxhounds would not chase rabbits.

I wanted an excuse to take a break from stooping over picking cotton so I said, "I'll walk down the field and see what the dogs are barking at." I took off the strap of my cotton sack and proceeded to walk toward the barking dogs. When I got within about twenty steps of the dogs, I could hear the rattles of rattlesnakes. It was a frightening sound and I could not see the snakes among the grass and tall cotton stalks. Not being able to detect just where the rattling was located, I turned and ran back to where Dad was picking cotton.

"It's a bunch of rattlesnakes, Dad. I could not tell how many but it sounds like a bunch!"

"Son, run to the house and get the shotgun and some Number 6 shotgun shells and hurry," said Dad.

Mom had taken off her cotton sack and gone to the wagon where Lucille was playing.

The house was about 300 yards away but I ran all the way and back, bringing the double-barreled shotgun and six shells. It was a lot for me to carry and I was exhausted by the time I got back. Breathing hard, I handed the gun and shells to my dad. He ran down into the field toward where the dogs were continuing to bark. We could hear him calling the dogs away from the snakes. Then he fired the shotgun twice and all was quiet. I had rested enough that I was breathing normal, so I walked down to where he was standing among the tall cotton stalks.

"Joe, you take the shotgun and I will bring the snakes," he said, handing me the gun. We started walking out of the field to the end of the rows where the wagon was parked. Dad had two diamondback rattlers that were each more than five feet long -- the largest that I had ever seen.

They were such beautiful specimens with the perfect black diamond designs down the center of their backs from head to tail.

"One has twelve rattles and a button and the other has thirteen rattles and a button,' said Dad, holding up the snakes so I could see their tails. "This time of year the rattlesnakes are blind just before they shed their skins. They could not see to escape the dogs," he explained. As I looked up from the snakes, I saw the backs of Mom and my sister walking toward the house. They were more than halfway there.

"Well, son, it's you and me until the first frost. Your mom will not come back to the field till the leaves are gone."

"Maybe she'll put on her rubber boots and come back and help us with the picking," I said hopefully.

"Son, I think it will take more than gum boots to get her back in this field. Come on, we got a bale of cotton to pick," said Dad as he walked down the row to the spot where we had left our cotton sacks.

# IT'S A PLANE

It was June of 1945 and it was a hot summer. My dad had always wanted to raise alfalfa hay to feed the horses, but the acidity of our soil was not the best for growing it. Mr. Jesse Peterson, the agent from the County Extension Service, determined we could add lime to the soil and correct the problem. It was successful. If we had a good year, we would get six cuttings of hay from the field on the ridge behind our house.

"Joe, I know it's a little early. We should let the alfalfa grow another two weeks but the baby is due," said Dad.

I was eleven years old. It was early in the morning and we were in the barn milking. We could hear Mr. Ed Strong's rooster crowing. His farm was next to ours. Down by the pond, Mom's gander goose was honking. It was also the home of several domestic ducks and two white geese.

Five years earlier Dad had dug the pond in the pasture to provide water for our farm animals. He borrowed a slip from a neighbor and -- using our team of horses -- he scooped out a hole about six feet deep and approximately thirty feet across.

The slip was made of heavy gauge metal. It looked like a metal box with the top and one end removed. Extending out the back were two heavy wooded handles, like a wheel barrow. With the horses hitched to the slip, Dad would lift up the handles, causing the sharp bottom edge of the open end to dig into the earth. When the scoop filled with dirt -- much like a drag line bucket -- it would be pulled some distance by the team.

By lifting the handles, it would flip over toward the team, landing upside down. The horses would continue slowly moving forward, empting the slip. This method was the common way of moving dirt with teams of horses or mules. Before mechanized earth-moving equipment, this method was used in the construction of highways.

"What does the alfalfa field have to do with Mom having a baby?" I asked. I put some cotton seed meal and cracked corn in the trough for the two cows to eat while we were milking.

"Dr. Biggs has a Piper Cub. When it's time for him to deliver the baby, he's coming out here in his airplane," said Dad. I could hear the streams of milk striking the empty milk bucket. He had started milking.

"He can't land his airplane in the road, can he?" I asked. I had never seen a plane land or take off.

"Oh no, but Doc told me that the alfalfa field is long enough. He flew over the other day and looked at it from the air. But the alfalfa can't be knee deep or the plane won't be able to land safely," he explained. We have to cut the hay even if it is a little early."

I hoped I could invite Jimmy Strong to come over and watch when the plane landed. His family lived on the farm that adjoined the back of our place. His dad was James Strong, an older brother of Ed. I would have bet that Jimmy had never seen a plane land and take off.

"Your Grandma Berry is coming to stay with us until your mom can take care of the baby," Dad said. The medical profession at that time insisted that women stay in bed for twenty-one days after giving birth.

It all happened on a beautiful, clear, hot Wednesday. I don't recall just how Dr. Biggs was notified that my mom was in labor, because there were no telephones in our area at that time. We didn't have an automobile so I assume that a neighbor drove the twelve miles to Oak Grove to notify the doctor.

"Joe, you stay here at the house with your mother while I go to the alfalfa patch," Dad said. He had a white pillowcase in his hand. "Dr. Biggs wanted me to signal him so he wouldn't land in the wrong field."

"But Dad, Lucille is here with Mom. I want to be up close when the airplane lands," I pleaded. My sister was six years old.

"You can watch the plane land from our back door," he said as he turned and walked toward the hay field. "You come for me if she needs me."

The landing site was only about 200 yards from the back of our house, so I would have a good view of it. At the end of the alfalfa field was a cotton shed. During harvest time, this building was used to store picked cotton until we had enough to take to the cotton gin. Dad took a hoe from the shed and tied the white pillowcase to the handle, making a white flag.

It wasn't long before we heard the drone of the engine of the doctor's small plane. It approached from the east, flying over Mr. Ed Strong's farm. I ran out into the back yard. Dad was waving his flag.

The yellow Piper Cub flew over the landing site and circled over the Del Rio family farm that joined us on the west. I could see it coming straight for the hay field, but it seemed to be going too fast. If Dr. Biggs could not stop the plane, it would crash into the cotton shed or go into the plowed ground of the adjoining cotton field.

I looked around and Lucille was standing in the back door clapping her hands. The plane landed in the field and stopped long before it got to the cotton shed. A small door under the wing opened and the doctor stepped out. Reaching back in the plane, he got a black bag as he spoke to Dad.

The 22nd of June was momentous: the plane arrived, the baby came and Grandma arrived.

Lucille and I had a new baby brother with a healthy set of lungs. "His name is Dwayne Eugene. Ain't he a pretty baby?" Mom announced as we stood by the bed looking at our two-day-old, crying brother.

A few days later, I walked into the house to get a drink of water. The baby was in his cradle in the living room, crying at the top of his lungs. Grandma was in the kitchen cooking dinner. Mom was in her bedroom. I was sure she had to be awake with all the noise.

"Grandma, is there something I could do to stop that baby from crying?" I asked.

"Just let him cry. That will make his lungs strong," she said, never looking up from the green beans she was snapping. The pile of fresh picked beans was lying on her apron in her lap. I went back to the garden to pick some tomatoes for dinner. Grandma had had fourteen kids -- seven boys and seven girls.

When Dwayne was about three years old, I caught a little striped green garter snake near the fig tree in the back yard. Mom was out in front of the house, taking advantage of the warm spring weather and working in one of her beloved flower beds. She probably feared snakes more than she feared death. Though these snakes were harmless, I didn't want her to see it.

With the little garter snake in my hand, I opened the screen door and looked in the kitchen. There was Dwayne standing by the table munching on a cookie, wearing only a pair of training pants. I quietly walked up to him and squatted down on my toes so he could get a good view.

"Hey, Butch, look. I caught a pretty little snake," I whispered. I don't know who gave him the nickname, but we all called him "Butch."

"Snake," he said, with no fear in his face. At that instant, the garter snake wiggled and popped out of my hand, landed on the linoleum floor and zipped under the refrigerator. In his excitement, Butch screamed and jumped up and down, laughing. Then I heard the front door slam. It was Mom rushing into the kitchen.

"What happened? Why is the baby screaming?" she asked. Always short, she had grown heavier through the years. She had on a print work dress and a bonnet to protect her head from the sun. I dreaded telling her I had let a snake loose in the house.

About the time I thought she was ready to go back out to her flower bed, Butch bent over, cookie in one hand and pointing with the other, said, "Snake! Snake!"

Instantly, Mom jumped up and stood on the seat of one of the ladder-back kitchen chairs. "Oh my God!" she screamed. "Joe, did you bring a snake into this house?"

Our refrigerator was an early model made by General Electric with the refrigeration coils mounted on top. The coil assembly looked like a large bucket turned upside down. It had four eight-inch-high legs on the bottom that created an open space under the appliance.

Butch pointed under the fridge, saying, "Look, snake! Look, snake!" I got on my hands and knees to reach under the refrigerator to retrieve the escaped reptile.

"Get that baby back!" Mom screamed. "He's gonna git snake bit." Trying to control my laughter, I finally caught the garter snake.

"Mom, it's only a harmless little green snake," I explained while walking toward the back door.

"I don't care, just git the thing out of this house," she exclaimed, still standing on the chair.

As I released the snake in the tall grass near the garden gate, I warned it, "If she ever catches sight of you, she will chop you up with her hoe."

Dwayne was seven years old when I left home. Like the rest of us, he also worked hard on the family farm. One summer when he was about twelve, he came out to visit my family when we lived in Houston, Texas. Growing up on the farm, in a sheltered environment, I wanted to show him a good time on his very first visit that far away from home.

We took him to the beach in Galveston for his first view of the ocean. He and I went to the Drag Races on the Gulf Freeway between Houston and Galveston, which sparked an interest in cars that he never lost.

After finishing high school, he joined the U.S. Air Force. He married his sweetheart, Martha, a very pretty woman. She had grown up in Greenville and had the loveliest southern accent. I could talk to her on the phone and think I was in Mississippi. Dwayne and Martha had one child, a son they named Dee.

The phone rang. It was early on Monday morning, July 20, 1981. It was my sister, Lucille. "I hate to have to tell you, but Dwayne was killed yesterday evening," I marveled at the calmness in her voice at such a tragic moment.

After a long pause, I asked, "What happened?"

"He was in his little Datsun pickup. He and Dee had been out in the country near Swiftwater to get some watermelons, when a drunk driver ran a stop sign and hit them. The force broke his neck," she explained. "He died instantly. Dee is in the hospital, but he is going to survive." (Swiftwater was a crossroads location near Greenville, Mississippi.) Dwayne and his son had been less than two miles from home.

"I'll get some things done here at the store so I can get away. I should be there late tomorrow," I said. My van would need new tires to make the trip from West Virginia to Mississippi. "I'll bring Andy with me." Andy was my seven-year-old grandson.

Dwayne had been a good man, admired by friends and family. He never drank booze or played music in bars and honkytonks like Dennis and I had. When my dad's health began to fail, Dwayne and Lucille took care of our parents. Because I lived so far away and was struggling with my own family, I felt bad that I could not provide any assistance toward their care.

Since Dad had passed six years earlier, and Mom lived alone, I felt I should call Mom. I was sure she must be devastated.

"Hello," she said into the phone. Her voice sounded the same as always.

"Mom, it's Joe. With Dwayne's sudden death, I'm worried about you. How are you doing?" I asked.

"Oh, I'm doing OK, but you should call Dennis. He's having a hard time," she said. And then, she added, "Son, it's the Lord's will."

All my life her reply to any question or event she could not explain was, "It's the Lord's will."

Mom only finished the eighth grade. With her limited education, the many questions that I asked as an inquisitive child were easily answered with "It's the Lord's will." For instance, as a preschool child, I asked why the yeast caused the homemade bread to rise. And as a child growing up on a rural farm in the swamps of Louisiana, I had all these questions about how farm animals reproduced and how the combustion engine worked on Mrs. Field's Maytag washing machine.

This answer applied to any question, regardless of the nature. Of course, it must have been her security in time of crisis. I realize there were times when the phrase was used as an escape, but in other times it was a symbol of her faith in God.

I told her that Andy and I were coming the next day and hung up the phone. I kept thinking how she got so much from her religion. That was what religion should to do -- provide needed strength during the difficult times in life.

Lucille called me back late Monday night.

"Joe, they're having the funeral tomorrow," she said. "The people at the funeral home suggested having the burial as soon as possible. This is often done with sudden, unexpected deaths."

"I can't believe they're burying him that soon," I said.

"They say it's much better for the family to have closure as soon as possible," she explained.

"I thought you had to wait three days to bury someone," I said

"Not in Mississippi," Lucille replied.

"Anything must be legal in Mississippi. If we left now, we couldn't get there in time for the funeral," I said.

Lucille offered to have the funeral postponed so I could attend.

I thought for a few seconds and made a decision. "No, it's not that important for me to be there. Funerals are for the living. Our brother is gone. I do appreciate you calling and thanks for all the help you're giving Mom."

Grieving is greater when death comes unexpectedly to one in the prime of his life. I did not have any regrets about missing the memorial service of my brother. It would have been better for me to have been with my family, but I certainly did not want to be responsible for them delaying the funeral.

Dwayne was the most successful of my siblings. He and Martha built a trucking business. He was highly respected by many of the family. Years later, at the Berry reunion, Uncle Lloyd, one of Mom's brothers, turned to me and said, "I just want you to know, Joe, I loved that Dwayne. I miss him. I still carry a picture of him in my billfold." He reached in his back pocket, took out his wallet and showed me a photo of Dwayne.

My first experience with death came when I was five years old and my Uncle Dewey died of diphtheria. He was six months older than me. We stayed at my grandparents' home near Greenville, Mississippi, for several days before and after the funeral. Some of my very first memories were of all the grieving the family endured.

It was a big gathering since Dewey was the youngest of fourteen children. Of course, the young ones all enjoyed playing with their cousins until the day of the burial ceremony. Witnessing the lowering of the small casket down into the ground, we realized why we were there.

In their grief, parents were unable to explain death to the children, possibly because it was never discussed until someone died. At such a time children are distracted by all the emotions that go with death. Seeing our parents and all the other grown-ups crying and grieving made a young child feel insecure.

It is possible that spending my youth on a farm and witnessing the birth and death of so many animals, plants and even large trees, instilled in me the fact that everything that lives eventually dies

A philosopher once wrote, "Anything that has a beginning has an end." The sorrow and grieving over the loss of someone you love, I experienced and I understood.

For some people, death is something that they totally ignore. Then, when it comes upon them unexpectedly, it leaves them in total shock and emotionally out of control.

In our society, death is primarily ignored and seldom discussed except when someone wants to sell us a life insurance policy. We search our vocabulary to find words or phrases that we can substitute for the word "death" that will soften the fact, like "pass away," "going to the other side," "meeting his maker," "crossing over," "only sleeping," "going to heaven" or "joining their friends and loved ones over there."

Many of our religions fail to prepare us to face the certainty of the death of a loved one, a dear friend, or our own demise. At a wake, people will still not discuss death but talk about the weather, the stock market, or some item in the news, with the assumption that "if I just keep my attention elsewhere, this will never happen to me." I always believed that we are all souls temporarily occupying a body until it is involved in an accident or we wear it out.

It was in Kinshasa, Zaire, that I witnessed a young woman being fatally struck by an automobile as she ran across a busy intersection. That was the first time I witnessed a human being killed. A cloak of sadness immediately covered me.

The people in the street and along the sidewalks became hysterical over her accidental death. A crowd quickly gathered around the still body. People began jumping up and down, swinging their arms and screaming. It was not anger, I was told. It was just the way some African tribal cultures reacted to death.

I have a dear friend who spent time in therapy because she could not continue life normally after her cat died. To some pet owners, the death of a dog or cat has an impact close to or equal to losing a human friend. It could also be that the amount of love and joy the pet or person gives us determines the amount and depth of our grieving at their deaths.

I heard someone in my family question God's decision to end a life. I just don't feel that I am capable of questioning God's decision. Maybe that's where "Thy will be done, not mine" is supposed to help us accept the things in life we don't understand. I like the phrase in the old Christian hymn: "Farther along we'll know all about it."

I believe that death is like a good dream. It's as natural as breathing and sometimes an escape from physical or emotional suffering. But the fact is, you don't know when it is coming, so many of us live life as if death would never come to claim us.

# MISTA' RED

Leon Berry, next to the oldest of my mom's seven brothers, was born in 1913 when my mother, Lillie, was three years old. Like the rest, he grew up as a sharecropper's child in the Mississippi Delta.

He married in 1955 when he was forty-two years old. Many years earlier he had planned to marry a young woman but she died of cancer at an early age. Mom always said that he was so in love with this lovely girl that he never got over her death, which was the main reason he never married until he was in his forties.

Leon was my favorite uncle. There were several things that contributed to his popularity with my cousins and me. The first was his genuine love for children. He always had a jolly, loving greeting for every one of us. As far back as I can remember, he would reach into his pocket and greet you with the gift of a quarter. That would buy you five candy bars.

It is possible that he was even more liked by the boys since he was a fisherman. When he returned home from the South Pacific after World War II, he became a commercial fisherman. Over the years he fished commercially in all the lakes along the Mississippi River in the Delta region. I spent several weeks during three consecutive summers living in his fishing camp and helping to bring in the catch.

On the farm, there was a period in summer between the last plowing of the fields and the actual harvest that was referred to as "lay-by time." This was sometime between the middle of July and the middle of August, depending on how much or how little it rained. Before families began using LP gas for cooking and heating, many farmers spent lay-by time cutting wood for the winter. With the use of gas, we had a short vacation from working in the fields before the extremely laborious fall harvest began.

The first time my father suggested I spend those weeks helping Uncle Leon was in 1948. The rest of the family would be visiting kinfolks in Greenville.

I couldn't believe it. This would be the most exciting thing to happen all year. Up to that time, all of my fishing had been done on the Beouf River, which was only a half mile from our house. I'd never ridden in a motor boat. Except for the times I could borrow someone's homemade boat, I'd always fished from the riverbank. This was going to be an opportunity for me to do some real fishing.

At Uncle Leon's, I'd get to fish and ride in my uncle's boat that was powered by an outboard motor on Lake Whittington. It would be hot out on the lake in July, working the heavy nets, but we'd catch a lot of fish. This type of commercial fishing would be great fun for a thirteen-year-old farm boy.

After my return home, I'd have all these wonderful stories to tell my friends. Not only that, Uncle Leon might put out some gill nets on Lake Ferguson, which was the beautiful lake near Greenville.

"We're driving over to Mr. Berry's house tomorrow morning," said Dad. Mr. Berry was my grandfather -- my mother's father. This was great news! I hurried to pack the things I would need for the next two weeks. With the excitement of anticipating the trip, I had trouble sleeping that night.

We had been at my grandmother's house about two hours when Uncle Leon's pickup pulled into the yard. The truck had some rust spots and looked as though it had never been washed except by the summer rains. In the back, the bed overflowed with a couple of fishing nets in burlap bags, several buckets, one washtub, more than a dozen cork floats used as buoys for the nets, two very worn boat paddles and an old raincoat. And it always smelled of dead fish.

"Boy, you look like a farmer, but we're going to turn you into a fisherman," Leon said as he stepped out, with a big smile on his round, sunburned face. Looking at his face and bare arms you could tell that he worked out in the sun. "I'm glad you're here, Joe," he said.

Uncle Leon was close to six feet tall, stocky built and even at thirty-five years old, had been mostly bald ever since I could remember. An old, worn and faded hat covered what little hair he had, which was bright red. His close friends and family knew him as "Red."

The percentage of sharecropper children in the Delta who finished high school was very low. We never talked about his school days, so I never learned the extent of his formal education.

During the Great Depression, there was no work so he joined the National Guard and served two years of active duty. Then he returned to Greenville, Mississippi, where he worked as a rigger for a company constructing the Greenville Bridge. That bridge connected Mississippi with Chico, Arkansas. It was completed in 1940.

Leon and four of his brothers served and returned safely from World War II. At this time, Leon was still serving in the National Guard on inactive duty.

"Uncle Leon, I'm excited about getting to spend time fishing with you. What's the biggest fish you caught today?" I asked.

"Well, I guess the largest one in the nets this morning was a gar that weighed ninety-four pounds. I think that he's the big one that's been tearing up my nets. One morning, there was a hole in it you could drive a car through. I'm sure he's the one who made the hole so I was pleased to catch him. He was a scissor-bill and about as long as you are tall," Leon explained while putting his arm around my shoulders.

"Tomorrow we'll get up real early and go up to my camp on Lake Whittington. You can help put out two more gill nets," Leon said. "The fish are running good on that lake so we should catch a lot of fish."

"How long are the gill nets?" I asked as we walked toward my grandmother's house.

"They're about 100 yards long. Running those nets is hard work and sure makes you hungry. I hope Mama has something cooked," Leon said opening the door and looking toward the kitchen. I could hear Grandma in the kitchen. The house smelled of fried chicken and fresh baked blackberry cobbler.

In the early morning light, the surface of Lake Whittington was like a mirror. There wasn't a ripple anywhere. Because of the mist hanging just above the water, you could barely see the willows on the bank almost a quarter of a mile away.

"You know, Joe, at one time this was the Mississippi River. She changed her course and left this beautiful lake," Leon explained. We were up early to run the nets before the summer sun became intense. "That was a good spot where we set those nets yesterday. We could have a boatload of fish this morning," he said.

"I hope we catch a big one today," I said. I was at a place of pride for me, the helm of the flat-bottomed fishing boat. Uncle Leon let me operate the outboard motor, which left behind a wake that interrupted the glassy surface of the lake.

We caught a variety of fish, buffalo, spoonbill catfish, drum and several other species of catfish. There was also the occasional gar and large turtle. Even in the unkind summer sun, I was having the time of my life. The hard work was nothing to a farm boy. I had never seen so many fish.

Looking at the bottom of the boat that was covered with fish, Leon said, "I told you that was a good spot. I've set nets there before. Just look at that load of fish."

"Where will you sell them?" I asked. We had arrived back at the shore near our fish camp. It was still morning but the temperature was rising.

"We'll dress out the spoonbill catfish and pack them in barrels of dry ice and ship 'em to New York," he said while he was sorting the fish and placing them in different large containers. "The remaining fish we'll sell to families out in the country."

"New York?" I asked. "Who in New York buys fish caught in Mississippi?"

"The spoonbill is sold in restaurants in the big cities, where it's considered a delicacy," Leon said. "Spoonbill is probably my favorite fish when it's prepared properly. It has no bones," he added.

After the barrels were filled and shipped to New York, all the remaining fish were packed in containers of ice, which were placed in the back of that old pickup truck. We headed out of town for the rural farm area. Other than the actual removing of the catch from the nets, this was my favorite part of the fishing experience with Uncle Leon.

Scattered throughout the Delta along the country roads were old farmhouses. Some of these were the homes of poor black families who supplied labor for the same fields their ancestors had worked as slaves. When farm labor was replaced by newly developed farm machinery in the 1950s, these families migrated to the towns and cities in order to find work.

Leon brought the truck to a stop on the side of the gravel road in front of a run-down, old wooden, four-room farmhouse, and said, "This is a family that has bought fish from me for years." Immediately the screen door opened and out came a black woman wearing a faded print dress but no shoes. There was a white cloth tied around her head.

"ista Red, I am sho glad you come by, cause we-all hongry fur a mess o' fish," she said, walking toward the truck. A girl wearing a soiled dress, not even ten years old, followed her, a baby on her hip.

"Sissie, how y'all doin'?" Leon asked. "I got a nice load of fish." Without answering him, Sissy turned and looked at the girl. "Child,

you take dat baby back in da house, rhat now." Then, she turned to Leon and explained, "Mista Red, my man ain't had much woik lately. I thought I might give you some butter beans that I picked this moning fa a small fish," she offered.

"Sissie, we got a big garden and I don't need the butter beans, but you just take one of them buffalo fish and feed the family. You can pay me next time," said Leon with his big smile.

A small boy ran from behind the house and up to the truck to see the fish. He was only five or six years old.

"Is this boy yours, Sissie?" Leon asked.

"Yes sa', Mista Red, that my little Johnnie," she replied.

"Come here, son," said Leon. "This is fa you," he added, handing the child a nickel. The boy took the coin and smiled, revealing two missing front teeth.

"Johnnie, what you pose' to say?" scolded Sissie.

"Thank you, sah'," said Johnnie.

Taking the fish, she placed it on the scales to see just how much money she would need when Leon came back. "Mista Red, I sho do thank you for letting me slide. You knows I always pays."

"Sissie, I sold yo mama fish. By the way, how is she doing?" he asked.

"She ain't doin' no good a'tall, Mista Red," said Sissie.

"I hope she does betta and you tell her that I asked about her," said Leon. "Yo mama is a good woman and raised a big family."

"I sho will, Mista Red. Now don't you forgit to stop at dat next house 'cause Becky and Tom moved in there and she wants a mess o' fish."

As we drove away to our next customer, Leon said, "Joe, I very seldom lose any money giving these poor people credit. Somehow they find a way to pay me. And if they don't, that's all right, too."

I have often wondered if Leon was aware of the love that these struggling families had for him. He must have sold fish like this for over forty years. He wasn't just supplying much-needed protein to their diets, but trust in his fellow man.

That summer was three years after the end of World War II. Leon talked very little about his time in the service though he did share a few things. For instance, since he had spent time in the Soloman Islands and the southern Philippines, he told me how beautiful it was in the islands of the South Pacific.

Just before he was to be discharged from the National Guard in 1940, his service was frozen and he was put in the Army as a sergeant. Soldiers that had National Guard experience became non-commissioned officers training new recruits. It was their job in boot camp to prepare them for fighting.

Uncle Leon told me that he was one of the first to go through this training. One of the drills was to crawl across a field with a machine gun firing over their heads. Of course, he thought they were firing blanks. When he rolled over onto his back to go under a wire, he saw the tracers. Then he realized that it was live machine gun fire.

Uncle Leon expressed some regrets of giving ten years of the prime of his life to the government, and went as far as saying that if any of his sons did not want to go to war, he would support them.

But I shall always remember walking places with him and hearing some friendly voice call out, "Mista Red, how you doing?"

In November of 2003, I planned a trip to Louisiana to visit my sister, Lucille, who was recovering from surgery for colon cancer.

"Lucille, how are you doing?" I asked her on the phone.

"Just fine," she replied.

"How's Parnell?" I asked. Parnell was her husband, who had suffered with severe crippling arthritis for more than twenty years. He had taken so much pain killing medication that now he was experiencing heart failure.

"About the same. He has good days and bad days," she answered.

"I'm planning to come and visit with you and Parnell about Thanksgiving," I said.

"Well, I had a call from Greenville this morning, and Uncle Leon is in the hospital. He's not expected to live long enough to come home. You might want to come earlier if you want to see him while he's still living," she said.

I asked how old Leon was.

"If he makes it until December the 10th, he'll be ninety," she answered.

On November 11, 2003, I arrived at the hospital in Greenville, Mississippi. Several of my relatives greeted me and someone told me Leon's room number. I took the elevator up.

All of his sons were there in the room, Floyd, Dewey and Jimmy. Uncle Leon was not conscious. I was too late to say a last goodbye to my favorite uncle, but I stayed for a few minutes trying to think of something comforting to say to the grieving family. The next day Mista' Red was gone.

Jimmy's wife, Helena, was one of the family that enjoyed my playing and she asked me, "Did you bring your fiddle? Dad would have wanted you to play at the funeral services." One of the sons also asked me if I would play.

"I would be more than honored to play during the services," I replied. "I would rather play for my Uncle Leon's funeral than perform at Carnegie Hall."

The funeral services were conducted in a local Church of Christ. I met the minister who had been chosen to conduct the services for my favorite uncle. He was most comforting to me and the family and I liked him.

As I sat in the chapel watching family and friends gathering to pay their respects, I thought about when I was a kid and my folks would not allow me to own a violin. They thought the fiddle was evil. Our church only had unaccompanied singing and permitted no musical instruments.

I wondered too, what the preacher's feelings were concerning my violin being played in his church. Did he think it was evil? Had there ever been a musical instrument played in this church? Though I had no intention of making anyone uncomfortable because of their religious beliefs, I was going to play my very best for Uncle Leon.

I was startled by someone gently tapping on my shoulder. It was the funeral director.

"What song are you going to play?" he whispered.

"Amazing Grace," I answered.

"After Mrs. Vera White reads a poem she has written especially for her brother, you play your song. There will be no introduction," he whispered, then walked away.

People were still arriving and taking seats in the chapel. I looked out over the crowd and did not see one black face. Where were all those black folks who loved and supported him when he had entered county politics years ago? Where were the blacks who had purchased his fish for years? Surely three or four would show up for his funeral. But no, not one African-American was there. I knew that his obituary was in the

Greenville newspaper. If you were black and lived in the Mississippi Delta, did you have to have an invitation to attend a white friend's funeral?

The minister conducted a wonderful service. Aunt Vera, Leon's sister, stood up and read a poem she had written for his upcoming ninetieth birthday party. At such a difficult time, she read with strength and conviction. I was proud of her.

I stood and played "Amazing Grace" on the violin that had been so good to me for the past ten years. I pressed hard on the bow and made a special effort to play my very best.

While I played, I thought about the times Uncle Leon and Aunt Vera had danced while my youngest brother, Dennis, and I played those old swing tunes at the Berry family reunion.

After the first verse, I moved up into the third position. Letting the drone strings sing, I did my bagpipe imitation. The chapel was filled with a sweet sound. Uncle Leon would have been pleased.

"Joe, would you play at the graveside? I would like that very much," said Aunt Thelma, Leon's widow. Her health was poor and she had lost so much weight that I didn't recognize her. Her frail body looked almost lifeless in the wheelchair.

"Yes, I will," I assured her. "Thanks for asking me."

At the graveside, I played a song that had been made popular in the 1950s by the late Red Foley, "Peace in the Valley." After the burial ceremony, I drove across the Mississippi River to Louisiana to be with my sister and her family. Along the way, I kept thinking about all those African-Americans that lived in Washington County, Mississippi, who so admired my uncle but not one had attended his funeral.

It is ironic that "Amazing Grace" was written sometime during the 1790s by a slave ship captain, John Newton. After being converted to Christianity, he became a minister of the Church of England.

"Peace in the Valley" was written by an African-American, Thomas A. Dorsey, who was from Georgia. He is considered to be the father of black gospel music.

The poem that follows was written by Vera Berry White for her brother, Leon Berry, to celebrate his ninetieth birthday on December 10, 2003. A party had been planned for the occasion. Sadly, Leon passed away on November 12, 2003. The poem was read at his services as a tribute to his life.

OUR BROTHER, LEON
By Vera Berry White

The year was nineteen hundred and thirteen,
When a baby boy appeared on the scene,
He was the second son to bless the house,
Of Rube Berry, and Lizzie his spouse,
Both parents the father and mother,
Were happy to have for Arthur, a little baby brother.

The new baby was named Leon and grew to be a nice boy,
To the whole Berry household, he has brought so much joy.
From boyhood to manhood, he was the same wonderful guy.
So the reason we love him, you don't have to ask why.

Many fond memories I have of Leon.
But the one I'm relating is a very special one.
Home from the War, he took each one to the store.
To let us buy something special we had not had before.
He helped care for us younger siblings, and sure didn't mind.
But was always helpful, loving and kind.

He was a fisherman, hunter, and the best joke teller in town,
In fact our brother was one person we enjoyed being around.
If you were ever downhearted lonely or blue,
Just ask Leon for a joke or two.
A good one to ask for is the one about the bear.
The man in that story sure got a good scare,

A lot of slipping and sliding but I won't tell you the rest.
Because brother Leon could sure tell it the best.

I thank everyone for coming, glad we could be here today.
The floor is now open, if you have something to say.
As I'm ending this poem, I have something to say.
Dear brother Leon, Happy, Happy birthday.

# SEEDS OF DISCONTENT

It's always hot in Louisiana in August, and on the day of my tenth birthday, it was hot. This was the day that Dad chose to teach me how to pull my end of a crosscut saw. No air stirred where we felled an oak tree in the woods of the slough that ran through our property.

In the intense heat we split the log to make fence posts. Dad was most kind and patient in carefully teaching me how to pull the saw with the desired rhythm. He did all the splitting because I was just too small to swing the axe with any power. At the time I sensed the pride he took in enjoying teaching his son how to split oak fence posts. In spite of the heat of the swamp I was not angry. It was just not the way I wanted to remember my tenth birthday.

I think my dad worked the hardest in my early years. The happiest I ever saw him was when he was working in the fields. Before we purchased a used farm tractor and equipment after WWII, he did all the heavy plowing with a pair of gray draft horses. Their names were Mack and Prince.

"Joe, get that jug and take your dad a cool drink of water. He's breaking land in that field at the end of the pasture," said my mother. "I know he's tired."

The jug she was referring to was a large mouth glass gallon jug that originally had contained molasses. The burlap bag that was wrapped around it was held in place with baling wire. I went out back of the house, primed the pitcher pump, then pumped water until it was cool and filled the jug. The burlap was soaked with the cool water to keep the contents cool as long as possible.

It was over an eighth of a mile to the field. The jug seemed very heavy by the time I arrived at the end of the row where my dad was plowing. (I was probably in the third grade.) The horses pulled the plow out to the end of the row and then he turned them back to make another furrow. Dad had already plowed several acres. From the waist up, his faded bib overalls and blue chambray shirt were wet with perspiration. On his head was a straw hat with sweat stains around the brim. The horses were lathered with sweat and seemed to enjoy the rest.

He took a long drink from the jug of cool water. Then he bent down and took a handful of the fresh plowed soil and raised it to his face.

Looking at me, he said, "I just love the smell of fresh plowed ground, son." Even as a small boy I knew that he was tired but he was smiling. He loved his farm and never cared for traveling. Being a land owner he had control of his time and made all the decisions about crops or methods of farming. I guess it was the independence he enjoyed.

As we worked in the fields, I would wonder why my dad never took me fishing. Mom loved fishing, so when I got old enough I would take her to the Beouf River for a day of fishing.

During the school year, farm children would miss about the first three weeks of school because of harvesting, picking cotton. Then we would miss most of the last three weeks of school because we were hoeing cotton.

The school kids never got a break. But during the winter when it was raining, the adults on the farm got a break. There were a lot of wooded swamps and wild game was abundant. Many men took this opportunity to go hunting.

When we picked cotton, Dad taught me all the skills of hunting. He was thorough in teaching me the proper way to safely use a gun. He told me the location of the hickory trees where the squirrels fed. Very precisely he described how to walk through the woods without being seen or heard. Though we worked side by side in the fields, he never took me squirrel hunting.

Dad went deer hunting every year I could remember but I was not permitted to go. I don't think he ever killed a deer but he loved going hunting with our dogs.

My parents were very religious. Regardless of what happened Mom's comment was *It's the Lord's will.* There is something to be said for a family who worked together in the fields and in the home to survive. This formed an invisible bond and instilled respect for each member. I worked very hard but so did everyone else. No one complained. I would be an adult before I could look back and understand that I grew up in a very loving family. We all loved one another. I never heard my parents swear or have destructive arguments. For these reasons I was not a rebellious teenager.

I was thirteen years old when Aunt Kate died. I remember it well.

"Walter, there is a car driving up in our front yard," Mom exclaimed as she was peeking out one of the living room windows.

This was most unusual. Our farm was on a gravel road and it was a rough road most of the time. We did not own an automobile and neither did many of our neighbors.

The dogs started barking. Patsy was our shepherd dog. Spot was a mongrel that I took rabbit hunting. Neither of the dogs would bite.

"Who in the world could that be this time of night?" Dad asked. "Lillie, it's nine o'clock."

He went to the door and scolded the dogs as a tall well-dressed man got out of the car and walked toward the house.

"Mr. Dobbs, my name is Calvin Simpkins and Arthur Berry sent me to bring you folks to Ruleville. I'm a close friend and live near Arthur. It troubles me to have to tell you folks but Kate died shortly after giving birth. The baby was a little boy. Stillborn."

Mom began to sob loudly. She and Aunt Kate had been very close. Dad put his arm around her and said, "Please come in Mr. Simpkins and have a chair. The dogs won't bother you." He turned toward the dogs and said, "Get under the house." Both dogs stopped barking and ran under the porch.

The tall man sat down in a rocking chair in the living room. He looked relieved to have delivered his tragic message. Mom was still crying. She and Dad went into a bedroom and closed the door leaving my sister Lucille and me standing in the room with Mr. Simpkins. Lucille would soon be eight years old.

After what seemed like a long time Dad emerged from the bedroom, closing the door behind him.

"Mr. Dobbs, I have this new Buick four-door sedan and there is plenty of room to take all of your family to Arthur's house in Ruleville. I can assure you that we will see to it that you get back home after the funeral."

"This is so sudden. We knew that Kate was expecting, but we didn't know there were complications," said Dad.

The closest telephone was twelve miles of gravel road away in Oak Grove. The only way to contact someone in case of an emergency was to call the sheriff's office in that Parish. They would send out a deputy with the message but it could take a couple of days in remote areas. There was no way to reply.

"I'm busy with the farm. We have a lot of animals that have to be fed and watered each day. Lillie and I have decided that I will stay here. She and the kids will go with you. Mr. Simpkins, it is so kind of you to do this for us. Lillie needs to be with her brother and his family at a time like this," explained Dad. "She's packing now and will be out in a few minutes. Would you like a cup of coffee?"

"I sure would," said Mr. Simpkins.

Dad loaded bags containing our clothes in the car. I'd never seen a new car and we were going to ride all the way to Mississippi in this new Buick. Mom was still crying when Dad kissed her goodbye.

"Joe, you and Lucille take care of your mother," instructed Dad. As the car pulled out on the gravel road, I could still see Dad standing in the darkness of the front yard.

The Buick was so elegant and inside it still had that new smell. There was a fold-out ashtray on the back of the front seat with a cigarette lighter mounted on the right side. I listened and the engine was so quiet, I could hardly hear it running.

I wished it was daylight and maybe some of my friends could see me riding in this new Buick. They would never believe me. Lucille was lying down on the seat and had gone to sleep. But up front in the passenger seat, I could still hear Mom sobbing.

As far back as I could remember it was the same. We would work hard, doing backbreaking labor, hoping that this year would be the year. But after harvest came in the fall, we would still be poor. Something would always happen and we would not be able to pay all the debts we had incurred raising the crop. It rained too much, there was a drought, the rains came too soon, the rains came too late, the boll weevils destroyed the cotton crop, it rained on the fresh cut hay and molded, or the army worms came through and stripped leaves from every plant. Every year something happened.

One season we had about forty head of hogs that we had worked two years to get. Dad said we could market them and not have to depend entirely on the cotton crop. It wasn't too long before two of the older sows became sick. The County Agent, Mr. Jesse Peterson, came out and ran a test. We learned that the hogs were infected with cholera.

"Mr. Dobbs, you have to destroy all the hogs," he said. "You have no other choice." We shot and killed every animal and stacked them in piles. The dead bodies were covered with logs and brush and burned. Watching the burning pile I was devastated, but Dad seemed never to be discouraged. He had a very positive attitude. We would just try some other type of crop to make up the loss.

Those rare years that we had a great crop there would be just enough money to pay the debts of the failing years. Many of our neighboring farmers took jobs in town. They seemed to do a lot better. Once, a neighbor asked Dad if he would like to work in the International Paper Company Mill in Bastrop, Louisiana, about thirty miles from our farm. Dad wasn't interested. I was disappointed when he declined the offer. Any work other than farming he referred to as "public work," which he often said he did not like.

Many of our neighbors were part-time farmers and held a job in some other industry. These families prospered while we remained poor. I thought the work would be much easier on Dad than back-breaking jobs like baling and hauling hay. After I left home, he worked part time as a truck driver.

I believe that until I moved away from home at seventeen, Dad was unaware of my discontent. Though he said I'd be back in a month, I never returned except on visits. It would be over forty years before I would understand his love for farming. When I worked long hours building a business, a Music Store that I loved, I understood why he was so engrossed in owning and making a success of his family farm. Interesting to note, none of my children share my passion for the music store business.

My father was so respected in the community. The only disagreements he and Mom ever had concerned his helping some neighbor, when she thought he should be working in our fields.

Looking back, I realize that there was no one that he regularly hunted or fished with. He never had any real close friends except a church member. Reminiscing, I came to the conclusion that Dad was a loner.

My dad died in 1975, but my mother lived another ten years. After he was gone and I would go to Louisiana to visit, there would always be someone telling me how my dad was a good man. At my brother-in-law, Parnell's funeral, I saw Doug Strong. I hadn't seen him since I left home in 1952 when he was a child. Doug insisted on telling me how much he thought of my dad.

During my last visit with Mom in the summer of 1984, we talked about us kids growing up. There were four of us all born five years apart. I was the oldest, then my only sister Lucille, Dwayne, and then my youngest brother, Dennis. We were traveling out to Palestine, Texas, to visit Dennis and his family.

"Mom, we all worked hard on that farm," I said. "I don't understand how you had the strength to work in the field picking cotton all day and then coming home and cooking a big meal."

"Joe, you worked a lot harder than the other kids. After you left home, Walter thought he was too hard on you," she said. "The other kids went on their class trips and didn't have to work in the fields as much. Walter thought he had made a mistake and he was easier on the other kids."

Her statement lingered in my mind

I spent a week with Dad several months before he died of cancer. We talked about all kinds of things. Living in the swamps, his childhood, the big war, politics, the 1927 Flood, the time Uncle Jesse shot off part of his hand while they were rabbit hunting in Mississippi, but he never mentioned my field work. *I wish he had. I would have told him it was OK.*

# LEAVING THE FARM

*The spring of 1952 had arrived and the farmers were preparing the fields for planting. The smell of fresh plowed ground was in the air. I was having difficulty hiding my anxiety. I would graduate from Forest High school in May and some way or the other, I was leaving the farm.*

I don't know exactly when I knew I was not going to be a farmer like my father. But the older I got, the more I knew it to be true.

The compulsory Agricultural classes at school were the only vocational training available. During four years of those classes I made very good grades. Knowing deep down that I was never going to farm, I really had no interest in the vaccinating, castrating, or artificially inseminating of farm-animals.

I detested all the never-ending hard work of the farm, so I counted the days until I could leave. One could be sure that I would not be there during the fall harvest. Could this be what one endured while serving in some prison? Just counting for the day when you could leave?

"What a pretty day," said Uncle Arthur as he got out of his 1950 Nash station wagon. The small car was a two-tone green color that looked new.

All the doors opened and out came my Aunt Mae, holding the baby in her arms, while Sidney and Katherine got out of the back seat. They had come from Clarksdale, Mississippi, to our farm near Goodwill, Louisiana, for a weekend visit. Sidney, Katherine, and one-year-old Millie were my first cousins.

"Lillie, what are we having for dinner? We're all hungry," Arthur said to my mom, joking.

Mom was coming out the front door. "I'm so glad to see all of you. I'll find something to cook," she replied, hugging her brother. "Mae, bring that baby and come on in the house. This is such a pleasant surprise."

We seldom had visitors, so this was a special occasion. Relatives from across the Mississippi river would make the trip over about once each year. I can remember years during WWII when no one came.

Arthur Berry was two years younger than Mom, but he was her oldest brother. He and his first wife, Kate, had lived on the adjoining farm back in 1939, when we all first moved to Louisiana.

When Arthur joined the Navy in 1943, he became a barber and served on a ship in the Pacific. When he came home after the war in 1946, he went to work in a barber shop in Ruleville, Mississippi.

Aunt Kate died in 1947 of complications during childbirth, leaving Arthur to raise their two children. Sometime later, he moved to Clarksdale, where he worked as a barber and married Aunt Mae. Their first child, Millie, was born in 1951.

"Joe, you're really growing," Arthur said. "Just how old are you?"

"I'm seventeen and I graduate from high school in May," I said as we walked toward the house.

"What are your plans once you've graduated?" he asked.

"Joe's enrolling in Louisiana Tech this fall," said Dad.

"I need to come up with some kind of job for the summer. My scholarship only pays part of my tuition," I said. Sydney and Katherine went inside the house. Arthur, Dad and I sat down in chairs on the front porch.

During the Graduation Ceremonies, I had been presented with two small scholarships that were more ceremonial than actual financial value. I was the class Salutatorian and was also presented with the American Legion Award. Since there were only eighteen graduates in my senior class, I did not think this recognition was significant.

One of my teachers told me that it was possible to get a better-paying scholarship, but I would need the help of my Senator. I mentioned this to Dad. With his Southern pride, he considered it to be some type of welfare. He said something about us not wanting a handout.

However, I went to talk with Senator Allen Haley at his home just east of Oak Grove. He was eager to help and his friendliness quickly erased my fears. I liked the Senator. In addition to a better scholarship, he offered to sponsor me as an applicant to West Point. After explaining all the procedures, he gave me some papers that would have to be filled out and signed by Dad.

Wanza Drane had been two years ahead of me in class and we were Boy Scouts together. He had gone to West Point but dropped out during his first year. After learning when he would be home from college, I visited with him in Forest, Louisiana.

Wanza was very intelligent. After listening to his description of his life as a cadet and his reasons for leaving West Point, I determined that I was not interested. I have never regretted that decision. With the help of Senator Haley, I did get a better-paying scholarship to Louisiana Tech at Ruston.

"Joe, why don't you just come up to Clarksdale after you get out of school? I know a lot of people in town and I will help you get a good summer job," said Arthur. That sounded exciting to me, but Dad didn't say anything. I knew he was expecting me to stay on the farm and work all summer. But I knew if I did, I would not have any money when I went to Louisiana Tech in August.

"Hey, Sidney, let's go down to Beouf River and I'll show you the swimming hole," I said, as I looked in the front door.

"I'll be right out," he said.

Our Senior Class trip was scheduled for a couple of weeks before graduation. All of our class was going to Vicksburg, Mississippi, to spend the day exploring the Civil War Battleground. A couple of days before the trip, Dad told me that he needed me to take the farm tractor and plow the large field of corn on the north side of the alfalfa field. I knew this would be the end of me going on the trip.

"Dad, this could be the last time I would get to spend any time with my classmates," I said.

"You've been to Vicksburg before." He added, "I'm afraid it will rain before we get the corn plowed."

That sealed it for me. I knew then that I would leave for Clarksdale and Uncle Arthur's family the day after I graduated.

True to my resolve, the day following graduation, I packed an old metal suitcase. Since my fiddle playing was rather poor I left my fiddle at home. I said goodbye to all of the family. One of my friends gave me a ride across the Mississippi River.

I had lived a very sheltered life, spending all my time working with the family on that remote farm. We never had the opportunity to travel and meet people. One of the very few times I left the farm was when I was in the seventh grade on a school field trip to go to Jackson, Mississippi.

My family and I went to a small country church, but I was not accustomed to meeting people outside my small world. This was years before television. I had seen less than a dozen movies. Back then, we were not as aware of the world as the kids in the eighties or nineties.

When I arrived in Clarksdale, Mississippi, Uncle Arthur and his family made me feel most welcome. After Aunt Katherine died, Uncle Arthur was left with Sydney and Katherine. Aunt Mae had two boys, Eddie and Blake, by her first husband. (Blake lost his life rescuing flood victims while serving in the National Guard in the late 1950s.) Then she and Arthur had Millie.

When I arrived, there was Uncle Arthur, Aunt Mae and five kids in the family and Mae was pregnant again. They all lived in a three-bedroom home but made room for me. I will never forget Uncle Arthur or his family's kindness for letting me live with them part of that summer.

Arthur was an accommodating man all his life. He always had numerous friends, which seems to go along with being a barber. He went on to live a full life, outliving three wives. The last time I saw him was at my Mom's funeral. He was seventy-three years old.

After a couple of days of playing with my cousins and learning my way around Clarksdale, I was ready to go to work. After all, I was going to college in August.

One night at the supper table, Uncle Arthur handed me a piece of paper. "Mae will drive you down to this address tomorrow morning. You go in the office and ask to speak with Max Reed. He does the hiring at the Rubber Company. They manufacture automobile inner tubes. He has a job for you. His name is on this piece of paper," Arthur explained.

I was a bit apprehensive, but also excited about finally going to work at a real job. It would be better than hoeing cotton in the hot sun for $3 a day.

The next day, I walked into the office of the Royal Rubber Company. Down a small hallway, I found the office that had a sign on the door that read 'Personnel,' and walked in. A big man was sitting behind a desk. He reminded me of my high school shop teacher, Mr. Joyce. There was a little wooden sign on his desk with the name, Max Reed. The whole place smelled of burning rubber.

"What can I do for you, young man?" He looked up from some papers that were lying on his desk and removed his glasses.

"Arthur Berry is my uncle, and he told me to come and talk to you about a job." I answered.

I was conscious that I was very small for my seventeen years and looked much younger. My weight was probably less than one hundred and twenty pounds. I never weighed a hundred pounds until I was sixteen years old. That heavy work on the farm like hauling hay and splitting wood had made me exceptionally strong for my size.

"You look like a kid, but Arthur is a good friend. I was down at the barber shop and he told me you are a good worker. Be here at four o'clock tomorrow and we'll get you started. You'll be on the evening shift from four till twelve and we'll pay you eighty cents per hour," he explained.

That was the minimum wage. I thanked him and walked briskly out of the building. I was so happy that I wanted to run. I had a Job!

My new job was working on an assembly line folding new inner tubes and placing them in a small box and closing the lid. The person across the work table from me made the boxes.

All around me, the factory was dark from the black materials that were used to manufacture the rubber. The strong odor of rubber was all through the plant. In one area, there were big machines that were like a giant ringer washing machine. This was the area where they mixed the ingredients. Those big aluminum rollers were very hot.

Shirtless men stood in front of the hot machines, adding all the materials between the rollers. In addition to several sizes of inner tubes, they also made the big rolls of rubber that were sold to plants that recapped tires. It was called "camel-back." This was years before tubeless tires.

Two weeks later at the breakfast table, I said, "Yesterday was payday."

"Hey, that was your first paycheck," said Aunt Mae. She was so good to me. Though she was obviously pregnant and Millie was not yet two years old, each afternoon she would pack me a lunch before I left for work. I appreciated it, but I did not want to add to her work.

"I don't know why, but I didn't get all my wages," I said.

"What do you mean?" asked Uncle Arthur.

"Well, I worked forty hours at eighty cents per hour. But my check was less than thirty two dollars," I explained, handing my paycheck across the table to Uncle Arthur.

He looked at the check and said, "Oh, they took out for Social Security. That money goes to the government so you can draw a retirement check when you are old. No need to worry, because there won't be any left by the time you reach sixty-five," he said.

Each afternoon, I rode a bus to the rubber plant. When I got off at midnight, the buses were no longer running. Two men who worked in my department would drop me off at home after work. Curly and Red were all the names that I knew them by.

"We go right by Arthur's house, so it's no trouble at all to give you a ride. Arthur cuts my hair," said Curly. He was stocky and less than six feet tall with a head covered with curly black hair.

Red was very freckled, with a ruddy complexion and dark red, straight hair. He was somewhat taller than Curly. They were buddies. Only a couple of weeks prior to my starting work, they had been discharged out of the US Army and had gone to work in the plant.

It was Friday, payday, and I had been working about three weeks. I had plans to go fishing with Sydney the next day and it seemed that twelve o'clock would never come. When I pushed my time card in the time clock to punch out, I was in line right behind Curly and Red. When I got to the parking lot, Curly and Red were both sitting in the well-used 1941 Ford sedan. The car belonged to Curly, who was driving. I slid into the back seat and we pulled out on the street.

When he drove out to where Main Street crossed Highway 61 and turned south, I thought he was going the wrong way, but maybe that was a different way home. We proceeded south on 61 until we were out of town. In the moonlight, I could see the rows of huge cotton fields on each side of the road.

"Where are we going, Curly?" I asked. "This isn't the way home."

"Red and I have a stop to make. It won't take long," he said, looking over at Red. Both were grinning at each other.

No one spoke as we kept going south on 61. Curly drove a little over the speed limit, but after twelve at night, there was no traffic. In that flat Mississippi Delta, you could see for miles.

As we slowed down and went through the little town of Shelby, I said, "This is taking us farther from home. I just wish you guys had let me out back in Clarksdale, and I could have gotten home somehow."

"We'll have you back in Clarksdale in no time," assured Red. "We're going to a whorehouse in Mount Bayou, the next town, and we're almost there." They both laughed.

Mount Bayou was all black. There were no white folks living in the town. The mayor and all the town government were black.

I was really frightened. I had never been inside a bar or beer joint. My mom would turn her head and look the opposite way when we drove by that beer joint directly across the Beouf River. That was in Morehouse Parish. West Carroll Parish, where we lived, was dry, no booze.

It was after midnight, and I didn't know what I was going to do. Mom said if you went in those saloons and drank whisky, you could go to Hell. She never mentioned the word "whorehouse." I just assumed that would be worse. I wondered if the whorehouse would be in a bar run by colored people. This was not good.

We turned right off Highway 61 onto a gravel street. On the right, I saw the sign that read "Mount Bayou." After we drove a couple of blocks, Curly pulled over in front of a frame house that was painted white. He stopped the car and turned off the engine.

Seemed like the crickets were chirping loud and I heard a dog barking several blocks away. It looked like any nice neighborhood. The houses were far apart, on big lots, and appeared to be like any average three – bedroom homes.

The area was not well lit, but there was a street light at each crossing.

"This is it," said Red. "Come on, get out."

"I ain't going in there," I said. "There ain't no way. I'll just wait here in the car." I was so scared, my heart was pounding.

"Hell, you can't wait in the car," Curly said gruffly. "This whole town is colored. What if a cop just happens to drive by, and sees a white boy settin' in a parked car in front of this house, at one o'clock in the morning? Get out, Joe, you're going in."

"I'll just lay down in the floor," I said.

"Get out of the car!"

There was no traffic in the area. It seemed as though the whole street was asleep. They got out of the car and walked up on the porch, with me close behind them. You could see dim lights through the windows.

They did not knock. Red simply opened the door and we walked into what looked like an ordinary living room. There was a couch against one wall and a coffee table in front of it. On either end of the couch, there were two big comfortable chairs that matched. On the wall behind the couch was a painting of some western mountain landscape. I wondered if they could hear my heart pounding. I was really frightened.

There was a shuffle behind a purple curtain that hung in the doorway leading out of the living room area. A heavy-set black woman entered the room from behind the curtain. I wondered how she knew we had come in. She was wearing a beautiful print dress that came about half way to her ankles. It was emerald green and covered with big magnolia blossoms. She was dressed as though she was going to church.

As she entered the room, her face lit up and she said, "Lawd, have mercy, my little soldier boys has done come home!"

I sat down in the chair that was near the end of the couch. I wanted to just disappear.

"When did ya'll get out of the service," she asked while she was hugging Red.

"Luella Mae, it's so good to see you," said Curly. "We've been out about a month now."

"Honey, you jes make yo self at home," she said, looking at me. "Ya'll come with me," she said, turning to Curly and Red. The three of them disappeared behind the purple curtain.

I sat there for what seemed to be forever. My mind was racing. But then, my thoughts were interrupted by the opening of the front door. In staggered a tall, thin, African-American man. He was very dark with a well- worn fedora hat cocked on the back of his head. You could tell that his white shirt had been starched and ironed when he first put it on. But now his clothes were all wrinkled, as though he had slept in them for several nights. On the front of his shirt were drops of dried blood.

He came to stand directly in front of me. All I could think was that *I am so young, and I'm going to die here in this Mississippi Colored Whorehouse. I hope that this drunk man cannot see my leg shaking.*

My heart was pounding, and I pressed my foot against the linoleum floor to stop my leg from shaking. I took a quick look around the room, but saw nothing with which to defend myself. *He's towering over me and I'm going to have to get up to hit him with force.*

He began mumbling at me. I just sat there looking blank and scared. He was so drunk that I could not understand what he was saying. *Maybe he wants money. Today was payday, but all I have in my pocket is eighty-three cents.*

I knew that wouldn't be enough to satisfy him. All I could think of was, *Surely, I'm going to die. My folks will be so ashamed to know where my life ended.* He started mumbling again and shaking his finger in my face, when Luella Mae came through the curtain.

"You leave that white boy alone!" she exclaimed. "You git yo ass out of here right now or I'll have you locked up." He staggered out and slammed the door, still mumbling.

Luella Mae turned to me and said, "You'll be alright, honey, he won't be back."

I wanted to get up and hug her neck, for I was sure she had saved my life. Then the curtain opened and Curly walked into the room tucking in his shirt. Red followed.

I was so relieved that we were leaving.

"We'll see you next time," said Red. Luella May was smiling big enough to show her gold tooth.

"Ya'll welcome anytime," she said, closing the door.

Everyone was quiet as we drove back to Clarksburg. I thought about being in that Colored Whorehouse, but not seeing any of the prostitutes. I guess they were all in rooms behind that purple curtain.

They dropped me off at Uncle Arthur's house and I entered the house as quietly as I could. No one woke up. I didn't want to have to lie about why I was late.

The next week, Mom forwarded me a letter from Cletus Tally, one of my senior classmates. He was working in Houston, Texas. I opened the letter and learned that he had me a job lined up in a machine shop that paid one dollar and 45 cents per hour.

Tex Hawkins was the night foreman and my boss. I punched the time clock to begin my shift and immediately went to Tex's office.

"Mr. Hawkins, this is going to be my last shift here. How can I get my paycheck?" I asked.

"Joe, I know this is your first job. Maybe I should explain some things," he looked at me with concern. "In order to have a good work record, you have to give two weeks notice before you can leave. That gives the company time to train someone to do your job. "

"I have to leave. I have a better job," I explained. "I'm trying to make enough money to help with my college expenses, so I can't give you two weeks' notice. I can send you a letter when I get located, so you can send me my last check."

"Where are you going to work, Joe?" Tex asked.

"One of my classmates in Houston, Texas, has me a job that pays more money, in a machine shop."

Mr. Hawkins got up and left the room saying, "Let me see what I can do." He was gone about ten minutes and returned with an envelope in his hand. Handing me the envelope, he said, "I'm from Ft. Worth. Here's your check. Good luck," he said, reaching out his hand.

That last week I worked at the Rubber Plant, any time I caught Red and Curly alone in the washroom, I would say in a falsetto voice, "Lawd have mercy, my little soldier boys has done come home."

On my way to Texas I went by the farm and got my fiddle.

# THE TALL TEXAN

In the fall of 1952, I enrolled as a freshman at Louisiana Tech in Ruston. One day I was bent over my desk studying for an exam in my Qualitative Chemistry class the next day. There was no air conditioning in the dorm, so all the windows were raised and the door was open.

I was startled by a male voice saying, "Are you Joe Dobbs?"

Standing in the doorway was a tall, slender, well-dressed young man who looked more like a salesman than a student. He was wearing a pink dress shirt, pressed slacks, shined shoes and a pleasant smile.

"That's me," I answered, as I laid down my slide rule and looked up from my chemistry calculations.

"I'm Merle Kilgore and I need a fiddle player. I've heard you play and you're probably the worst I've ever heard, but you're the only fiddler on campus. I have to have one. Do you want to play some jobs with me?" he asked.

Everybody had heard of Merle Kilgore. He billed himself as the 'The Tall Texan' and played hillbilly recordings on KRUS, the local radio station. Painted in bold letters on each side of the Chrysler he drove around campus was "The Tall Texan."

I was well aware of just how poorly I played. But if he thought I played well enough to accompany him, I would do it.

"I'd like to play fiddle for you," I replied. Regardless of how bad I played, I thought, "Since I am the only fiddler on campus, I'm also the best."

At that time, the Louisiana Hayride was broadcast over Radio Station KWKH in Shreveport, Louisiana, and was one of the most popular Saturday night radio shows in the country. The Hayride had so many top artists, it rivaled the Grand Ole Opry. Hank Williams, Jim Reeves, Faron Young, Webb Pierce and the Maddox Brothers and Rose were among the regular performers. Every week, there were special guests and upcoming stars like Johnny Cash and Elvis Presley.

Merle was the most focused young person I had ever met. While Merle was still in high school, he sang on the Hayride several times. He would hurry and finish with his morning paper route, then ride his bicycle down to the KWKH Studios and help musicians carry their instruments upstairs to the studio. That was where they played live early morning radio shows.

As a teenager, he became acquainted with a lot of Country Music stars, such as Hank Williams, Sr., who was a regular on the Louisiana Hayride. Merle graduated from Fair Park High School and at the age of eighteen, he knew exactly what he wanted to do with his life.

"Joe, would you see if Jim and Ronnie would like to play in the studios of KRUS? Ed wants us to do an hour show on Saturday," said Merle.

I had been playing in a trio with Ronnie Crain and Jim Landrum, the Hogback Mountain Boys. There are no mountains in the swamps of Louisiana, so I guess the name was just a bit of humor. Ronnie, from Shreveport, was a student who played guitar and sang. Jim was a geology student from Minden, Louisiana. He played the Chet Atkins' finger-picking style on his Gretsch guitar. We often played with Merle on shows where he needed a band.

"I'm sure they'll play," I answered. "We always enjoy working with Ed."

Ed Hamilton was the program director at KRUS. Being a Korean War Veteran, he was attending Louisiana Tech on the GI Bill. Ed was of average height, very thin, and always wore his dark hair combed straight back. He had the wonderful deep, smooth voice that was so desired for radio. Up until 1955, most small town radio stations programmed a variety of local live musical entertainment.

While attending the 1964 Disc Jockey Convention in Nashville, I ran into Ed in the old Andrew Jackson Hotel. "Joe, I hope you're having a good time in Nashville. It's so good to see you again," greeted Ed. "By the way, did you ever learn to play the fiddle?"

I guess he was remembering our college days. That was the last time that I saw him. I heard that he became a popular Radio Personality in Music City.

"These college classes are interfering with my career," Merle said. "I know that I can get a good job as a DJ at a larger radio station or maybe a TV Show over in Monroe."

"I'm working all those hours in that grocery store and trying to carry two classes with four-hour labs," I complained. "This is just too much work to be doing when I'm not even sure what I want to do in life."

We both dropped out of college after the second semester. Merle enthusiastically pursued a musical career while I had no direction. My advisor at the college saw my high scores in math and chemistry and decided I should become a nuclear physicist, something in which I had absolutely no interest.

Looking back, I think that I was just elated to be away from the family farm where I had worked so hard as a youth. The only real career decision I had made was "*I am not going back to that farm*." So Merle went full time into his music and I went to Houston, Texas, where I got my old job back in the machine shop.

Several months later as I was traveling from Houston to visit my parents, I stopped in Monroe, Louisiana, and contacted Merle. He was always excited about his career.

"Why don't you hang around here for a while? I have this TV show on KNOE here in Monroe. You could play fiddle with me," Merle offered. "I've booked Saturday afternoon shows at the local movie house where we play for kids after the cowboy picture ends," he explained.

"Well, I really don't have any plans. It sounds like fun and I'm willing to give it a try," I said.

"How would you like to play the fiddle on my TV show Saturday night?" he asked.

"I've never played on TV." I answered. "I'll do it."

On the way to the studio, Merle coached me as to how to look at the red light on the camera and keep smiling.

"You gotta imagine that you can see all the folks out there watching and just keep smiling," he said.

Merle was focused on being a recording star. He always wore the proper western clothes and the big white hat that was customary with Country Music singers. During his high school years, he had observed the stars playing on the Louisiana Hayride and had learned the proper ways to dress and conduct himself in a professional manner.

"Twenty seconds," said the TV director. The red light came on the camera and we began smiling and playing.

Merle was born a performer and his show was well received. The Tall Texan was on TV.

I hoped that the folks at home watching couldn't see my legs trembling. It was a blessing that I was not required to talk. I was shaking with "stage fright" and was so relieved when the show finally ended.

As we walked off the lighted stage, there was a person that came through the door into the studio. I didn't recognize him because he was behind the bright studio lights.

"Joe Dobbs, I knew it was you. I stepped out of the shower and I heard that fiddle on TV and I knew it was you," he said, walking up to me with his hand extended. "I'd recognize your fiddle playing anywhere." Then he said he lived near the TV station studios.

Holding my fiddle and bow in my left hand, I shook hands with him. I refrained from asking if it was because I played good or was it because I played bad. "Jim Vaughn!" I said. "Boy, it's good to see you."

"I just couldn't believe it was you on the TV," exclaimed Jim. He had attended Louisiana Tech with me and we had played together in a band where he played bass.

I knew I was a poor player, but Jim always had nice, encouraging things to say to me, and remember, I was the only fiddler on campus. The "Tech Southernaires" was the first group I played with at Tech. Sonny Montgomery played lap steel. Jerry Edmonson and Philip Misenheimer each sang and played guitar and Tom Head, who was from my hometown, Oak Grove, played piano. The next time I saw them was forty-six years later in 1999, when we had a reunion. I hardly knew them, for they were all a "bunch of old men."

The Tech Southernaires played a series of concerts at high schools in the northern Louisiana area as part of a variety show to interest high school graduates to enroll at Louisiana Tech. We were also the band that accompanied Merle Kilgore during his performances.

One night, we were gathered in the dressing room backstage at the Rayville, Louisiana, High School auditorium.

"Merle, would you sing a sweet love song and dedicate it to someone in the audience for me?" asked Jim Vaughn, the bass player.

"Jim, I'd be happy to do that for you," answered Merle, while pacing the floor and tuning his guitar. "Write her name on a piece of paper and I'll put it in my pocket," he said, looking in the mirror.

"Her name is Carolyn and she's sitting in the second row," explained Jim. "I'm very fond of her, so don't forget."

"You boys are on next," said a voice just outside the door. We went out on stage and Merle was MC. He sang several songs that were well received by the capacity crowd.

"Hey, Merle, don't forget my request for Carolyn," whispered Jim. "I told her there was a surprise for her during our show."

As the applause ended, Merle nodded to Jim and turned back to the microphone. "Thank you so much! We've enjoyed singing for you. This last song is special and I almost forgot. Jim Vaughn, our bass player, wanted me to dedicate this song to Carolyn, who is sitting right down there in the second row. So this song is for you, Carolyn, "Bessie, the Heifer, The Queen of all the Cows."

Merle had planned to end the show with an uptempo song and "Bessie The Heifer" was an old Western Swing song that Merle sang well. Just as he started singing, he realized he had made a dreadful mistake. He turned and looked at Jim apologetically.

After the applause that followed the last song we went into the dressing room. Merle was greeted with the band echoing "I can't believe you did that!"

From the time I began to learn to play the violin at the age of ten, Mother and Dad tried to discourage me from playing music. Due to their religious convictions, they were sure that it was evil to play the fiddle. I bought my first instrument from a friend with $10 that I had earned working in the neighbor's cotton fields. My parents had prohibited me from buying a fiddle, so I lied and told them it was borrowed. They never knew that I had bought the instrument.

However, an unusual thing happened after they saw me play that first time on TV. For some reason my playing on TV made my musical interests acceptable in the eyes of God. After that TV appearance I could play the fiddle without my parents having the fear of me going to Hell. With this change in God's attitude, my relationship with my parents improved.

As we drove out of the TV studio parking lot, Merle said, "I have a job booked tomorrow afternoon. We'll be playing for the opening of a Dairy Queen out on Highway 82."

"We can take my car," I offered. I had a well used '46 Ford convertible automobile.

"No, TV stars have to arrive in style," Merle explained. "I know this guy, Ed Stokes, that has a late model DeSoto convertible and he's going to drive us to the Dairy Queen after he washes and polishes the car. We're going to show up at this job in style. You have to present yourself as an artist," he explained.

"Do they have a stage or maybe a flatbed truck where we'll perform?" I asked. "Is there room to play inside?"

"It's a Dairy Queen and there is no inside," said Merle. "The owner wants us to play on top of the flat roof so we can be seen by the passing traffic. Maybe we can get the attention of some of the folks driving down

Highway 82. The weather is supposed to be clear, so we'll ride up with the top down. Now, that's class."

As we drove up in the classy DeSoto convertible, we could see several cars parked in front of the Dairy Queen.

"Look, they already have the sound system set up," explained Merle as we pulled up to the building. Ed got out and went around to the rear of the car and opened the trunk so we could remove our instruments. I reached in and picked up my fiddle case as Merle removed his guitar from the trunk.

"Look it's Merle Kilgore, the Tall Texan," said this tall, dark-haired girl to her friend. She was wearing sunglasses and had on a pretty summer dress with a yellow floral design.

Merle immediately set his guitar case on the ground and greeted his fans, "Hello ladies, and thanks for coming. The show begins in about twenty minutes. We're glad you are here."

"I'll be back and pick you up after the show," said Ed as he began to move the car backwards. There was a crunch and I turned and saw the rear wheel roll over the upper part of Merle's guitar case.

"Oh, my God!" exclaimed Merle. "My guitar!"

"I'm so sorry," said Ed getting out of the car. "I had no idea that the guitar was behind the car.

"It was my fault," said Merle, opening the guitar case. "I should have been more careful." There was a crack down the middle of the back of the neck. The lower half of the headstock with the three treble tuners was broken off.

We managed to borrow a guitar and finish the show. When we returned to Merle's house, we examined the damage done to the guitar.

"Faron (Faron Young) bought that D-18 Martin new at J & S Music in Shreveport," said Merle. "I had this old beat up Martin D-28 that I had bought from Johnny Bailes. Faron was invited to play on the Grand Ole Opry and he didn't want to go to Nashville without a D-28 so we traded guitars. I really hate that it got broken."

"I think that I can repair that guitar," I said. "You'll still see the crack but it will play as good as new." I took the guitar and repaired all the damage done to the neck. After I was sure that it played well I took it back to Merle.

"A TV star can't be seen playing a guitar with a repaired crack in the neck," he said. "I'll just have to buy me a new guitar."

He wasn't interested in the repaired guitar so I purchased it for $35. That was in 1953. I cherished the instrument because it was a Martin and it had an interesting history. In 1961, I loaned it to a friend in Houston who carelessly left the guitar in its case on the back seat of his car. It was in the summer and the windows were down. Someone stole the instrument while my friend was inside a bar having a beer.

I talked with Merle only three or four times down through the years but he always asked me about the D-18 Martin that had belonged to Faron Young. I never located the stolen Martin.

"I want to sing you this song that I wrote," said Merle taking his new guitar out of its case. "This is going to be a hit."

I wasn't really interested in new songs. I was desperately trying to learn to play the old songs on my fiddle; however, I respectfully listened.

Merle was a very talented singer and as he finished he said, "The title is 'More and More.' What do you think?"

"I don't think it's that great," I said, giving him my honest opinion. He was so excited about his writing that I don't think he heard my criticism. Was I ever wrong! That song was later recorded by Webb Pierce, Charlie Pride, and Guy Lombardo and sold over a million records. Merle went on to write six more million sellers.

It was difficult for Merle to book enough work so he could pay me and I felt like I was a burden on his career.

"We're just not making enough money so I've applied for a job up in Arkansas keeping the field office books for a pipeline contractor," I said.

Merle tried to convince me to stay and play music with him. He was sure that we were just beginning. I was tempted to stay.

As I walked out to my car to leave for Arkansas, Merle was standing on the porch.

"You should stick with me, Joe, and you'll fart through silk," he said.

We went in different directions and I would not see or talk with him again for almost nine years when we were backstage at the Louisiana Hayride in 1960.

After that, I never saw Merle again. I thought about going to visit him several times when he traveled with the Hank Williams, Jr. show but I never wanted to endure the crowds of people.

George Walker, of West Virginia Public Radio was the producer of my program, 'Music From the Mountains,' which was on the radio for over twenty-five years. Since Hank Williams, Sr. had died in Oak Hill, West Virginia, George suggested that we do a Hank Williams memorial on that New Year's weekend.

He had heard me mention my association with Merle Kilgore and suggested that we get Merle involved since he knew Hank back in Shreveport, Louisiana.

I contacted Merle and he was excited about the idea. He was Hank Williams, Jr.'s manager at the time and they were always on the road. Near Merle's home in Paris, Tennessee, was a small recording studio. George suggested that we set up a time when Merle could go into that studio and I would be in George's studio in Cross Lanes, West Virginia.

We would record the interview and it would sound like we were both in the West Virginia Public Radio broadcasting studio. Thanks to George, it worked just as he explained. Merle told wonderful stories about being around Hank Williams, Sr. back in 1953. It was a great show and as they say, the rest is history.

The last time I talked with him on the phone was in 2003. He asked me to promise that the next time I was in Gallatin visiting my daughter, Diane, I would come to his offices so we could visit. I never went and I never saw him again.

Without a doubt, Merle could have been successful in any profession he chose. He died of cancer on February 6, 2005. The memorial services were held in the Ryman Auditorium. A friend told me the funeral was so large that it held up traffic on Interstate 40.

This is a list of the songs Merle wrote that sold over a million records:

"Ring of Fire"

"Johnny Reb"

"Wolverton Mountain"
"More and More"
"Folk Singer"
"Old Enough to Love"
"The Easy Way"

# THE WHITE PELICAN

After leaving Merle Kilgore in Monroe, Louisiana, I went to work laying pipeline for R. C. Cudd, a contractor. The first location I worked was in Murfreesboro, Arkansas, at the only operating diamond mine in the United States. That job was completed in about three months. The next job was laying a gas pipeline in St. Joseph, Louisiana, a small town on the west side of the Mississippi River about half way between Vicksburg and Natchez. This was where I met my first wife, Amy.

I worked with Troy Turner, her father, several months before I met Amy. Troy was well liked by his fellow workers and he worked in the pipeline crew at several different jobs. During World War II, he had served in the US Navy on an LST Ship. He always had great stories about his time aboard ship. When the Philippines were being taken over by Japanese invading forces, his ship evacuated General McArthur. In order for the general's furniture and personal property to be loaded, he saw U.S. soldiers left standing on the beach. Troy was not a fan of General McArthur.

Another story he told was when his ship sailed out of San Francisco Bay for the Pacific. This was in 1943 when the fighting in the Pacific was intense. So many vessels were being sunk by Japanese submarines, many of the sailors wondered if they would be fortunate enough to return home safely. As the ship sailed out of the bay it passed Alcatraz. Just as they were going by, a young sailor stood up on the rail, waved toward the rocky prison and screamed, "Goodbye, Daddy!"

By 1955, Amy and I had been dating for over a year and we got married in May. I thought she was such a pretty young woman. We were two young people in love in the Ozarks. We both enjoyed outdoor activities and during the summer we were somewhere in the mountains almost every weekend.

For some time I continued to work for the R. C. Cudd Company. Most of the jobs were for the Corp of Engineers along the Arkansas River from Ft. Smith to Pine Bluff. I started out as the field office bookkeeper, paying accounts receivable and doing the payroll. Then, I discovered that I could make more money driving a truck or operating heavy equipment such as bulldozers, side booms, or graders. My experience on the farm driving tractors and working with other farm equipment proved to be an advantage.

Amy and I lived in Barling, Arkansas, which was the home of Fort Chafee, an artillery unit of the US Army. The soldiers in training would begin firing their 105 mm cannons at 4a.m. It sounded much like thunder.

Sunday, May the 13th was Mother's Day. I had mentioned seeing some fishermen catching fish off the dike we were building and Amy decided she wanted to go fishing. I reminded her that the doctor had said she could have the baby any day, but she insisted on going that Sunday afternoon. Early on I had learned not to argue with a pregnant woman so we drove six miles to the Arkansas River.

Before sundown that evening we left with a bucket filled with fish. Amy had worn shorts and a short sleeve shirt and became very sunburned. Her mother, Lorene, had come up from Nashville, Arkansas, to stay and help with the new baby, the first grandchild in the family. When Lorene saw Amy, she was furious. After treating her sunburn, we went to bed. Sometime during the night Amy woke me. She was in labor. Inside I was frantic, but I made an effort to appear calm.

With Amy, her bag of clothes and Lorene, I drove to the hospital in Ft. Smith, which was about five miles from Barling. I was really frightened. When the doctor saw her, he was concerned as well. Obviously, the sunburn was severe enough to affect her giving birth.

On Monday, May 14, 1956, our son Dale was born. Mother and baby were both fine. Lorene was happy and I was relieved that it was over.

We continued to live in towns along the Arkansas River for another year. The first two years we were married, we moved eight times. When the job moved to a location where it was not feasible to commute, we would rent another apartment. Amy never complained. I knew this was difficult for a mother with a baby, but she had seen her parents do it for years. That was just one of the inconveniences that went with construction work.

After Dale was born, the company moved across to the north side of the river to the small village of Alma, Arkansas, where the Alma Cannery was located. Every morning, I drove along vegetable fields to get to the job site. The only bridge across the river in that area was up at Ft. Smith. Rather than make the drive each work day, we moved to an apartment in Alma.

One night, I received a phone call from a Corps of Engineers inspector I'd worked with on several jobs, Sam Jones. He had funny stories about the times when he was stopped by the police and they asked him, "What's your name, sir?" He always dreaded telling them it was "Sam Jones."

Mr. Jones told me that the McAlister-Davis Company had so many jobs on the Mississippi and Arkansas Rivers that they needed to hire someone to run the job at Pine Bluff. He had recommended me and suggested I go to Pine Bluff for an interview.

Mr. Davis was a small man with white hair. He was dressed as though he were going to the golf course. A dress straw hat with a wide cloth hatband was cocked on the side of his head.

"Joe, I am one of the Davis brothers that own this company," he explained. "Normally I work in accounting, but they sent me out on this job temporarily as superintendent until we hire someone. I don't really know anything about the construction site."

"The job is yours," he informed me. "You come highly recommended, but you sure look too young for the job. You don't look like you shave more than twice a week, but maybe you could grow a mustache so you look old enough to be the boss," he said laughing. "That pickup over there is your company vehicle," he said as he pointed to a new 1955 green Chevrolet truck.

I thanked Mr. Davis and told him I would do my best. Then, I went back to Alma to work another week before changing companies.

Some evenings on my way home from work, I had stopped at a roadside produce market and bought the fruits and vegetables that Amy needed. This market was owned and operated by an older couple, Mr. and Mrs. Carter. Amy and the baby had met them as well.

"Well, Mr. Carter, this is the last time I'll be stopping. I'm going to miss you folks. I have a boss' job with McAlister-Davis in Pine Bluff," I said, proudly.

Thinking back, Mr. Carter must have liked me. When I stopped by, I was dusty and sweaty like any construction worker who had been outside working in the sun all day.

"Come back here and let me explain a few things before you go running off to be a job superintendent," he said, pointing to the back of the shed. We went behind a big stack of empty wooden crates that had been used to hold apples or vegetables. He turned two of the heavy crates upside down and said, "Have a seat." He sat on one and I sat on the other. Mrs. Carter was out front waiting on customers.

"I'm retired from Phillips Petroleum in Bartlesville, Oklahoma," he began. "I just want to give you some vital information that I learned by being a supervisor for thirty years. Please don't think I am trying to be smart but you are very young and I like you. I want you to be successful and I hope that you and Amy have a good life."

During the next hour, he gave me a crash course in personnel management that I would continue to use the rest of my life. He gave me examples of how to gain and keep the respect of much older employees.

"For example," he continued, "When you get on that new job, there is probably an older man who operates the dragline. The first day you go up and call him down off that big machine. Look him in the eye and tell him, "Mr. Smith, I'm your new boss. I'm sure you've been farther around this big machine than I have been around the world. I have no idea how to operate this thing, but I do know how many yards of dirt it is capable of moving per day. I'm depending on you. I need your help so we can make this project a success. If you need anything, you just let me know." I did exactly as he told me. Mr. Carter was right because it worked.

One morning on the job, I was walking by the dragline and the machine stopped. Mr. Clarence Pope was the operator and my father-in-law, Troy, was his oiler or helper. There was activity all around us. Large dump trucks loaded with stone drove along the temporary road on the river bank. The dragline was removing the dirt out of a deep cut that was to be filled with stone to stop the river from eroding the bank. But now, Mr. Pope got out and walked toward me.

"Joe, I think the watchman you have working here on weekends is sleeping on the job. A couple of times when I got here on Monday I noticed that the dragline wasn't exactly as I had left it on Friday. Someone has been tinkering with this machine. I'm concerned because this is a very expensive piece of equipment and as the operator I feel responsible."

"Mr. Pope," I said, very humbly, "that was me. Amy and I came out to the job a couple of Sundays and I started the dragline. I'd like to learn how to operate it. I'm surprised you noticed because I thought I was leaving it just like I found it."

He grinned, "What in the hell for? So you would be like me and spend the rest of your life sitting up there?" He pointed to the cab of the dragline, then turned and went back to work. I did not continue my efforts to learn to run the dragline.

I used Mr. Carter's advice with all of the employees and we finished the job far ahead of schedule. Two months after the job was over and I was no longer an employee, the company sent me a sizeable Christmas bonus. When I opened the envelope and saw the bonus check, I immediately thought of Mr. Carter. The wisdom he had shared was priceless and I was grateful.

During the first two years of our marriage I did not play any music. We had my fiddle and a D-18 Martin guitar that I had gotten off Merle Kilgore. Merle had gotten the guitar in a trade with country music star Faron Young when they both lived in Shreveport. But I seldom picked up any instrument.

Amy asked me why I never played the fiddle. Construction work had long hours and I came home tired. I didn't have the opportunity or desire to play.

In the fall of 1956, we moved to Pine Bluff, Arkansas. I was the superintendent for an Arkansas River bank stabilization project for McAlister-Davis, a large company with home offices in Memphis, Tennessee.

My little family lived on the north edge of Pine Bluff on highway 365. Directly across the street from our garage apartment was a restaurant owned by the Brown family. The Browns were parents of Jim, Ed and Maxine Brown, popular RCA Country Music Recording artists. Occasionally, I saw their father in the restaurant. He had a peg leg.

While we lived there, I played fiddle on a Saturday night stage show near Pine Bluff. I don't remember much about the musicians or the show. There was also a live radio show that I played for. The singer had stardust in his eyes but I was not impressed with his performance. I don't recall his name.

Had it not been for Amy encouraging me to play I'm sure that I would have given up my music. I thought I should concentrate on providing for our young family. My attitude could have been a result of me growing up in a family with no one playing music. In the back of my mind, I was still dealing with my parents thinking that playing the fiddle was evil.

While working along the Arkansas River I met several local farmers. These men would come out on the job location on rainy days when the weather prevented them from doing their farm work. Some came because of curiosity, and some were interested in our work on the river. They would stand around and watch the trucks hauling stone and big machines building the dikes. I found these hard working farmers most interesting.

I started a collection of old firearms. I bought one gun from a farmer in his seventies. It was an 1873 model 45/70 Springfield rifle, the same gun used in the Spanish American war. He didn't have the bayonet.

With the gun the old man included several old black powder cartridges which were the same size as a .410 shotgun shell. He'd had this ammunition since sometime back in the 1920s. I asked if the cartridges were still good and he told me about shooting down a Canadian goose on the river the previous winter.

One day it rained, and everyone went home except Troy and the Hall brothers, Cletus and Dusty, and me. We were at the top of the Arkansas River bank, standing beside my company pickup. Our job was to pave the bank with stone to prevent erosion.

We were just getting ready to leave when Dusty said, "Look at that white pelican down there in the river. I've never seen a white pelican in this part of the river before."

"I've seen brown ones before, but that is the first white pelican I've ever seen," Troy said.

"How far is it to the bird?" I asked. There were markers placed along the bank every one hundred feet.

Cletus said, "It's eleven markers to where the pelican is swimming. So that would be eleven hundred feet. That's almost four football fields."

Reaching behind the seat of the truck, I said, "I have an old 1873 model rifle here that can shoot that bird." I pulled the old relic out of the leather gun case. Then the harassment began.

"You're crazy," said Dusty.

Troy had taken his cap off and was scratching his head said, "Hey Joe, that's almost four hundred yards."

Before purchasing the rifle from the old farmer I had done some research. This model had been used to compete in fifteen hundred yard shooting matches (the same distance as fifteen football fields). I knew I wouldn't hit the pelican, furthermore, the pelican was a protected bird and the last thing I wanted to do was kill it.

"You guys don't know much about firearms, do you?" I said, jokingly. "Why with this gun I can nail that pelican in one shot."

As I opened the trap door on the old rifle I said, "I'm going to give you guys a lesson in marksmanship." I pushed the cartridge in the chamber and closed the trap door.

"First I have to set the windage," I explained. On top of the barrel was a rear sight over two inches long that lay flat, but could be flipped up in an upright position. There was also a sliding mechanism calibrated for twenty-five hundred yards.

"Before I set the windage, I must set the distance," I explained while moving the sliding sight up near the four hundred yard mark and tightening the thumb screw. "This sight is calibrated in yards instead of feet, so I will set it just below the four hundred yard mark. That should be eleven hundred feet." I was enjoying my performance.

"Joe, I don't think it is going to make any difference where you set the damn sight," said Troy, walking around the front of the pickup.

"This is a bunch of crap!" said Dusty. "Before you fire that piece of antiquated junk, do you want to make a little wager?"

"I want in on that bet," said Cletus.

"Joe, I don't think I would bet, if I were you," muttered Troy. "I'd hate to see you lose that money. You got a family to feed."

Reaching down to the ground, I picked up some dirt in my left hand and threw it up in the air. The wind caused the falling dust to drift over toward the river. "Well, there is a little breeze from the west, so I'll have to take that in consideration setting the windage," I bragged as I screwed the adjustment so the rear sight aimed off to the side, trying to make it appear that I knew what I was doing.

"That should do it," I said, with confidence.

"Let's just put $20 on this shot," said Dusty. He was getting excited, for he just knew it was a sure thing.

"You couldn't hit that pickup at eleven hundred feet with that old gun," said Cletus, "I want in for twenty."

"Joe, you're a gonna lose your money," warned Troy.

"I'm going to do you guys a big favor," I said, walking over to the truck. "I just can't find it in my heart to take your hard-earned money." I could tell that Troy was relieved.

Cletus was still mumbling about me being "chicken" as I rested the gun across the hood of the pickup. I knew I couldn't hit the pelican, but I was going to shoot the gun. I had only shot it a couple of times before, but I knew that the old black powder cartridge would fire. I reached up with my right hand and pulled back the big hammer until it clicked twice.

To add to the intrigue, I spent a long time looking down the sights at the white pelican. At eleven hundred feet, the pelican was so small that the sight covered it.

Finally, I squeezed the trigger. There was a big explosion and a large puff of smoke came out of the barrel, created by the black powder. The muzzle velocity of that old gun was about one thousand feet per second and it was a .405 grain bullet, about the size of a small marble. For about a second after the explosion you could hear the bullet buzzzzzz through the air and then there was a plop.

The white pelican exploded. It looked like someone had busted a feather pillow on the water. I was momentarily shocked. I could not believe that I had killed a protected bird.

"Well, I'll be damned!" said Troy. "Joe hit that bird. Let's get out of here."

I never told any of them it was just luck. Controlling my surprise, I said, "Let that be a lesson to you boys. Never bet with a guy with an old gun."

Thankfully, there was no one else on the river and we all went home.

Up until the end of his life Troy would say, "Did I ever tell you about the time Joe shot that white pelican on the Arkansas River?"

I loved that man.

His last years were spent in their home on Highway 27 just north of Mineral Springs, Arkansas, near the Texas and Oklahoma border. His parents had moved there from Fort Worth, Texas, when he was about five years old. The house was next to an old country church, though I never knew of Troy attending church. However, on one occasion, he went over to the church and complained to the preacher about people parking in his yard during the Sunday services. That same minister preached his funeral.

# TEXAS

In November, the job was finished in Pine Bluff, Arkansas. McAlister-Davis, the contractor, laid off all the workers. The job had gone so well, I was assured that I could work with them in the spring. Considering all the long hours I worked on the Arkansas River that summer, the time off would be a welcome vacation.

My wife, Amy, and I moved temporarily to a farm house that Amy's parents had rented near Mineral Springs, Arkansas. It was located across the state near Oklahoma. We owned a '53 Chevrolet two-door sedan, so we had a good car to travel around the area. The next two months, we spent visiting relatives, celebrating Thanksgiving and Christmas.

During this time, I played music with some local musicians. Amy tried learning the fiddle, but I proved to be a poor teacher and it was short lived.

In January, I had a call from Joe Nutt, who lived in Houston, Texas. I had met him when we worked for Houston Pipe & Steel, which fabricated piping for refineries, chemical plants and power houses. We had become very good friends before I returned to Monroe to play music with Merle Kilgore.

"Joe, what are you doing now?" he asked. Joe and his wife Opal had three children. At work, he was a pipefitter and worked as a welder foreman. There were several musicians that he knew. He did not play, but we all enjoyed weekends at family outings.

"Well, I'm married and we have a little boy," I explained.

"The main reason that I am calling is to tell you about a job. Where are you working now," he asked.

"I'm out of a work at the moment, waiting for a construction job to begin."

The job he offered me was an office position at the Houston Pipe & Steel plant. I would be running the shop office under the supervision of the Plant Superintendent, Leonard Kauf, who had been my boss the summer that I had worked there. The shop was a huge structure with an overhead crane, known as the Hughes Strut Plant. The Howard Hughes Company had constructed the building to manufacture airplanes.

After talking it over, Amy and I agreed that this was an important opportunity for me. It was a large company that could offer me a secure career, and we could settle in a home without the worry of moving when the job ended.

Amy and I and our son, Dale, moved to Houston and I took the job. A year later, I got a promotion and Amy gave birth to a beautiful red-headed baby girl we named Diane. Not only did she have long bright red hair, but she was born with one front tooth.

When the nurse brought the baby into the hospital room, Amy looked at that full head of red hair and became very upset. She was convinced that the nurse had made a mistake and brought her the wrong newborn. To console her, Amy was wheeled down the hall so she could look through the glass window and see the new babies in the nursery. All of the newborns were either Mexican or African American. Amy settled for the redhead.

My promotion was a move into Accounting where I worked in the estimating department bidding on jobs where new plants were being built. It was office work, but I liked my job and my fellow workers.

I felt secure in my job, so we bought a three-bedroom home on the northeast side of Houston near my work. We were raising a family and enjoying life, living in a safe, suburban housing addition with lots of kids.

I had occasionally played in bars or nightclubs back in Louisiana. But now, since I only worked forty hours a week, a big change from the construction jobs, I had time on my hands. Music entered my life once more.

Bill Green lived just off Laura Koppe Road. He was a good ballad singer that I met at a friend's house where we were playing music. Bill was a stout-built man with graying black hair. His Indian heritage was obvious. He looked much like Navajos I had met.

Bill liked my fiddle playing and insisted that I play at a couple of bars with him. He had a Saturday night gig in a bar somewhere out on the Beaumont highway.

The truth was, though secure, my office job did not pay as well as I would have liked, though it did offer the incentive for promotions. I decided that the bar jobs would be good practice and we could use the additional income. After a few weeks, Amy and I began to depend on the money that I earned playing. I had become a "weekend warrior."

That bar was where I met Bob Priest. He and his wife, Vanita, became friends with our family. They had no children. Though Bob was legally blind, he played guitar and pedal steel very well. He taught me music and we played in bands for over five years.

Our daughters, Susie and Jani, were born at the Northshore Hospital during the years that I worked for Houston Pipe & Steel.

In the early afternoon of a day in May 1962, Amy answered a knock at the door. Standing just outside the door was a young girl and her brother, dressed as if they were going to church, and the little girl had a wrapped gift in her hand.

"Hi, Alison," said Amy. "Did you need something?'

"We're coming to Dale's birthday party," answered Alison. Dale, our oldest son, was six years old that day.

Looking down the street, Amy noticed there were more children coming with gifts.

"How do you know that Dale is having a birthday party?" asked Amy. She was having trouble understanding how such a mistake had occurred.

Dale had just enjoyed his birthday party with his sisters, Diane, Susie and Jani. Amy had baked a two-layer cake with Dale's name across the top in red icing. We only had a small piece remaining because the family had just finished celebrating his special day.

"He told every kid on the street that his birthday party was at 2:30 this afternoon," said Alison.

Amy called Mrs. Mitchell across the street to come over and help with all the children, while she hurriedly went to the market and bought cake, cookies and ice cream. When she returned, Dale was enjoying his privately planned birthday party.

"I will deal with you when this is over, young man," threatened Amy as she went into the kitchen.

After the shock was gone a couple of days later, I asked Dale, "Was your birthday party really worth the trouble you had with your mom?"

"Sure, just look at the gifts I got," he replied with a mischievous grin.

There were many live music performances broadcast on local radio stations throughout the country well up into the 1950s. Since leaving high school, I had occasionally played on live radio shows. While in Houston, I got my first radio experience as a broadcaster when Bob coaxed me into joining him on the radio at Station KTLW in Texas City, Texas. We bought an hour of radio time on Saturday morning and sold advertising spots. Bob had difficulty seeing the record titles so I helped him in the control room during the time we were on the air. I didn't enjoy playing records, because I was more interested in playing music.

December 15, 1962 was a big turning point in my life. Up until that time, I thought I was set for life. I would work in the accounting office until I was sixty-five, retire and live happily ever after. We all thought our employment was secure. However, our company was bought by the Crane Corporation and I was included in the twenty-five percent of the office personnel who were terminated.

Mr. Ryerson was the president of our company. He could have had the department heads give us our final check, but he chose to have each employee come into his office alone. What a terrible duty he had telling all these workers that they no longer had a job. He said that he had no control over this decision and regretted this happening, just ten days before Christmas. When he handed me my final check, he had tears in his eyes. I respected him for taking the time to talk to every terminated employee.

Amy and I were in shock. This was totally unexpected. I had been replaced by an IBM machine. Finding a job before the first of the year was not likely so I took every music-playing job offered during the holidays. I sent out resumes and went on interviews.

Because I had acquired a special skill of being an estimator, I hoped I could stay in the same field. However, the several employment agencies I talked to said that because I did not have a degree they would not send me on interviews, regardless of my experience.

Amy and I started a company that promoted stage shows in the south Texas area. Some of these shows were used as fundraisers for charitable organizations. Considering it was our first year, we did well. Our big show was to be in the Beaumont area on November 22, 1963. That fateful day, President Kennedy was assassinated and no one came to the show. Once again, I was broke.

Looking back, I realize that the loss of my secure job at Houston Pipe & Steel was a blessing. Had I stayed at that job until I was sixty-five, I would not have had the opportunity of traveling all over the world playing music. And I would have never discovered West Virginia.

# NEW MEXICO

Being well established as a country fiddler in Houston, I knew I could do well playing during the December holiday season. There were private and company parties that paid well and the ballrooms and New Year's Dance were all profitable. I planned to work through December playing and then find secure employment.

Amy and I sold some of our household furniture and appliances. Then she took what money we had, took the kids and moved in with my parents in Louisiana until I could get our lives reorganized. For about two weeks, I lived in my car in the Houston area, taking my showers in truck stops.

I was the fiddle player for the Larry Butler band, playing at Dance Town USA, a Houston ballroom, when Eddie Noack came in the door. It was unusual for Eddie to come to a club. A successful songwriter, he had been playing cowboy bars for years and performed somewhere every weekend. He walked up to the bandstand and asked me to come over to his table when we took an intermission.

"Eddie, how are you doing?" I asked. Eddie had light red hair and a fair complexion that looked as though he had never been in the sun.

"Guess you lost your ass on that show down in Beaumont," he said, with a gleam in his eye. "That's what you get for booking Sonny Burns instead of me."

Sonny Burns was a country singer who played the clubs in Houston and Galveston. Sonny, Eddie and George Jones had all performed and drank together when they were in their teens. All three had serious alcohol abuse problems and each one blamed the other two for their addictions.

I liked Eddie. You could always count on him telling exactly what he thought. He was smiling, but you never knew if he was sincere or joking.

"Are you saying if I had booked you, President Kennedy would not have been shot?" I asked.

"You never know," he said. "I got a call from a booking agent named Bob Cunningham. He booked a job for me in Farmington, New Mexico, at the Somewhere Club," continued Eddie. "There's enough money in this deal for me to take you with me. You could play fiddle and sing harmony. I'm getting a lot of radio play on my latest record out there."

I didn't have to think twice. I could get out of Houston, make some plans and earn some money. Until then, I had never been farther west than San Antonio and that was how I got to New Mexico.

Eddie was really too drunk to drive when we left his house. Though we traveled in his car, I did most of the driving. We spent the first night in Tucumcari, New Mexico.

As we traveled, Eddie told me many musician stories. For a time, he had worked out of Nashville as the rhythm guitar player for Hank Snow. He was also a big Jimmy Rodgers and Hank Williams fan.

One of his stories was about attending a memorial conducted in Mobile, Alabama for Hank Williams in the late '50s. A local disc jockey interviewed him as one of the singers on the show. The announcer told Eddie that the local people did not think that Hank Williams was that great.

Eddie remarked that the local folks didn't seem to object to the money spent by all the crowds of people who came to pay their respects to the great country singer.

Back at the hotel, Earnest Tubb, also a Country Western artist, called and invited Eddie up to his room. Earnest was impressed with Eddie's answers for the local disc jockey and when Eddie met with Earnest, he was given a custom-made leather covered guitar case. The leather was hand-tooled with "Earnest Tubb" embossed in three-inch letters on the top.

Eddie cherished that guitar case. He told me that sometimes when his guitar was in the pawn shop, he would carry the empty case to a performance. When he opened it, it would be empty. He would call out, "Hey, I must have left my guitar at home. Will someone loan me an instrument so I can do this show?" Someone always would.

Eddie drank so much on the trip that I feared that he would be unable to perform when we arrived in Farmington. That meant we would not get paid. I hid his half-filled whisky bottle in the hose of the air duct under the hood of the car. When he could not find his bottle, he became furious. Later he told me that was the worst thing I could have done to an alcoholic.

We spent the night in Albuquerque. He was in such a difficult condition that he asked me to get the telephone number for AA. I made the call. When someone answered, I told them about Eddie's being drunk, but he had stopped drinking and wanted help. In about thirty minutes a man was at the door. I left them and went down the street for coffee. Later, Eddie told me that they would always come and help as long as you were not drinking.

New Mexico and Arizona were totally different from any place I had been. I had always lived near sea level and the elevation at Farmington was over 5,000 feet (a mile high). The country was very arid and actually a high desert. I'd lived most of my life in the Gulf Coast area where the humidity was greater. I had some trouble singing at that southwestern altitude, and it took some getting used to.

The job with Eddie lasted one week. But the local band at the Somewhere Club offered me a job playing the fiddle and doing some singing. I called Amy and she came out. We spent a week traveling around the area. We decided to move the family to Farmington. Amy went back and moved the family out to New Mexico. Eddie paid me and drove back to Houston.

The singer of our band at the Somewhere Club left and I became the singer and fronted the band for a few weeks. I also got a job as a truck driver. In the East, I'd gotten experience driving semi-trucks. I'd also driven dump trucks hauling granite on the Arkansas river projects.

On this job, in Farmington, New Mexico, I was lucky enough to be hired to drive a large diesel tandem dump truck hauling hot-mix or asphalt to a big coal powered power plant on the Navajo Reservation.

Later, I went to work for Radio Station KHAP in Aztec, New Mexico, which was located about ten miles east of Farmington and fifteen miles south of Durango, Colorado.

After a few months, the Federal Communications Commission (FCC) closed the radio station. We learned that the station was owned by a minister and he had failed to pay his taxes, which resulted in the shutdown.

Chip Bradiger called me from Silverton, Colorado. Chip was a bass player. While working with Rex Allen in Reno, Nevada, he had fallen while getting off the bandstand. It was a freak accident where he tripped and tried to break his fall with his left hand and fractured his wrist. He would not be able to play the electric bass guitar until his wrist had healed. He was also a trained bartender.

"Joe, they need a musician to work here in Silverton when the Narrow Gauge Train arrives each day. The pay is excellent. You can play the fiddle in the band and be the sheriff in the gunfight," he explained. "I'll be tending bar in the Bent Elbow Saloon."

Silverton was about fifty miles north of Aztec. I took the job hoping the radio station would be back on the air soon. This was my first experience with drama. I worked with some talented college students. It was their summer job. Each day at noon, we staged an entertaining gunfight in the street. About an hour later, the old steam engine train left Silverton to wind its way through the snow-capped mountains to Durango.

At the end of the tourist season, I returned to Farmington and worked at a variety of jobs while waiting for the radio station to open.

Jr. Meeks, who lived nearby, offered me a job in the oil fields south of New Orleans, Louisiana. He was the boss on a rig. We worked seven days a week and the pay was good. I worked a few weeks, sending all of my money home to Amy and the family.

On Pearl Harbor Day, December 7, 1964, our son, David, was born. He immediately drew a lot of attention. In the Farmington Hospital there were mostly Navajo Indians. Some of them had never seen a blue-eyed, blond-haired baby.

One day soon after, Amy decided to lie down to rest for a few minutes while David slept in a bassinet that sat on the floor.

"He's such a pretty baby," said Diane to her sisters. All three girls were standing around the bassinet admiring their newborn brother. Diane was seven years old, Susie was five, and Jani was three. David was asleep but his lips were moving as though he was nursing, a normal action for any baby.

"He looks red and wrinkled to me," said Susie. "Diane, look at his mouth moving," said Susie. "I think he must be hungry." Jani was squatting down by the bassinet to get a closer look but said nothing.

"Maybe we should give him something to eat," suggested Diane, trying to think of what to feed a new baby.

"I know," said Susie, "I'll put some peanut butter on a cracker."

She went into the kitchen and returned with a cracker which had a large blob of peanut butter on top.

"I'll give it to him," said Diane, reaching for the cracker.

"You will not," warned Susie, holding the cracker behind her. "I got the cracker and I'm going to feed him."

All three girls squatted down around the bassinet and watched as Susie touched the baby's mouth with the peanut butter and cracker. David immediately awoke, and began smacking his lips very loud to try to get the peanut butter off his mouth. He kept smacking.

The girls didn't hear their mother walk into the room. She had heard the loud smacking sound the baby was making.

"What in the world are you girls doing," asked Amy. Then she saw Susie holding the cracker with the peanut butter to the baby's mouth. "Oh, my God, he will choke!" she exclaimed, pulling Susie away from the bassinet.

"Susie, you're never to give him peanut butter! You could choke your baby brother. Never, never do that again, it is so dangerous for the baby," Amy scolded.

"But, Mom, he was hungry, so I fed him," explained Susie.

It's scary to think what small children might do to one another if an adult isn't watching.

Radio Station KHAP in Aztec finally opened. It had been bought by the San Juan Broadcasting Company. Finally, I had a job that was not seasonal.

# MUSIC

It was a Saturday night and I was playing the Hitching Post in Albuquerque with the Dave Kirby Trio. Dave was a DJ on a local country station and later became a recording session guitarist in Nashville. He was also a talented songwriter and wrote "Is Anybody Going to San Antone or Phoenix, Arizona?" which was a country hit for Charlie Pride.

This cowboy bar was on the south side of town on old Route 66. It must have been there since the '40s, but I would not be surprised if it still exists. There were a couple of neon beer signs on the front of the old, wooden, flat-roofed building. Along the sidewalk in front was a hitching rail made of cedar posts. It looked like the hitching rails in the old western movies where cowboys tied their horses. As you entered there was the usual odor of stale beer. The bandstand was against the right wall and the bar was directly across the dance floor on the opposite wall. Half of the dance floor was littered with small square tables each with four chairs. Exit signs and lighted beer advertisements provided the only light in the bar.

I had ridden out to the club with Hal Bynum, who lived in Albuquerque at the time. He later became a very successful song writer with songs like "You Picked a Fine Time to Leave Me, Lucille," which was a big hit for Kenny Rogers.

Sometime during the second set a very drunk, older woman staggered up to the bandstand and in slurred speech asked, "Would you play 'The Wildwood Flower'?" We played the song.

I think that was the time I decided that I was tired of performing for drinking audiences. I didn't object to anyone drinking if they wished. I just preferred playing for sober groups. On the way home, I came to the conclusion that if I did not want to play the selections that my paying audience requested, I should quit.

The next day, I called Dave and told him that I had been working bars and nightclubs for over eight years as a weekend warrior. I was tired of playing in that atmosphere and thought it best just to quit. He sympathized with me and was very kind. The last time I saw Dave (except on TV) was several years later in the parking lot of Capitol Studios on Music Row in Nashville when he was going to a recording session. He had a guitar in each hand and told me he had been fishing all day.

I'd been thinking about giving up my professional playing for some time. I think that it began back in Houston in 1959, when I was playing with a country band a club on the Galveston Freeway. Generally, a recording artist appeared with the band each weekend. I don't remember all of the band members. But I do know Benny Whitton was the bass player because I rode to the club with him. (Benny was later one of Earnest Tubb's Texas Troubadours.) My old friend Bob Priest played pedal steel.

As I closed the car door, I asked, "Benny, who is the star playing with us this weekend?"

"On the way home from work this evening I heard it is Roger Miller," said Benny as we pulled out on the street in front of my house.

"Who is Roger Miller?" I said.

"He has a new song out on RCA called 'When Two Worlds Collide'," explained Benny. "He also wrote 'Invitation to the Blues' that Ray Price recorded."

"I never heard of him," I said.

When Roger and his manager arrived at the club, I was surprised. His manager was an old friend who had attended Louisiana Tech at the same time I was there, Ed Hamilton. That had been eight years earlier. I thoroughly enjoyed visiting with Ed, who had moved to Nashville and was a very popular DJ. He was also managing the careers of several artists, one of which was Jeanie Sealy, who recorded for the Monument label.

Roger Miller was a gentleman with an abundance of wit and very gracious to work with. He would ask the band member first, but then he played every instrument on the bandstand.

Before the last set, he asked, "Joe, would it be OK with you if I played a couple of tunes on your fiddle?"

"Sure, here's my fiddle," I said, as I handed him the violin.

The first song he did was 'Me Oh My, Miss Molly.' This was an old Bob Wills tune recorded back on a 78 during the 1940s. The original recording contained three very complicated jazz violin breaks. One was by Jesse Ashlock and one by Louis Prima. I don't remember the third fiddler, but it could have been Joe Holly. Roger Miller not only sang the song but he played all three different jazz breaks exactly like the recording. I couldn't believe he was such an accomplished fiddler. I couldn't even hum those improvisations.

"Roger, that was just super. I didn't know you were such a good fiddle player," I said.

"Joe, I just play at the fiddle. That was the first job I had when I went to Nashville. I played fiddle for Minnie Pearl," explained Roger.

On the way home, I thought, *Here is a guy who is not known at all for his fiddle playing and he is so much more accomplished than me.*

During the winter of 1964, I went down to Safford, Arizona to play in a club with this four-piece country band from Farmington. Chip Bradiger, who was from Minnesota, played bass. Ron Hoskins was the steel guitar player and he was from somewhere in Arizona. I was playing fiddle and we were breaking in a new drummer from Show Low, Arizona.

When we arrived, we were told that Roy Clark would be playing with us for three nights. He was out of California at the time and had a song on the charts, 'Tips of My Fingers.' We knew Roy as Wanda Jackson's guitar player and as being easy to work with. I had also seen him on TV some years before when he played on the Jimmy Dean Show out of Washington, DC.

"Roy, we have a new drummer," I said. It was an hour before the show and we were on the band stand setting up equipment. "I'm not sure our drummer can follow you on some of your fast show tunes," I said.

Roy had a recording of his guitar playing that I'd heard. On several tunes he played extremely fast at the end. This was an exciting part of his performance and one of his trademarks.

"Joe, don't you worry about a thing. It will all work out," said Roy.

There was no rehearsal, but before the show Roy told the young drummer that he would play some very fast pieces in his show. It was not necessary for the drummer to try to accompany the tune at that fast pace. He should just sit back and enjoy the picking.

It was a joy to work with Roy. And his performance with us was most enjoyable. He told our new drummer that he played well. The remark made the kid feel good about his first job as a musician.

At the time, I did not know that Roy played fiddle. On the last set that first night he asked if it would be all right if he played my fiddle. I was blown away, for here was another musician who just picked up my instrument and played better than I could.

It was about 1995 during the Vandalia Gathering in Charleston, West Virginia, that I saw Roy Clark, Jr. He was living in Parkersburg and was a regular customer at the Fret'N Fiddle music store.

"Roy, I would like for you to know that I worked one weekend with your dad back in 1964 at the Safford Hotel in Safford, Arizona. We had a five-piece country band and not an exceptional musician among us. We were just a bar band, but your dad treated us like we were royalty. I know it was a challenge for him to do his show with us, but he complimented every one of us. He was just great. I never met your dad after that job."

"He's playing over at Laidley Field just across the street, tomorrow. Why don't you go to the show and I'll take you up to see my dad," said Roy, Jr.

"That was over thirty years ago. Your Dad wouldn't remember me."

"You wanna bet? My old man has a mind like a steel trap. He never forgets anybody," said Roy, Jr. "You really should go."

I didn't go.....

There was another time this happened. I was playing with the same country band in Farmington, New Mexico, at the Somewhere Club. At the time, I was working at a radio station, but I would play weekends with the band. Frequently, the club would book some very famous people on their way back east from Las Vegas to perform with our band. One Saturday, our guest artist was Jeanie Shepard, who was traveling with her guitar player, Jackie Phelps. He accompanied Jeanie on her part of the show. Many years later, Jackie was a regular on the Hee Haw TV show.

I invited Jackie out to my house to have dinner with my family. The best thing you could do for a road musician, was to invite him into your home for a good meal, and my wife, Amy, was an excellent cook. After the meal, we got out our instruments and played a few tunes. Jackie played the guitar while I played the old fiddle tune 'Leather Britches.' When I finished the tune, Jackie said, "Do you mind if I show you another version of 'Leather Britches'?"

"Not at all," I said, handing him my fiddle. Well, it happened again. I had no idea that he was a fiddle player and here he was far more accomplished than me. *You know,* I thought, *I should just quit.*

# SONGWRITER

"Joe, we've purchased a station in Albuquerque," said my boss, Tom Moyer, of KHAP, a Mutual Radio Network affiliate. "We would like for you to be the Station Manager."

Tom was a thin man with slumped shoulders. He and his wife, Barbara, who appeared to be several years younger, raised Appaloosa horses. She had grown up in Phoenix, Arizona, and possessed a great love for horses. Her mother worked for the station as a bookkeeper. Her father was a real cowboy and had a corral outside of town where he boarded and trained horses. I liked him.

On our farm in Louisiana I had plowed with horses until 1948. When Dad bought our first farm tractor, he sold the team of grey horses we had used on the farm. Since I had worked with horses, I would occasionally hang around the corral.

One time, we were all riding in a parade in Aztec, and Barbara's father, Bob, had chosen an Indian pony for me to ride. When I first got on him, he was a bit skittish. Halfway down Main Street, someone in the crowd along the sidewalk waved a black cowboy hat that spooked my horse. He jumped sideways, but I was prepared. I kept talking and trying to console the pony, realizing he had never been ridden out in public.

For a moment, I thought I just might end up lying on the concrete street. After the pony settled down I looked over and saw Bob, who was riding in the parade beside me, hiding behind his hat and laughing to himself, trying to conceal his cowboy humor.

I liked Bob, but he was a mischievous character. He hadn't told me the pony had just been brought in off the Navajo Reservation, where it had spent its life out in the dry desolate country. It certainly was not used to the crowds of people that lined the sidewalks and hats being waved. However, I survived the parade, pride and body intact.

"Tom, I appreciate your offer, but I don't want to move to Albuquerque," I said. I had been back to work at KHAP for about eight months and wasn't keen on moving. "My family is happy living in Farmington and we have kids in school."

"Just do me a favor and go down there and work during the week until I can find someone to take over," begged Tom. "I've already hired an engineer who can pull a board shift. The only catch is that the station has been off the air for over two years."

"Now that's a major problem," I said. "Albuquerque is two hundred miles away and I have to convince customers to purchase radio advertising for a station that's not even on the air."

"Joe, you can do it. Look at the sales you have here in Aztec," Tom said, trying to sell me on the job.

Reluctantly, I agreed to go to Albuquerque and work during the week and come home on weekends. I would help out until he could find someone permanently. Arrangements were made for me to stay in a motel that was one block from the station.

My engineer was Mike McKee, who had just been discharged out of the Marine Corp. He was a very small man. He told me that he had eaten several bananas before his physical for the Marines so he could pass the minimum weight requirement.

Mike's father worked for the Bureau of Indian Affairs (BIA) on the Navajo Indian reservation, and his mom was Italian. When Mike was a kid growing up in Gallup, tourists often thought he was Navajo because of his dark complexion and black hair. During the summer, he would wear a red sash tied around his head and speak a few words in the Navajo language. Thinking he was a Navajo boy, tourists would pay to have photos made with him. He enjoyed telling about all the folks back east who had photos of themselves posing with a Navajo boy who was actually Italian.

Being a capable engineer and working a shift as an announcer, Mike made my job much easier. He was also a very good copy writer.

One day when I was typing the log for the next day's broadcast, a tall man walked into my office. He was wearing a light brown suit and looked to be about thirty years old. What hair he had left was blond.

"You must be Joe Dobbs," he said. "I listen to your show every morning. I'm Hal Bynum," he said, extending his hand.

His hand was as soft as a woman's. *He has never picked up anything heavier than a pencil*, I thought.

"So good to meet you, Hal, and thanks for listening to KHIP," I said. "We just went on the air last week. How did you find us so soon?"

"I used to listen to this station before it shut down and I saw your ad in the paper," he explained.

"What kind of business are you in?" I asked. He was dressed like some company executive.

"I'm a social worker," he answered. "I work here in the city of Albuquerque."

"Hal, is there something that I can help you with? I have an appointment and have to leave soon," I said, apologetically.

"Well, there is one thing. I'm a songwriter. Have you received any new releases recently from Decca Records?" he asked.

"No," I said.

"Bill Monroe recorded one of my songs 'The Old, Old House,' that was also recorded by George Jones. I'd very much like to leave you one of my cards. Maybe you could give me a call when the record arrives."

I came to the conclusion that this wasn't some amateur poet but a real songwriter. He had written a song that George recorded. And George Jones was a big country music star.

"Congratulations. I'll sure call you just as soon as we get a copy," I said. "Hal, since bluegrass recordings are seldom big sellers, it's doubtful that you would receive a very big writer royalty."

"I know, but this is not about money, Joe. Bill Monroe has cut one of my songs! I can just see him in the recording studio now, looking over them little half lens reading glasses, glaring at the twin fiddles to see if they make a mistake," explained Hal with a broad grin.

"By the way, you could never guess who called me while I was on the air this morning," I said. "It was Merle Haggard. He and Bonnie were driving from California to some show."

"With I-40 coming through here, a lot of acts pass through on their way to Vegas or going back east," explained Hal.

"I've never met Merle, but he sounded like a friendly guy. He'd heard me play his record so he pulled off the road and found a phone booth to call and thank me. I thought that was nice," I said.

"He apologized for not coming to the station. Merle said that he and Bonnie had been driving all night and were tired. They were traveling in a pick-up with a camper."

I never met Merle Haggard in person.

It was not unusual for some famous person to stop in the station because it was located just a block off old Highway 66 on San Pedro Street. The new Interstate 40 was only about five blocks away.

Early one morning, I was on the air. It was before regular working hours so I was the only person in the studios. Through the big glass window I saw a yellow taxi back into the closest parking spot. A slim, well-dressed woman got out of the taxi even before the driver could get out and open her door. It was winter and she was wearing an expensive coat with a big fur collar. She came in the station and walked into the studio where I was sitting at the console doing my disc jockey thing.

"Hello, please excuse me for just barging in. I'm Mae Axton," she said. Before I had time to answer, she continued, "You may have heard of my son, Hoyt Axton. He has a record out and he's going to be a big star."

"It is nice to meet you," I said. "Thanks for stopping by." I had never heard of Mae or Hoyt Axton. I thought she was just some weird person from California.

It was just before sunup and too early for kooks, I thought. Mae Axton was wearing one of the biggest diamonds I had ever seen. Maybe she was from Hollywood. I looked out the big glass window and the taxi was still in the parking lot with the motor running. The driver looked like he was waiting for bank robbers to return.

"I live in California, and I'm taking this trip to promote my son's latest album. He is such a great entertainer. His name is Hoyt Axton and you'll be hearing a lot about him. He's going to be a big star," she continued without pausing long enough for me to respond.

"You know I'm one of the writers of 'Heartbreak Hotel?' Tommy Durden and I were sitting in this hotel with Tom Parker and we wrote that song. Of course, Tom made us include Elvis as a writer, so I only got a third. Here's a copy of my Hoyt's record," she said, without pausing. "He would certainly appreciate any airplay." I took the album from her. Above the photo of a man sitting in the floor singing and playing an acoustic guitar were the words *Mr. Greenback Dollar Man,* by Hoyt Axton.

She left as quickly as she came. Through the window I saw her get in the back seat of the taxi and they sped away. I never saw or heard from her again. *That's a great way to start your day,* I thought, as I placed the Hoyt Axton recording on the turntable.

(Hoyt did become a very successful songwriter. *Joy to the World* and *Never been to Spain* were recorded in the 70s by Three Dog Night. He not only became a well-known recording artist but also had bit parts in several movies. In 1999, he died at the age of fifty-one.)

Hal Bynum and I became very good friends during the short time I was in Albuquerque. He had an abundance of material he had written.

"Look, Joe, I'm under contract to Pamper Music. They publish every song I write. Let me make you a deal. I'm going to start a publishing company. Move your family to Nashville and you can run it and pitch my songs," Hal said. "We'll do well."

"Hal, that's a great offer. Let me discuss it with my wife this weekend and I will let you know," I said. I was just being kind to Hal. He was notorious for his lack of control when he was drinking. In the music business, I had known several alcoholics but sometimes Hal became very violent when he was drinking. I had no desire to work under those conditions.

Even though Hal agreed to pay the expenses of moving my family to Tennessee, I did not go to work for him. Looking back that is one of the times in my life that I wonder if I made the right decision. What direction would my life have taken if I had worked in the publishing business?

Several years later, when I was visiting Nashville, I stopped by the office of Glad Publishing Company, which was run by a friend I had known in Houston, Eddie Noack. I was just visiting because I was not involved with any part of the music industry. Eddie had written "*These Hands,*" which had been recorded by several artists including Hank Snow and Jimmy Dean.

"Well, your ole buddy is in town," said Eddie with a gleam in his smile.

"Which ole buddy?" I asked. Since I knew only a few people in Nashville I had no idea who he had in mind.

"Hal Bynum," said Eddie, reaching in the top drawer of his desk and writing down a number. "Here's his number if you want to give him a call."

I called Hal and we met in the Flaming Steer Restaurant near Music Row. We had a good meal and a good visit talking about the times back in Albuquerque. He was enthusiastic about his writing and focused on his creativity. With that talent, I was not surprised that he was extremely successful.

In April 2002, the phone rang and it was Buddy Griffin. "Hey Joe, I have to go down to Nashville Saturday to play the Opry with Jim and Jesse. Do you want to ride along? We will also be on at the Earnest Tubb Record Shop after we finish our show at the Opry."

Buddy Griffin was one of my dearest friends. His playing and friendship had enriched my life. We met in 1978 and later recorded a CD called "Friends, Fiddles and Favorites."

I'd been very busy and Buddy was busy, too. Between my store and his teaching at Glenville State College and playing fiddle with Jim and Jesse McReynolds, we never had time to visit. Though I didn't want to ride all the way to Nashville from West Virginia, I knew that going down and back would give us a lot of time to talk.

"I'd love to go, Buddy," I said. "Thanks for inviting me."

"Very good, we'll have a great time and I'm sure I can get you backstage at the Opry," he said. "I'll come by your house and 'holler you out' about nine o'clock Saturday morning."

It was late on Wednesday night after band practice with The 1937 Flood and I was driving home. The band had been gathering at Charlie and Pam Bowen's house in Huntington every Wednesday for several years, honing our skills as a jug band. There were no serious ambitions, just fun with a jug band without a jug.

Since I was going to Nashville with Buddy Griffin on Saturday, I decided to listen to Eddie Stubbs on WSM radio in Nashville. I very rarely listened to commercial radio. When I quit playing the clubs, I abandoned country western music, so I was not familiar with most of the current artists. Occasionally some road musician appearing in a show would drop in at the Fret'N Fiddle, my music store.

As I tuned the radio to 650, Eddie announced that Hal Bynum was being featured on the Grand Ole Opry that Saturday night. His latest recording "An American Prayer," was on the country charts.

Hal Bynum singing? When I had known Hal, he had no ambition to become a singer. However, he did have an old D-18 Martin guitar that he played while composing his songs. The announcer mentioned that Hal had several CDs out. Now this made the trip to Nashville more exciting.

Because it was Easter week-end, it was doubtful that I could get backstage at the Opry. However, Buddy and Jesse McReynolds insisted that I come to the back entrance at a specified time and they would see that I got in.

"Look, it's is not important to me that I get backstage," I said. "I was backstage at the Ryman years ago." Buddy, Jesse McReynolds and his wife, Joy, and I were sitting at a table in a restaurant near Opryland.

Jesse, a very kind man, leaned toward me and said, "We want you to have the opportunity of going backstage at the Opry. Easter Weekend is crowded, but we will get you in." *What a down-to-earth nice person,* I thought. I understood why he had so many fans and a career that went back to the early 1950s.

Backstage, Buddy introduced me to Michelle Voan, the Music Librarian. To me, she seemed to be the Stage Manager. Buddy then went to his dressing room to rehearse for their Opry performance.

"Is Hal Bynum here, backstage?" I asked Michelle. She was very busy keeping the performers informed about the show. I could hear Jimmy C. Newman singing out on the stage.

"He sure is, Joe. Hal is our featured artist this evening," she said as Eddie Stubbs walked by.

"I haven't seen him since back in the 60s. Could you tell me how I would recognize him?" I asked.

"He has a trimmed white beard and he's wearing a camel blazer and black pants. He's back here somewhere, I saw him just a minute ago," she said.

The stage area at Opryland was very modern. The lighting was well done and you got an excellent view from the wings looking out across the stage into the audience. You could see the performers that were currently on stage and I saw Little Jimmy Dickens, in his eighties, singing to the crowd.

Backstage directly behind the Main stage was a large open area. All around the wall, which was "U" shaped, were doors opening into dressing rooms. Performers, friends, roadies, and groupies were socializing throughout the open area. It was a festive atmosphere and the energy was very high.

I located Hal. He was talking to a gentleman wearing a dark suit, whom I did not know. I stood near Hal until they finished talking.

"Hal Bynum?" I asked. He turned and looked at me.

I returned his gaze and said, "I'm Joe Dobbs."

There was just a short pause, then his face lit up with a big radiant smile and he said, "Joe Dobbs! It's been a long time." We shook hands. I was always reluctant to approach someone that I had not seen in years, fearing that they would not or did not want remember me.

But my fears vanished when he put his arm around my shoulders and said, "This is just great. Come with me. There is someone I want you to meet."

We passed several doors before he said, "This is my dressing room," and opened the door. I don't remember just how many but there were several people in the room. Hal stepped in the room and said, "Folks, this is an old friend that I have not seen in years." With kindness in his voice he added, "We would appreciate a few minutes of privacy."

The visitors left and closed the door. Across the room sitting in a comfortable chair was a well-dressed lovely lady. She had black hair, dark eyes, and very pretty facial features. In her lap was a little long haired dog that looked as though he thought he was a human.

"Joe, this is my wife, Rebecca, and our dog Beau. This woman saved my life."

"Hi, Joe, it is nice to meet you," she said.

"My pleasure," I said.

"Honey, Joe and I knew one another years ago in Albuquerque. This man always liked my songs." Turning to me to me he said, "Joe, I just cannot tell you how good my life is. Thanks to Rebecca, I have some spiritual direction and life is just wonderful."

"My manager is Merle Kilgore. I remember you telling me that you and he were roommates in college," he said.

We visited a few minutes, but I knew he had a performance to do. I thanked him for taking the time so we could visit. He was one of those talented people that passed through my life so briefly and after many years our meeting again had touched me emotionally. To me, the experience of our lives crossing was priceless.

Walking away from Hal and Rebecca's dressing room I thought, *This is a good time and I am so glad I came.*

Hal Bynum was a most talented and prolific song writer. Some of his compositions are:

"Lucille" recorded by Kenny Rogers

"Chains" recorded by Patty Loveless

"Papa was a Good Man" recorded by Johnny Cash

"There Ain't no Good Chain Gang" recorded by Johnny Cash and Waylon Jennings

"Nobody's Fool" recorded by Jim Reeves

"The Old, Old House" recorded by George Jones, Bill Monroe, Ralph Stanley

Hal's book "The Promise" is excellent reading.

# GO EAST, YOUNG MAN

It was the summer of 1966 and we had been living in Farmington, New Mexico for almost three years. The local economy, which was tied to the drilling of oil and gas wells on the Navajo Reservation, had plummeted. Housing developments were eighty percent vacant because so many families were moving out of the area.

Though the radio station where I worked was a very good experience for me, they were not paying what we had agreed upon. The station, KHAP in Aztec and owned by the Moyer family from California, had hired me to sell advertising. After calling on clients all day I would then pull a three-hour board shift each evening as a disk jockey. In addition to my meager salary I was to receive a commission on all my sales. Since I was their only salesman, I should have been doing well.

One day after looking over my commission check, I walked into the bookkeeper's office. Margaret was a very pleasant middle-aged woman who was the boss's mother-in-law. She was very nice to me and told me that she listened to my show each evening.

"Margaret, I was looking over my commission check and I don't think I was paid for the Coca-Cola account," I said. "Could you please check on it for me?"

"Joe, I'm only supposed to pay your commissions on paid accounts and Coca-Cola has not sent us a check," she said, flashing her big smile. I thanked her and left the building.

The Coca-Cola distributing company was located about twenty-five miles north of Aztec in Durango, Colorado. Bill Hall, the manager of the company, had become a friend. He was a big fan of Anita Bryant, the wonderful singer from Oklahoma.

Since our station programmed only Country Western music and some Rock and Roll, they were disposing of the easy listening record library. I took all the Anita Bryant albums and gave them to Bill.

I liked Bill. His company was my largest advertising account. Their offices were on the second floor of a bank building and his favorite line was '*Our ass sits over a million dollars.*'

I walked into Bill's office and we talked about fishing for German Brown trout on the San Juan River and how good the fishing had been for the last two months.

"Bill, I would appreciate it if you could pay your advertising account with the radio station for last month. Man, I have five kids to feed and we could use the commission," I said.

"Joe, let me check, but I'm sure that invoice was paid over three weeks ago," he said. He walked into the next office and then returned showing me a canceled check.

"Thanks, Bill, sorry I bothered you. We'll go trout fishing next week," I promised.

I went back by the radio station and asked Margaret if she was sure that the Coca-Cola account was delinquent. She looked uncomfortable but assured me that she had not received the check.

That evening during my program, Tom Moyer came into the control room and said, "Joe, from now on if you have any questions about your commission check, you see me instead of Margaret."

For several months I had known that I was not being paid all of my commissions. I knew Tom had no intentions of paying me what I was due. Realizing the state of the local economy, I knew it was only of a matter of time until the radio station would close. We were one of three stations in a two-station market.

I had experience at several skills, but there were no jobs. I had worked as an accountant, salesman, truck driver and radio announcer to name a few. I could operate some heavy equipment such bulldozers and other types of dirt moving machines.

A very good friend, Walt Massey, had called several times offering me a job in sales with a firm in Nashville, Tennessee.

My wife, Amy, and I talked about the difficulty of making the move all that distance back east to Tennessee with five children. We had to make a decision about whether the move to Tennessee would be more than we could afford.

I had met Walt in November of 1963. I was driving near Beaumont, Texas, listening to several different radio stations because a country music show that I was promoting required radio advertising. One station caught my attention with a program called, "Morning Coffee with Walt." The announcer had a beautiful, resonant, network voice and he was playing what was called "easy listening" music. Which meant it was big band swing music with singers like Perry Como, Dean Martin, and Frank Sinatra.

Following a beautiful song by one of these crooners Walt interrupted with, "Throughout the morning I've been programming music for your listening pleasure. Now I'll play one for me." And in the middle of a program of "easy listening" music, he played Buck Owens' "Love's Gonna Live Here," which was a popular country song at that time, and was certainly not "easy listening."

I couldn't believe he played a country song during that program. Very likely, the station manager was out of town.

I just had to meet this person, so I drove fifteen miles to the radio station studios in Silsby, Texas. The station was located at the edge of town surrounded by beautiful, tall, Texas pine trees.

I walked in and introduced myself. Walt was of average height with a full head of black wavy hair. A well-dressed man of about forty-five years, he wore a big smile that set you at ease and carried himself with the confidence of a prizefighter. I immediately hired him to be the MC on the Country Music stage show that I was organizing. This began a friendship that would last for the rest of his life. He died of cancer in his home in Nashville in the late 1980s.

On November the 22nd, the day of the country music stage show, I was in the radio station with Walt and he told me to go back into the newsroom and get him some news off the AP wire.

All radio stations had a teletype machine that constantly ran printed copy of the world, state, and local news and also the weather forecast. If there was an emergency, a bell, much like the one on old typewriters, would ring several times.

As I approached the machine, the bell began to ring and did not stop. I read as it came over the wire, *"President Kennedy has been shot in Dallas."* I tore off the page and immediately took it into the control room. Walt interrupted his program and made the announcement that the president had been shot.

Well, no one except the performers came to the show that night. The entire country was in shock and mourning the death of our leader. I lost all of my money and our country lost a great president.

Almost three years later, I was out of a job and could not find work, so we made the decision leave New Mexico.

Living in the Southwest had been much like an extended vacation, because we spent many summer weekends camping in the mountains of southern Colorado. The thought of having to move from an area that the family thoroughly enjoyed was saddening.

We visited several families of good friends to say our sad "goodbyes." One such person was Speedy McClain, who was originally from Alabama. Speedy had an excellent four-piece band that played a variety of styles of music on the Nevada Circuit. His group often performed at the Golden Nugget in Las Vegas.

Once, Speedy offered me a job with the band. Some of the band members could play several instruments and he wanted me to play bass so the bass player could switch to saxophone or clarinet. On country tunes, I could play the fiddle. I told him that I was not a bass player, but he said that was no problem. It would be easy for him to teach me to play the electric bass guitar on their Rock and Roll selections. This would have added another dimension to their show. I declined Speedy's offer.

The band was out on the road a lot, sometimes two weeks at a time. My family was more important and I preferred to be at home. I never gave the offer a second thought. This was one of those memorable chances in life that I had to let pass.

Since I never planned to work again as a professional musician, I sold Speedy several instruments and some musical equipment. One was a Fender Bassman Amp that I had used when I played with country bands. (The 1959 Fender Bassman Amp that I sold for $150 would be worth $3,500 in 1998.) I know that he neither needed nor could afford the musical equipment he bought from me. Nothing was said but I knew it was his way of helping a musician and his family in need. This was a gesture of camaraderie among musicians I would experience many times throughout my life.

As I helped him load the gear into the back of his station wagon, he said, "Joe, it's a long way to Nashville, Tennessee. If you and your family have any trouble on this trip please call me. You know my phone number." I never heard from Speedy again, but he has been in my thoughts many times.

All that was left after selling or giving away unwanted items, we loaded into a trailer that we pulled behind the car. We left behind two five-gallon buckets of Indian pottery shards that we had picked up in the yard and garden.

Other than friends, the most difficult to leave behind was our two-year old German Shepherd dog. A friend had given him to the children when he was just a puppy. Our veterinarian advised us not to move the dog because of the risks involved moving from 5,000 feet elevation down to sea level. He was sure the dog would have health problems. Our youngest, David, was hurt the most when we made the decision to leave the dog with friends.

Early one morning, we set out fully-loaded to begin our trip back east to Tennessee. No one was excited about moving east. It was strictly a move for economic reasons. In my heart, I sincerely hoped we could return when the economy improved.

Somewhere along the two hundred mile distance between Farmington and Albuquerque, we crossed the Continental Divide. After crossing this point you could no longer see the snow-capped Rocky Mountains. I stopped the car and the family got out for a last look at the Rockies. I promised to return, but as life would have it, we never went back.

We left New Mexico and drove across Texas and Oklahoma to western Arkansas. As we traveled across Oklahoma, it was harvest time for the watermelon farmers. Every few miles there were folks selling their watermelons on the side of the road. Oklahoma watermelons are truly delicious.

"Dad, please stop and buy us a watermelon," begged Diane. She was the oldest girl. "It won't take us long to eat some watermelon."

"Yeah, Dad, it's been a long time since we've had any watermelon," said Dale.

"Please, Dad," said Susie.

I pulled over at the next stand, which had roadside picnic tables and purchased two big watermelons. The entire family stuffed themselves on delicious ripe Oklahoma watermelon. I forgot that watermelon juice is a diuretic. We weren't out of sight of the roadside stand until the kidneys began to do their thing.

I don't know how my times we had to make rest stops before we arrived in Arkansas. We even made rest stops where there was no rest stop. It was quite some time before anyone mentioned watermelon again. To this day, at our family reunions some one will say, “Do you remember the time that Dad stopped and we ate all that watermelon at the roadside park and us kids peed all the way across the state of Oklahoma?”

Amy's family lived in Nashville, Arkansas, just a few miles from the Texas and Oklahoma border. There were grandparents, great-grandparents, and numerous cousins to visit.

After settling in Nashville, Tennessee, it was very difficult to find work that would support our family. I took a sales position with H & H Distributors, a wholesale distributor of record albums, but I had to travel to neighboring states.

The company put racks of popular record albums in supermarkets, drug stores and other retail merchants with a variety of music selections on each rack. I remember selling Beatles, Tijuana Brass, The Mamas and Papas, Monkeys and Lawrence Welk albums. There were also Bluegrass and Country music records on the racks.

The company had accounts in eight states and my job was to open new accounts. This kept me on the road and away from home during the week, which was a disadvantage. Alabama, Arkansas, and West Virginia were among the places I went to open new stores.

I had never been farther east than Memphis, so all the eastern states were a new adventure. On one trip to northwest Arkansas, I sold accounts in Eureka Springs and other towns in the Ozarks.

It was a Monday morning and the boss, Ed Hoskins, called me into his office. "Joe, we have several accounts in West Virginia, but in order for it to be profitable for us, we have to open some new dealers," he said. "The folks in West Virginia have an interest in music and our sales are very good. I think you'll enjoy traveling through the mountains," he added.

"I'll do my best," I replied. The company had assigned me a 1966 Ford Econoline Van, so I could take a selection of record albums to service the existing accounts.

The Appalachian Mountains were different from any region I had ever visited. The steep hillsides and small, narrow hollows were so different from the Rockies out west. The extremely crooked roads required your constant attention.

Just after noon. I approached the little coal mining town of War, West Virginia, located in the southernmost part of the state. I was starting up another hill, when I noticed an old pickup truck parked on the side of the narrow road. The hood was raised and a middle-aged man was standing beside it, looking very disgusted at the engine. I stopped.

"Having trouble?" I asked.

"Yep, I think it's the water pump," he answered as steam continued to rise from the motor. He was dressed in work clothes and I just assumed he was a coal miner. “Could you give me a ride down to War? It’s only about five miles over the next mountain.”

“Sure, I’m headed that way and you are more that welcome to ride,” I said. He opened the passenger door and got into the van.

In the Econoline van of those days, the vehicles were box shaped and once seated your feet were not more than eight inches from the very front of it. The small, six cylinder engine was under a hood between the two front seats.

As we started up the mountain road he was obviously a bit uncomfortable. He looked out the windshield and down at the road, then over at me and I could tell that he had never ridden in a Ford Van.

Then he said, “Well, if a feller was to have a wreck in this thang he’d be the first one there.”

I didn’t say anything but I thought; *Now these are my kind of folks. I think I am going to like West Virginia.*

Most nights on the road were spent in some inexpensive motel or old hotel. I would work until late and many times I would spend the evening doing my paper work.

One winter night, I stayed in an old hotel in Beckley because it was very inexpensive. After going to my room I could see why. I had to share the bathroom down the hall with the other guest. Not only that, the steam pipes made so much noise that I had trouble sleeping. I stayed there only once.

If I was anywhere near White Sulfur Springs, I would stay at an old hotel operated by two lovely older ladies, driving longer if I had to. It was located on Route 60, which was the main street. When you walked in, the furniture and drapes were much like a Bed and Breakfast and not a hotel. It was furnished like a living room in the 30s or 40s and the lobby made you feel so at home.

If you had been driving crooked mountain roads all day it was a very homelike, inviting atmosphere. The rooms were very clean and the ladies served breakfast. I stayed there only twice, but the following Christmas they sent me a Christmas Card. Obviously this was to impress their customers. I don't think I ever convinced Amy they were two ol and my relationship with them was only that of a hotel guest.

I opened a sufficient number of new accounts throughout the state and my company was pleased with my work. However, I disliked being away from home during the week. After a few months, I knew I had to find work that would keep me at home with the family.

On my second trip to West Virginia, I met a record album distributor in Huntington and he offered me a job. Even though it meant moving to West Virginia, it was appealing because I would not have to be away from my family.

We had not done well economically in Nashville, Tennessee. My income was not sufficient and the summers in that city were very hot. After much discussion, it was decided that I would take the job in Huntington and move the family to West Virginia.

I left Louisiana when I finished high school and only returned to the swamps for visits. In my earlier years, I had some guilt about not appreciating where I spent my childhood. But never in my life have I been homesick for Louisiana.

The people were great, but the climate was most uncomfortable for me. I have learned that people are about the same anywhere you live. Customs, traditions and speech may vary but folks are folks. It was the hot, humid weather and all the insects that made living in Louisiana a challenge.

One of my earliest memories was looking at a picture of the snow-capped Rocky Mountains on a calendar in my mom's kitchen. I wondered why God had me get born in the swamps instead of those beautiful cool mountains. I was about four years old.

After about a year in the mountains, West Virginia was home. It was the first time I had felt at home. For the first time in my life, when we would take a trip, I experienced the feeling of wanting to be home. I often tell people *I wasn't born in West Virginia, but I got here as soon as I could.*

# WELFARE LINE

Before the family came to Huntington, West Virginia, I worked for Toy House of West Virginia long enough to rent a house and make the necessary arrangements for them to move. The company serviced record racks and a variety of non-food items in grocery stores. We had accounts throughout the Tri-State area of West Virginia, Kentucky, and Ohio. Kroger and A&P were our two largest customers.

Our first house was on Auburn Road, in the west end of Huntington. It was located a block from the levee or floodwall (as it is called in West Virginia) that protected us from any flooding of the Ohio River.

The neighborhood children used the floodwall as a recreation area. Kite flying in the spring was best done on top of the flood wall. In the winter it became a slope for snow sledding. Any time a family purchased a new appliance such as a refrigerator, stove, washer or dryer, its cardboard box would become a sled to ride down the floodwall. This was especially popular in the summer when the grass was green and slick.

After a few months on Auburn Road, we moved several blocks to a much larger house near Camden Park. This was also near the Toy House Company warehouse where I worked.

David, our youngest son, was in the first grade. He acquired a taste for fresh grapefruit and almost every morning for breakfast, he would eat a half sprinkled with sugar.

"Dad, where do grapefruits come from?" asked David. We were at the breakfast table.

"Dave, grapefruit is a citrus fruit and it grows on small trees," I answered. "Oranges and lemons also grow on small citrus trees."

"I don't like oranges or lemons but I love grapefruit," said David getting up from the table to get ready for school. First, he went out the back door into the backyard but returned shortly.

I soon forgot about the incident. Then a couple mornings later, I noticed that after finishing his grapefruit, he went into the backyard again.

"What are you doing in the backyard this time of the morning?" I asked him as he came in the back door.

"Every morning, I save the seeds out of my grapefruit and plant them in the backyard," he explained. "I'm going to grow my own grapefruit tree," he said, with confidence. I did not want to tell him that grapefruit trees would not grow in West Virginia. Maybe later.....

"Joe, if you will run the outside, I will run the inside," said Frank Hawkins. He was the owner of the company and my boss. "You oversee the three truck drivers making our deliveries and sell new accounts. I'll make sure you have plenty of salable merchandise and I'll run the warehouse and keep the trucks loaded."

Frank had explained to me how he had wanted to retire and had turned the company over to his brother-in-law. Sales dropped drastically. The company was on the brink of bankruptcy when he took it over.

"Joe, with your sales experience and my warehouse management skills, we can make this a very profitable company," Frank said. He gave me a figure for the volume of sales that was a "breakeven point."

At the end of the year, we would split the sales we produced over that amount. He could only pay me a meager salary, but with my bonus at the end of the year, I would be doing well. Even the salary was enough for my family to get by on, but I thought this was a good incentive.

Everything depended upon my sales and customer relations. I would work hard and reap the benefits in the form of an annual bonus.

Frank lived up to his word. He kept the warehouse stocked with items that sold in the supermarkets. I worked six days a week and during that first year, we tripled the sales.

Although I was working a lot of hours, we as a family played together. The house was always busy with five children. Everyone had a bicycle and we lived in an area where it was safe to bike ride.

About this time, Diane decided to run away from home. She was ten years old and something happened that made her feel unloved. Neither she nor anyone in the family can remember what caused her to come to this conclusion.

We lived in the west end of Huntington where our house was about a block away from the railroad tracks. It was a suburban neighborhood with a lot of kids.

Diane took the white purse someone had given her because she thought it was pretty, and packed a pair of shorts, a shirt, and a peanut butter-jelly sandwich. She zipped it closed and left home forever just before dusk.

Diane decided to spend the night with her best friend, Jean Coder, and decide her future tomorrow. Jean lived about nine blocks away, across Route 60, which was a busy four-lane road. It was getting dark when Diane approached Route 60 and with all the traffic she became frightened. She decided it was too scary to try to cross so she started walking back home.

As night approached, she became afraid and knew that by then, the family would have discovered that she was gone. The more she thought about it, the more she realized her parents, brothers and sisters would be worried. As it got darker, she became more scared and the idea of the family missing her weighed on her.

Even though she did not feel loved, she made the decision to return home. By now, they must have called the police and the entire family would be worried out of their minds.

When she got to the backyard, she hid behind our two garbage cans and watched through the windows as the family members moved about.

It took a lot of courage to walk up the steps back into the house that she had left forever just two short hours ago. She was prepared for the family to be crying and just knew they would run and hug her after discovering she was safe.

As she walked into the house, the TV was playing loud, someone was at the refrigerator looking for food, and the boys were in their room playing a game. No one had noticed her enter the house.

Amy came walking through the room and without stopping said, "Diane, you need to clean your room."

It was terrible. Evidently, no one knew she had ever left. She went to her room and put the white purse on the bed, feeling crushed.

"Should I even tell them?" she wondered.

Amy and I were very excited about my bonus. I didn't have all the figures for the last two months of the year, but I knew it would be between $25,000 and $26,000. During the first four months, I had opened so many new accounts that we had difficulty getting merchandise delivered on time. With my success our family would have enough money to make a down payment on a house. Amy and I talked about which part of town we wanted to live in.

Sometime between Christmas and the end of the year, Mr. Hawkins called me into his office. Frank was a short, average-sized man. He never dressed to where you would know that he owned so much rental real estate in the Huntington area. Most of the time, he looked like a laborer on some construction job. Once he boasted to me that he had never owned a pair of shoes that cost over eight dollars.

One day a salesman stopped me outside the office and asked if the guy sitting behind the junky desk eating a baloney sandwich could really pay for one thousand dozen Halloween masks.

"Check his credit with Dunn and Bradstreet," I suggested.

"I did," said the salesman. "After meeting him, I still can't believe it."

Frank had a spreadsheet lying on top of the papers that cluttered his desk. I knew that it was a matter of days that I would receive my bonus.

"Joe, I find it hard to believe that we tripled the sales in this company the first year. We have merchandise in stores that we never serviced before, thanks to your ability for opening new accounts," he said. "You have done a remarkable job."

"Mr. Hawkins, we all worked hard. It requires a team effort throughout the company to achieve this level of sales," I said. Then, thinking of the future, I said, "Amy and I have been talking about buying a house as soon as we get the bonus." We were renting a house that he owned, which was just around the corner from the warehouse.

"Joe, I've been thinking about your bonus. You're a good employee and without you maintaining the customers out there, the company will dwindle again. I need some security that you won't go out and take a job with one of our competitors," he said. "After considering everything, I've come up with the decision that the company should hold back your bonus for a year."

My heart sank! I could not believe that he was doing this to me and my family.

"Mr. Hawkins, you know that I have a big family. In order to survive on my pay, we've been very conservative. And, we've really been looking forward to the time we can finally purchase the household items we need," I pleaded.

But Frank held firm. He went on to say that if I quit, I would forfeit my bonus.

Walking around the corner and up the street toward our house, I tried to think of some way to tell Amy that we wouldn't be getting the bonus. I couldn't believe that I had so misjudged this man. Now I knew he had no intentions of ever paying me the money I was due.

Frank and his wife flew to Las Vegas to a product show where they bought merchandise the company would need for the next year. When he returned, I quit. I gave him about a minute's notice.

It was about two years later that I was talking with someone in Nick's News book store in downtown Huntington. This man told me he was in town to build up the business of a tile company that was approaching bankruptcy.

I told him about my disappointment with the toy company and a radio station in New Mexico that I helped avoid going out of business. In both cases, the owners had agreed to pay me handsomely if I could make the companies solvent.

He very kindly explained that you must have a contract in these ventures. It doesn't matter how much you trust a person. When the money starts rolling in, they all get greedy. Without a contract, you will go without your earnings. These were expensive lessons.

Looking back, I think that Amy handled the misfortune better than I did. Our car was very old and undependable, so I could not take a job that required me driving out of town. During the next three years, I made several bad decisions concerning my work which caused the family financial hardships. This was also the time that our youngest child, Scott, was born. It was not the best time to add to our family.

Sometime in the early 70s, a couple of days before Christmas, we were out of money. We had just enough food. Amy and I tried to keep our desperate situation from the children, but our teenage daughter, Diane, knew we had no money.

All five children were expecting Santa Claus, and Diane kept telling me that something would happen and there would be toys for Christmas. I couldn't imagine how. On Christmas Eve, there was a delivery from the Calvary Baptist Church that was a miracle for our family. I still have no knowledge of how they knew about our desperate situation.

Our oldest son, Dale, helped the family by giving us the money he made on his paper route. We had no personal items that we could pawn. I'd sold my two violins. The small children never knew what a difficult time this was. At that time, all we had was our good health.

After a discussion, Amy and I came to the conclusion that we had to get help. There was no one in either of our families we could ask for help. Neither of us or our families had any experience with applying for welfare.

One morning, she and I went to the welfare office and filled out the necessary papers to acquire some assistance. It became a very positive action. They gave us food stamps that day so we could buy food. Medical care was immediately made available for the entire family. After filling out some forms we were told that they could place me in a job immediately. There were employers that were subsidized so they could hire me.

For us, welfare was not only a lifeline, but it was a leg up. It got us started on the road to being self-sufficient once again.

# BACK ON THE JOB

We received the food stamps for a very short time. Once I knew how the welfare system worked, I could understand why some families just stay and make no effort to get off the dole.

For the first time since I had lost my job at Houston Pipe and Steel back in 1962, my family had full medical coverage. In 1971, I would have to earn approximately $25,000 per year to purchase all the benefits I had on welfare while I was not working.

After all the theology, theosophy, and spiritual paths I had studied, there was one thing that I found consistent. You reap what you sow. Down the road there would be a price to pay if I abused the help my family received from the government.

The day after we applied for welfare, I interviewed for an auto parts salesman's job at Lavalette Auto Parts in Lavalette, West Virginia. It was located about eight miles from our house. The old car we had would be able to make that drive each day.

Wearing dress pants, a shirt and tie, I entered the store. I had to have this job. The owner was Joe Stultz, a slim, stoop-shouldered man with curly hair that was turning grey and made him look older than his age. As he looked me up and down he had a funny look on his face. I wondered if my fly was unzipped.

After introducing himself, he said, “Joe, I could put you to work today, but you’ll have to go back home and change into something more casual.”

I thought about how far it was back to Huntington. “Well, could I make it for just one day in these clothes?” I asked. “I could take off the tie.”

“I’m furnishing you an automobile and you’re going out to make sales calls on garages and car dealers. You’ll be talking to greasy mechanics and they’re not going to buy anything from you dressed up like that.”

Joe Stultz was probably the most honest and best employer I ever worked for. He had so much passion for people. The hard attitudes one needs to survive in the competitive business world were difficult for Joe. I worked for him about two years and then went into business on my own. He later closed his business and went to work for the US Postal Service.

It was the desire to get our family out of the busy city and find a more affordable house that prompted us to move out to Harveytown in 1973. This location was close enough that the children didn’t have to change schools. The house was small, but I was allowed to do some improvements in lieu of rent. The place we rented was up on the hill behind our landlord, Mr. Turner's house.

Mr. Turner was a delightful old man of eighty-seven years who had outlived two wives. He had been retired for over twenty-five years from the railroad. During his time with the railroad, he worked in a section gang that built and maintained the railroads that hauled coal out of Mingo, Logan, and Wayne counties. After we moved, I wished that I had spent more time with him for I am sure he had a lot of stories to tell about the “good ole days.”

Our driveway was beside his house and we parked our vehicle just up the hill from his back door.

"Good morning," he greeted me as I came down the hill to go to work. "Would you care for a little nip to start your day?" he asked, lifting a pint bottle of whiskey.

"No. Thanks, Mr. Turner. I think I'll pass," I replied. "Sure is a pretty day. I noticed the honeysuckle blooming. It smells nice and reminds me of my childhood. My mom always loved the smell of honeysuckle," I said, getting into my car.

Mr. Turner's house was a square cinder-block, four-room bungalow with a lot of large windows. The cinder-block walls had never been painted on the outside so it was rather plain. He lived simple and didn't own an automobile. You could see a black and white TV in one of the small rooms. He didn't seem to read or have any interests, but just waited patiently, waiting to go on to the next world.

His youngest son, Harry, would sometimes come and take him to run his errands. The kids said that Mr. Turner drank a pint of M&M (Matting & Moore) whiskey every day.

"I think that you kids are exaggerating," I said. I knew he gummed Brown Mule tobacco. He had no teeth.

"Dad, just go down and look in those weeds by the mailbox and count the bottles. That's where he throws his empties," said Dale, our oldest son.

There were a lot of stories about Mr. Turner. Some folks claimed that after an argument, he fatally shot a son-in-law who was sitting across the breakfast table back in 1910. And as the story goes, he never went to jail.

I found him to be a very genuine and good person who enjoyed the children, especially when they would stop and talk with him.

One evening when I arrived home from work, David met me as I got out of the car. David was the next to the youngest in our family of six children. He was a skinny kid of eight with natural blond hair and crystal blue eyes that were the envy of many of the young girls.

"Well, how was school today?" I asked.

Without answering my greeting, David asked, "Dad, would you buy me some chewing tobacco? I think that I'd like to try some."

Through trial and error, I had developed some parenting skills that seemed to work in a situation like this. I would just put it off as long as I could, in hopes that he would lose interest. This seemed to work a lot better than just immediately saying "No" or reprimanding the child.

"When did you decide to start chewing tobacco?" I asked, looking him straight in the eye.

"I don't know, I just thought that it would be fun," he said. "Will you bring me some when you come in from work tomorrow? I want to get started."

"I don't think you'll like it, but I guess you just have to try it," I said.

I thought this would be the last of the chewing tobacco, but when I drove in from work the next day, David was standing there. As I got out of the car, his first words were, "Did you get me my tobacco?"

"Dave, I'm sorry, I was busy working today and I forgot all about it," I lied. "I will get it for you tomorrow."

When I arrived home from work the following day, David was not there, so I was sure that the tobacco episode was over. Then, as the family was all sitting at the supper table that evening, David said, "Oh Dad, you didn't forget to buy me my chewing tobacco again, did you?"

David had three sisters, Diane, Susie, and Jani. They all picked up on the conversation.

"Dave, that stuff is filthy, surely you don't want to try chewing tobacco," said Diane.

"David, you're crazy, that tobacco will make you sick," warned Susie.

"Well, I hate to tell you this, Dave, but I forgot it again," I said.

"Dad, I just can't believe that you are going to let him try chewing tobacco, that's disgusting," said Jani.

The three girls had a strong bond with David. They had practically raised him. When he was small, he was often their "baby" when they were "playing house." Once I walked through the room where they were playing, and David, who was about two, was crawling around on the floor on his hands and knees barking like a dog.

"What's going on?" I asked.

Jani, holding a doll in her arms, looked up and replied, "David is our dog and be careful because he will bite." There was a special closeness he enjoyed with his sisters.

The next morning, David was up early to remind me to get his tobacco. It was unusual for him to get up this early because it was an hour before he caught the school bus.

"You know there are several kinds of chewing tobacco, so I really don't know what kind to get you," I said.

"What do you mean, Dad?" asked David.

“Well, there is the chewing tobacco that comes as a plug and some that comes in a bag. I don’t know which one you want," I said.

"Oh, I want the plug. That’s the kind that Mr. Turner chews," he said. "Every morning when I go by his house, he is sitting on the porch and just chewing and spitting. You can tell that it must be good."

It seemed that I was going to have to get that kid some tobacco so I said, "Now Dave, the tobacco that comes in the plug is very strong. I’m sure you would do better trying the pouch."

Just as I expected, when I came home, there he was waiting for me. "I got you some Mail Pouch tobacco, Dave," I said, before he could ask. “I think that it would be better if you just start out with a little chew." I wanted to discourage him, not make him ill. "Is it alright if I have a chew with you?" I asked.

"Sure," he said, opening the tobacco pouch. Smiling with excitement, he took a very small amount in his jaw and I took a small chew also.

Amy had a garden up next to the trees on the hill behind the house.

"While we are chewing, why don’t we go up and see how your Mom's garden is doing," I suggested.

The garden only got about two hours of sunshine a day because it was so close to the trees and the morning shade kept the sun out. I’d told her I didn’t think she would have a very good garden in that location. But she loved tilling the soil, so I did not argue. David and I walked through the garden looking at the small tomato plants and just chewing and spitting as we walked.

"How are you doing, Dave?" I asked as we walked by the row of onions. I could occasionally hear him ridding his mouth of the juice.

All at once he said, "Dad, I think I’m going to have to let mine go." He was walking behind me so I turned around and saw that his face was white. Not just around his mouth, but his whole face. I never dreamed that small amount of chewing tobacco would make him so sick.

"Spit it out, Dave, and let's go to the house and wash out your mouth," I said. He spit out the tobacco, but before we could make it to the back steps, he lost his lunch. He was very sick and still heaving when Diane ran out the house with a wet wash cloth in her hand.

As she ran, she said, "My Gosh! I just cannot believe that you would give him a chew of tobacco, knowing it would make him sick. This is just awful." And about that time David heaved again.

"Honest, I had no idea that it would make him sick, maybe a little nauseated, but not that sick," I said, apologetically.

It was several days before David's sisters could begin to see the humor in the episode. Some years later, David and his family were at our family reunion in Tennessee and I asked him if he remembered the chewing tobacco.

"Dad, that was my first and last chew," he said, smiling.

After being on welfare, for some reason that I never understood, we were eligible to purchase a new home from the Federal Housing Administration (FHA). They did not even require a down payment.

So we purchased a new home in Midville Heights in Lavalette. Shortly after that, I went into the music business.

It is true that I was never paid the money that I was due me by Hawkins, but I never held any bitterness. That will surely defeat you. Had I not had the experience of that situation, I would not have survived in the competitive business world. You don't soon forget expensive mistakes.

I went on to start and establish an international music business, entertained as a musician on several continents, created and produced a Public Radio Program for over twenty years, and acquired a substantial amount of rental property.

Is this a great country or what?

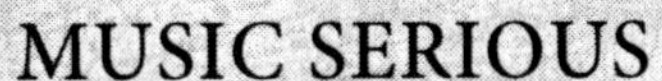

# MUSIC SERIOUS

After moving to West Virginia, I did not play for about two years.

I worked long hours and did not make the effort to locate musicians. At home, I had two fiddles in a double case that I never played.

On weekends, we enjoyed family activities like fishing at the roller dam on the Ohio River and camping. I was also the bicycle mechanic for the neighborhood. Most of the kids brought me their bikes that needed attention.

At this time, we lived in the west end of Huntington, about five blocks from Camden Park, the regional amusement park. One evening, while riding bikes with some of the kids, I noticed a sign on a vacant restaurant building that read "Bluegrass Show Friday Night." This older building, located across Route 60 from Camden Park, looked like it had been a very prosperous restaurant at one time.

"Amy, there's a stage show Friday night at that old restaurant down the street," I told my wife. "Would you like to go? It's a local bluegrass show."

"Not really," she answered. "I need to prepare some food to take with us fishing on Saturday. I want to leave early." Even as a kid in Arkansas,

Amy had liked to go fishing. It took a lot of food to feed five hungry kids, especially the growing boys.

"Well, I always wanted to learn to play the banjo. I think that I'll go and try to meet some of the players and see if there is a banjo for sale," I explained.

Once, someone out in New Mexico had given me an old Vega open-back five-string banjo, but I never found anyone to give me any instructions. After plunking around for some time I became discouraged and gave it to a friend.

Friday evening, I rode my bicycle the few blocks down the street to the old restaurant building. There were several cars and pickup trucks in the parking lot. I leaned my bicycle against the fence.

The sun had gone down but there was still some light. Two young boys ran around outside, throwing rocks across the railroad tracks that ran parallel with the street. Two men dressed in Western attire were outside, smoking. I was sure they were pickers.

As I walked up to the door I could see inside. There were about twenty men and women in little groups, talking.

I paid the lady at the door the one dollar admission. Inside, I felt a bit out of place, because everyone was dressed like it was Sunday morning in church. *These mountain folks take their music serious*, I thought. I was dressed in jeans, a tee shirt and tennis shoe, and wished I'd at least worn a clean shirt.

Two groups performed that evening. One was a six-piece bluegrass band, "Eck Gibson and the Mountaineer Ramblers." The other performers were a trio that lived in Huntington. I could not believe how well they all played, especially the trio. They sang in excellent three-part harmony.

Halfway through the show, there was an intermission. I had sat in the very back, wishing I was better dressed. I decided to slip out, get my bike, and go back to my house.

"How are you doing?" a friendly voice behind me asked as I stepped outside into the fresh night air.

"Just fine," I replied to this rather small man wearing a western straw hat and cowboy boots. He wore a starched western style shirt and a black western string tie. The way he was dressed, he could have been from New Mexico or West Texas. I recognized him as one of the banjo players in the show.

"My name is Elmer Byrd," he said, "And this is my wife, Beulah."

Standing beside Elmer was a lovely lady dressed like she was going to prayer meeting. Her salt and pepper grey hair looked as though she had just stepped out of the beauty shop.

"It's very nice to meet you," she said with a smile.

"My name is Joe Dobbs and I live down the street. I just wanted to come down and hear the music. I realize now, I should have dressed better," I said apologetically.

"I'd like to buy a used banjo," I said turning to Elmer.

"I don't know anyone that has one for sale. Do you play?" he asked.

"No, but I'd like to learn," I answered.

"Do you play an instrument?" asked Beulah.

"Oh, I scratch around on the fiddle," I said.

Elmer said he was finished with his part on the show and wanted to hear me play.

"I love the fiddle, but I never could play one," he said.

Looking down the street, I pointed out my house. Elmer went back inside and got his banjo.

"Beulah and I will meet you there. Maybe we can play a few tunes," said Elmer.

At the house, I introduced the couple to Amy, then got out my old fiddle case. I tuned the violin and we played fiddle tunes until two in the morning. I hadn't played in a long time and felt like my playing wasn't up to par. Regardless, they seemed to appreciate my playing and wanted me to come to Milton, West Virginia, and play for Eck Gibson.

"We really need a fiddle player," said Elmer. He gave me directions and invited me to come to practice on Monday night.

That first night I played with Elmer, he used his claw hammer style of playing banjo. In the bluegrass band, he had used a two-finger style. I told
him he should be using the old time style. His playing reminded me of Grandpa Jones and I thought it was just beautiful.

During the 1980s, he became acquainted with John Hartford. John admired his playing and encouraged Elmer to start performing as a solo artist. By this time, Elmer had worked over thirty years at Union Carbide and he was retired. So he and Beulah went on the road.

Elmer, the "Banjo Man from Turkey Creek," played his banjo at bluegrass and folk festivals throughout the U.S. and Canada. He and Beulah were loved by many fans all across the country.

Elmer and I remained very dear friends until his death in 1997. He and Beulah were my guests on the radio show "Music from the Mountains," several times. His first album was on my Fret 'N Fiddle Music label. I still miss the "Banjo Man from Turkey Creek."

John Hartford canceled several shows to come and be with the family and also played at Elmer's funeral. The viewing was held in Elmer's home town of Hurricane, West Virginia. His friends were many and I waited in line over an hour to get inside the chapel.

When I practiced with Eck and his group, he immediately invited me to join the band. I enjoyed playing in the band. The camaraderie was just great, but on Saturday night we would sometimes drive over a hundred miles one way just to play for about an hour. I had been driving all week and I would have preferred just playing. In the West, I had played bars where you played four or more hours a night. There was more actual playing than socializing.

I was working for a company in Huntington that serviced supermarkets with non-food items, such as housewares, toys, sewing needs, record albums, etc. We covered the entire Tri-State region which included parts of Ohio and Kentucky. This job required me to work long hours so playing music became too much.

With Eck, their music playing was a social event. I would have enjoyed more playing and less traveling, but I never discussed any of this with the band.

Eck was a bit disappointed that I was leaving the band for he did not know of another available fiddler. But he was a family man and sympathized with my decision to leave.

There was another reason to drop the music. My children were not interested in going to see me play a stage show. I told Amy that I didn't want my boys to grow up without me taking them fishing and camping. The beach was only about eight hours away and we tried to go each summer. There would be plenty of time to play music after the kids left home.

Later, I needed some money for something and I sold both fiddles to Elmer Byrd for $100. He sold them to someone else and I never saw them again. So from 1968 until 1973, I did not own a musical instrument. This was the only time since I was ten years old that I was without a fiddle.

In 1973, our oldest son, Dave, and I were at the Tri-State Drive-In theatre in Chesapeake, Ohio, at a flea market. Our items were displayed on a table. Most of them had been left in this old house we had rented.

"Dad, there is a fiddle over on that table at the end of the row. The man is asking $50, but I think you could buy it for less," said Dale. "You should buy it and start playing again."

After buying the fiddle, I spent some time getting it into good playing condition. While I worked on it, I decided that I had no desire to play in bars or county music. I didn't want to worry with a band so I would stay home and practice the old fiddle tunes that Grandpa Berry played. This way, I wouldn't have to deal with searching for someone to accompany my playing. That winter I gave up TV and practiced my music.

In the spring, Amy planted a garden just a few lots down from our house. We lived in Midville Heights, a new housing development just south of the Dixon Dam. The builder had told Amy she could plant a garden on one of the vacant lots. We had both grown up on farms and gardening was something she enjoyed.

We argued about what distance to space the tomato plants. I told her the rows she had made were too narrow. Wider rows would make it so much easier to walk among the plants during harvest time. There was plenty of space.

She didn't want me working in *her* garden. I was banned. I was only allowed to help carry tools and five-gallon buckets of fertilizer and water.

One Saturday, she planned to work in the garden. I tried to be very helpful and carried her garden tools and water to the area. I also took my fiddle. I turned an empty plastic five-gallon bucket upside down. Then I took my fiddle out of the case, sat on the bucket at the end of the garden rows, and proceeded to play.

On this particular day, my boss, John Trimble, came to visit. He saw us down in the garden. He walked up to the edge of the garden, placed his hands on his hips and said," I wish I had my camera."

John had a business of selling surplus Ka-Tel records and tapes. After the TV promotion had ended he would buy the surplus merchandise and we would sell them to accounts, including the Heck's Discount Stores in West Virginia and Kentucky. He was a large man with gray hair, about seventy years old. John was a friendly, pleasant person who also enjoyed practical jokes.

As long as I knew John, he enjoyed telling the story about when he walked up to find me sitting on a bucket, playing the fiddle, while my wife was stooped over slaving in our garden.

One day, John said, "Joe, my mother sings old mountain songs. She's ninety-two and I wondered if you knew anyone who could come out and record her singing before these old songs are lost."

"I'm going up to see her tomorrow," John said. "She lives near Summersville. Bring your fiddle; I want you to play for her. I'll ask her to sing some songs."

Mrs. Trimble lived alone in the community of Birch River on US-119. She was a spirited, small woman who enjoyed excellent health despite her age. When we drove up, she was outside, working in her garden. John introduced me and she invited us into the house. I carried my fiddle case under my arm.

"Joe plays the fiddle, Mom, and I asked him to come with me and play for you," said John. "Then I want you to sing some of those old songs for him."

Taking my violin out of the case I asked, "Mrs. Trimble, do you have a favorite tune?"

"Not especially," she said. "Just any old fiddle tune."

Leaning back in my chair I played "Soldier's Joy." She patted her foot and I thought she would get up and dance, but she went to the telephone. I ended the tune as she was dialing the phone.

"Beverly," she said into the phone. "John brought this man over here and he's a fiddler. He ain't as good as Senator Byrd, but he plays well." Looking at me with a twinkle in her eye and still holding the phone to her ear she said, "Beverly wants you to play one for her."

I would never have guessed this lady was ninety-two years old. She held the receiver up to my fiddle and I played the old square dance tune "Too Young to Marry."

Putting the phone back to her ear she said, "I told you he was good. But he ain't as good as Senator Byrd."

That was back in the early '70s, so I concluded that Mrs. Trimble would have been a young woman around 1900. I decided to play a song out of that era to take her thoughts back to her youth and played "The Old Spinning Wheel."

She told her friend goodbye and hung up the phone.

"Mrs. Trimble, I want to play you one more song," I said, and began to play. I had just gotten to the chorus when I noticed she had tears running down both cheeks.

At first I thought, *I cannot believe that out of all the songs I know, I chose a tune that brought sad thoughts to this nice little old lady. I could stop but it's too late. I'll keep playing.* After playing the song through twice I stopped. She was crying.

Quietly, I sat there until she gained control of her emotions and then I said, "I'm sorry that I chose a song that brought you sad memories."

"Oh, no, no" she said. "You couldn't have picked a better song. That music took me back to the time when I was a young woman, and there was a nice young man sparking me. He was so handsome and such a gentleman." Looking over at her son, she said, "And it wasn't your father either!"

Mrs. Trimble sang several songs. "Barbara Allen," "The Baggage Coach Ahead" and "The Little Rosewood Casket," were among her selections. On the way back to Huntington, I explained to John that those were old English ballads common throughout the Appalachian region.

# THE BIG APPLE

Before 1970, there were very few quality music teaching aids that one could purchase, even in the local music store. Most fiddlers depended on their ear and dedication to learn to play difficult fiddle tunes. The folk movement of the '60s changed the thinking of music book publishing companies and new books of instruction were introduced.

Sometimes, the learning fiddler would think that the reason he wasn't progressing as a player was due to the quality of his violin. He dreamed of finding an old Italian violin that had been lost for a couple of centuries. Stradivarius and other Italian Master violinmakers produced instruments for special orders. They had commissions from the wealthy, the church, and even the European royalty. It is doubtful that any of those valuable old instruments were ever found in a farmer's attic in Arkansas, but one could always hope.

"How would you like to visit New York?" I asked Amy. We had lived in several areas of the Southwest, but had never traveled the East Coast north of Norfolk, Virginia. We both grew up in the country and preferred rural areas rather than the large cities.

"New York! Are you joking?" she exclaimed. "New York City or New York State?"

"I really had Manhattan in mind. That would be a new experience and maybe exciting," I answered. "That old fiddle that Dale found at the Flea Market, the one with the worm holes and a short neck; I think there's a possibility it could be worth some money." Dale was our oldest son who had spotted the instrument on a table at the Flea Market. We had purchased it from a lady who had bought it some years earlier when she lived in England.

"What in the world does that have to do with Manhattan?" she inquired. "School is in session, and we couldn't take the kids." We had five children in school and the youngest, Scott, was only four years old.

"We would only be gone a few days. I thought we could take Scott with us and the neighbors would help look after the others," I said. "I've always wanted to see Harper's Ferry and we could also visit Gettysburg."

Amy interrupted, "I don't understand. Why New York?" By the expression on her face, I could tell that going to Harper's Ferry had caught her interest, but she wasn't convinced that a visit to New York was necessary.

"We have to take the old violin to someone I trust," I explained. "Someone who has the ability to determine if it is really valuable. The only shop I know anything about and consider reliable is Wurlitzer, which is located in Times Square," I said. While it was true that evaluating an old violin is a very specialized field, I knew of others who could do it. I just wanted an excuse to visit Manhattan.

"What makes you think that old fiddle is worth a lot of money?" she asked. "It just looks like another fiddle to me, and it certainly isn't pretty with all the worm holes."

I suddenly realized that this was going to require some persuasive explaining. "Sometime about 1800, people involved in music in Europe came up with 'standard pitch,' which we know as A 440 today," I began. "Before that time, pipe organs in churches and opera houses were tuned to the pitch that the maker thought sounded pleasant," I told her.

"This was a problem for singers and performing musicians, because they never knew what the pitch would be when they went to another music hall or church. Today all instruments are tuned to that standard pitch. So if you are a singer and you sing a song in the key of C in Cincinnati, you could go to Sydney, Australia, and the piano would be tuned to the same pitch and you would sing the song in the key of C," I explained.

"After arriving at a standard pitch, those famous composers, such as Beethoven and Mozart, began writing arrangements that required playing in very high positions on the violin. It was discovered that the neck designed by the Italian Masters around 1700 was too short." I looked at her to make sure that I had her attention and she was grasping this bit of musical history. After all, it was my effort to justify a trip to the Big Apple.

"That made it necessary for all those old violins to go to a very skilled violinmaker or repairman and have a new section grafted, lengthening the neck about 1/4 inch," I continued. "The graft is visible and the fiddle is referred to as having a 'grafted neck.' Then you know that it was probably made before 1800."

"So does this junky ole fiddle you bought at the Flea Market have one of those 'grafted necks'?" she asked.

"Would you please not refer to this violin as a 'junky ole fiddle' because who knows, it could be worth a lot of money," I cautioned. "No, it does not have a grafted neck but it has a short neck and just maybe it was never taken to a craftsman to have the neck lengthened. I remember Mr. Miller, who has the repair shop in Lexington, showing me several old violins that he had found over the years that still had short necks." Looking at her facial expressions I could tell that she was becoming more interested in that 'junky ole fiddle.'

"Just how much is a lot of money?" She asked. "Any amount of money would be a lot to us," she added, before I could answer. I could tell by the gleam in her eye brought on by the thought of the fiddle being valuable, New York Here We Come!

In the fall of '74, we made the trip to New York and Scott, our four-year old, went with us. We had a 1967 Ford Van that was more of a camper than just a van. Since there was just the three of us, we took out the seats and put in camping equipment. This would save a lot on motel bills.

"Are we going to Harper's Ferry and Gettysburg on the way up to New York or on the return trip?" Amy asked. She was checking to make sure that we had all our camping supplies and some food. We would have to make the trip as economical as possible. After putting the other five children in school, we had very little money.

"I thought we would do that on the way back home. I'm getting anxious to see just how much this junky ole fiddle is worth," I said. "If it happened to be worth a lot of money, we could give the van to someone and fly back to West Virginia."

"Now, just what do you mean by a lot of money?" Amy inquired. I could tell that I really had her interest.

"Well, I read somewhere that the Stradivarius violin that belonged to Jack Benny sold for over $300,000," I replied.

Amy said, "I saw Jack Benny playing on TV once, and his violin was shiny and pretty and looked nothing like that junky ole fiddle you have." To that observation, I chose not to respond.

This was a great time of year to travel in the eastern states. We camped somewhere in eastern Pennsylvania, beautiful with all the fall colors. I decided to drive through New Jersey and try to arrive in New York after the rush hour. I thought that with any luck we would get into the city about 10 o'clock in the morning. Not having made exact plans as to how to get the violin appraised, I wanted to have one more evening to think. So we drove across New Jersey and took the Staten Island route to Long Island.

As we drove along the deserted beach area of Fire Island, we noticed surfers. Scott kept looking out the window because he'd never seen the ocean before.

"I just can't imagine surfing in that cold water," said Amy. "I see that they're wearing wet suits," she said. "I still think it would be too cold."

We camped out on Long Island and went to sleep listening to the sea birds and the sound of the Atlantic. There were very large sea gulls everywhere.

I woke up to Amy's greeting, "Wake up, this is the big day." She went on, "Today we find out just how wealthy we've become by you buying that ole junky fiddle at the Flea Market."

"How about, if just for today, we don't refer to our treasure as 'that ole junky fiddle,'" I begged. "If it turns out that the violin is valuable, you should have some reservations about trashing the instrument."

"After breakfast, I think we'll drive through Brooklyn to Manhattan and try to arrive somewhere around 10 o'clock. Being so close, we wouldn't want to go back to West Virginia without seeing the Brooklyn Bridge," I added.

"I don't think I've ever seen so many people in all my life. I'm beginning to miss West Virginia," said Amy. "After we find out how much that violin is worth, I will be ready to go home."

Driving from West Virginia to Manhattan was more than cultural shock. At first, the hustle and bustle of downtown was overwhelming. The noise, and so many people apparently in a big hurry to get somewhere, grabbed your attention.

"There's a parking garage on the left," said Amy who had been keeping watch for a place to leave the van. "This must be what they call the garment district, because look at all those men pushing racks of clothes."

Some of these men and racks were going along the sidewalk and some were crossing the street. "Gosh! This sure is a long way from Lavalette, West Virginia," she said, while making a note of the address of the parking garage. We wanted to be able to find the van when we returned.

The street was crowded with people going every which way and taxicabs honking their horns as they tried to get through the racks of clothes. It seemed that no one paid any attention to them. "Just like in the movies," Amy observed.

The violin shops charged for appraisals and the usual fee was 10 percent of the appraisal value. Anyone would gladly pay the fee, even if it was a considerable amount, for with the appraisal papers the violin's authenticity would not be questioned and it would be easy to sell.

There was no way I had enough money to pay an appraisal fee, but I did have a plan. I had left West Virginia with only $200 to make the trip. If I had any problems with the vehicle, I would just have to call someone for a loan to get home.

"I cannot believe that you would dress like that and walk down the streets of New York," said Amy. "You really look like a hick."

I had on an old pair of bib overalls that were clean but faded and my red Chuck Taylor tennis shoes. My cap was something that Amy had made and was clean but worn. The blue chambray shirt was the most worn one I could find. I also wore a full beard that was black with streaks of gray but it was trimmed. Amy wore an unadorned print dress.

"I really don't feel that out of place. There are folks on these streets that look weirder than me," I commented. "I really wish you had dressed a little more hillbilly."

"Look, this is the plainest dress that I brought and I think that I look 'hick-y' enough. I'm sure I look terrible. This is the dress I wear when I work in the yard." Amy went on, "Here I am walking down the street of one of the most famous cities in the world, and I can't believe you talked me into wearing this dress."

"This fiddle had better be worth a lot of money," she said as we approached a big, wide street.

There were taxicabs everywhere and they all seemed to be in a hurry. I had the fiddle in an old, black, wooden-coffin case that was made about 1900. Then, I put the case inside an olive-green Army laundry bag with a big drawstring in the top. I held it under my arm so that no one could detect that what I was carrying could have been made by a famous Italian.

During our time on the street, Scott was frightened. He just could not understand all the strange, busy people.

"There's a taxi!" shouted Amy.

As I raised my hand, the cab driver pulled over to the curb.

"Come on, Sweetie," Amy said, comforting our son. "We're going to ride in the yellow car and you won't have to walk." She took him in her arms and held him close. He seemed to be reassured that everything was OK.

"Where to?" asked the cab driver. He was a dark man, very pleasant, and had a strong accent that I did not recognize.

"Times Square," I said as I closed the door.

Then, we were off down the street. The driver made the first light, but kept going faster. I peeked over the front seat at the odometer. The indicator was passing 50 mph.

"Wow! Can you believe how fast we are going in all this downtown traffic," I whispered to my wife. She, too, raised up so she could see over the driver's shoulder. I noticed that the speedometer needle was passing 60 mph.

"My God, I cannot believe this," she whispered. Holding Scott close to her breast, she moved down in the floorboard behind the front seat.

It seemed that all of the cabs were in a race to some unknown destination, with many of them honking their horns and switching lanes. Our driver was no exception. Suddenly he was caught by a red light and he stopped in the curb lane.

As we waited for the light to change, we watched the busy foot traffic on the sidewalk. I started to say something to Amy when I noticed a black woman who was over six feet tall. She was wearing extremely high-heeled platform shoes and a stunning tight black and gold satin dress trimmed in red. Her long hair hung in curls down to her shoulders. She appeared to have just stepped out of a nightclub.

"Hey, baby! How are you doin?" our cab driver called out his open window.

"I never felt better, Darlin'," replied the tall, black lady with a limp wrist gesture. She never stopped walking.

Turning to look at me, the cab driver said, "Hey, did you know that was a man? Yes sir, a man dressed like a woman! I love New York! Where else in the world could you see something like that, just casually walking down the street? Is this a great city, or what?" He hit the steering wheel with his open hand and laughed loudly, then the light changed.

All this time, Amy was on the floor with her eyes closed, clutching our son. This was exciting to me. Just as I was getting the hang of the driver's weaving through the traffic, he swung over to the curb and announced, "Here we are."

With the bag containing the fiddle case in my hand, I stepped up on the curb and paid the driver while Amy and Scott got out of the cab. We stood on the sidewalk, a bit shaken.

"That fiddle had better be worth a lot of money," was Amy's comment.

As I looked around, I discovered we were directly in front of the building where the Wurlitzer Violin Shop was located. "It's in this building on the sixth floor," I said, opening the door.

We stepped into the elevator and I punched the button for the sixth floor. As the elevator rose, I thought on my plan to discover if this instrument was of any value. The elevator door opened and before us was a large room with a glass front. Big gold letters on the glass door said, 'Wurlitzer Violin Shop.' We went inside.

By just looking, it could have been a doctor's waiting room. There were no signs or any violins or parts on display. The room was well decorated, with large potted plants in different locations. There were comfortable leather chairs which appeared to be very expensive.

A lady sat in one chair, her violin case on the floor beside her. It was a large, expensive case with an elegant canvas cover that had a zipper pocket to hold music. She probably played in the New York Philharmonic. I couldn't help but wonder what kind of violin she had inside. Could there be an old, Italian violin in that case?

Across the room was a gentleman wearing a dark suit with a similar violin case. A beautiful, cherry wood counter was in front of an open doorway, and behind it stood a man wearing a tailored expensive three-piece pinstriped suit. He wore a pale blue shirt with a red tie covered with intricate designs. To me, he looked like the host of a lavish Hollywood party.

At first, I noticed this place did not have the varnish odors or turpentine smell present in every violin repair shop I had visited. It was clean, as if someone had just scrubbed the place.

And here I stood in my faded bib overalls, my faded blue chambray shirt and my red Chuck Taylor tennis shoes. I walked up to the counter to the well-dressed gentleman and in my most practiced southern drawl said, "How ya'll doin'?"

With a look of -*I simply have to get these people out of here as soon as possible*- the gentleman said, “I am Harry Duffey, how may I be of service to you, sir?" He spoke with such a strong English accent that one would have thought we were in London.

"My name is Joe Dobbs," I answered, "And this is my wife and boy. We drove here all the way from West Virginny." Without giving him time to answer, I removed the old violin case from the Army laundry bag saying "I hear tell that you folks know ever’ thang there is to know 'bout fiddles. So I brought this'n fer ya'll to look at and maybe ya'll can tell a feller if it’s worth anythang."

The lady with the fancy violin case looked up from the book she was reading. I could not see the name of the book but she seemed to think we were far more interesting.

He began with, "Mr. Dobbs, it is true that we specialize in appraising valuable old instruments. Our worldwide reputation is unsurpassed. So if you wish, you may leave your violin and we will have one of our most qualified appraisers examine it and prepare a proper document. Of course you should know that the appraisal fee will be 10 percent of the appraised value." He had that confident look on his face of, *This should get rid of them-*.

I looked around at Amy and said, "What do you thank, hon? Now I don't see hardly how we could leave that old fiddle all the way up here in New York. We're kinda anxious to be a gittin' back to the house. Our youngin' has been fretin' ever since we got in this big city. And I shore don't mean to hurt yore feelings but we ain't a plannin’ on a comin' back. Hit won't take long fer someone to take a gander at it. It's got all these wormholes and the neck is short. I seen a lot a fiddles in my time but I ain't never seen one like this'n."

The woman who had sold me the violin had brought it to the U.S. from England. In England, wormholes are common in very old antique furniture. The holes on the violin were all over it and about 1/16 of an inch in diameter. I think the wormholes aroused his curiosity.

He looked at the closed case that I had placed on the counter and said, "Mr. Dobbs, would it be alright if I examined the violin?"

"Why heck, yea," I answered, opening the case. He gently took the violin in his hands and examined the holes.

Then, without looking up he said, "This is so unusual. Mr. Dobbs, would you object to my taking this back in the shop? We have someone here that I think would like to see this violin. I would only be a minute."

"Now, Mr. Duffey, ya'll can look at it as long as you want. I don' keer." He disappeared through the open doorway.

I thought that my plan had worked. It was seeing the wormholes that got him. After what seemed to be a long time he returned.

"Mr. Dobbs, I want to thank you for letting me take the violin for our specialist to see. The wormholes are so unusual and rare that I knew he would enjoy seeing it. I have to tell you though, that your violin is a Saxony copy. It really does not have any antique value at all. I wish I had better news for you."

"But did yore specialist measure the neck? How do you explain the short neck?" I asked.

In his very best English accent Mr. Duffey replied, "The chap had a short piece of wood."

I took a deep breath and said, "Mr. Duffey, I want to thank ye fer being so good to us. You are a kind feller and you've answered my questions so we had better be a gittin' back to West Virginny."

As I pushed the first floor button in the elevator, I said, "I had some doubts that the fiddle was valuable, but you never know. If you don't have it checked, you could spent the rest of you life wondering."

"I was right. It is just another junky ole fiddle," said Amy.

We stepped out of the building and back onto the busy sidewalk. I looked up and down the street for a taxi as I asked, "Amy, do you remember how far it is to Gettysburg?"

# THE WATER IS RISING

Each year in April, Huntington has the Dogwood Arts and Crafts Festival. Though it is now held in the Civic Arena, before, it was in two very large circus type tents downtown near the floodwall. Both tents would be filled with craftsmen and artists displaying their work for sale. Most years, there would be acoustic musicians playing in different areas, which added to the atmosphere.

"Amy, let's go to the Dogwood Festival. I think I'll take my fiddle and see if my playing has improved with all this practice," I said one April day in 1975. "Maybe I could locate a guitar player. If I play with a guitar, I could tell if I have the correct timing on some of these complicated old fiddle tunes."

Amy did a lot of sewing and thoroughly enjoyed seeing the crafts, so we went.

There are many musicians who play extremely well for their own pleasure. Many very good amateur musicians are shy. I thought rural fiddlers would be more apt to share some rare tune with me if I looked like the neighbor down the road.

By going dressed in my bib overalls and red Chuck Taylor tennis shoes, no one would know that I had played with recording stars. I kept my fiddle and bow in an old, wooden, coffin fiddle case that came with inexpensive violins around 1900. I would much rather be respected for my playing ability and not because of who I had performed with.

Amy and I walked around through the tents. She looked at the crafts and I, with my fiddle case tucked under my arm, searched for a guitar player. As we walked through the second long tent, I began to think that there was no one playing that year. Then I heard the faint sound of singing accompanied by a guitar.

We walked toward the sound and came to a booth where a woman wove cane in the bottoms of ladder-back chairs that she sold. Sitting in two of the completed chairs was a tall man playing a Guild guitar and a short guy playing an autoharp. An autoharp is a stringed instrument with a series of chord bars attached to dampers, that when depressed, mute all of the strings except those of the intended chord. Though thought of as a bluegrass or folk instrument, made famous by the Carter Family, other musicians have used them as well and in different genres.

Both of these musicians looked to be about thirty years old, a hippie version of Mutt and Jeff. The guitar player had medium long hair and an untrimmed beard. The autoharp player wore a beard but his hair was neatly trimmed. They seemed to be very good friends.

I was impressed, for they played extremely well. At first, I thought they were a couple of Folk musicians that were traveling and maybe appearing somewhere in town. Some of the tunes they played were Carter Family songs but others were folk tunes out of the 60s. A small group of listeners gathered around the front of the booth, enjoying the music.

The duo seemed to have a tight act. I knew if I asked if I could join them, they could say "no" and that would be the end. Not taking any chances, I pulled up a finished chair next to the autoharp player. I sat down and started taking my fiddle out of the case. I don't think a word was said, they just watched me.

The guitar player seemed to be thinking, if we ignore him maybe he will go away.

I looked at the autoharp player and asked kindly, "Would you play an A chord, please?"

He strummed the A cord. While I was tuning my violin to the A pitch, he turned to the guitar player and with a big grin said, "All fiddlers are strange."

I had the violin tuned and ready to play. The people standing in front of the booth waited patiently for us to play something.

The autoharp player asked, "Well, what do you want to play?" He was probably thinking, *If he plays as bad as he looks maybe we should just go home.*

My priority at this point was to not break up the playing session. I didn't know if the guitar player was accustomed to playing with a fiddle. He was a very good player but the fiddle is difficult to accompany if you have had no experience. The odds of me picking a fiddle tune they knew was risky. So I said, "Oh, just continue singing and I will play along."

After a couple of songs the autoharp player said, "Do you know 'Soldiers Joy'?"

"Sure, that's a good one," I replied.

"What key?" asked the guitar player.

"D," I replied and we played the old tune. The autoharp player had an unusual method of strumming and I found the rhythm of both musicians to be far above average.

After each song the audience applauded enthusiastically. This was most encouraging for our performance.

I don't remember how long we played, but I felt the duo become more comfortable as we went along. I asked them if they played somewhere locally and they told me they did not.

"I sure enjoyed playing with you guys. You are both very good musicians," I said, getting up out of my chair and placing my violin in the old wooden case. "I gotta go. Thanks for letting me sit in," I said, walking away.

"Where are you from?" the autoharp player called out after me.

"My name is Joe and I live in Dixon, Wayne County," I said, but kept walking.

Dixon was a small community south of Huntington on Route 52 which ran along Twelve Pole Creek. There was no post office. Dixon had an old stone dam across the creek that had once been part of a water mill. The mill had probably been gone for over fifty years. Kids would sometimes swim in the creek around the dam in the summer. Some folks in the community referred to it as Dixon Dam.

"In the beginning, I don't think they wanted you playing with them," Amy commented as we walked toward the parking lot.

"Probably," I agreed. "I knew I was being a bit pushy, but I wanted to see if I had regained my playing ability. I haven't played that much since we left New Mexico."

I thought about it a little longer. "I wouldn't have wanted some stranger barging in on my jam session. In a situation like that, you want to fit in with the other players, and not try to show them how well you can play. It's destructive to intentionally intimidate another player."

"It was interesting that the tune the autoharp player asked me to play was 'Soldier's Joy'," I continued as we approached our van. "That's the first dance tune I learned on the fiddle. Gosh, that must have been about 1946. Mr. Cox, who was a farmer, led the singing in our church. He was kind and patient enough to help a young boy learn tunes."

"What happened to him?" asked Amy.

"He's probably driving his farm tractor and plowing cotton or soybeans on that farm in Louisiana."

"Well, I think it worked out OK. It certainly felt good to be playing again," I said as we drove out 5th Street toward home.

At the time, I sold auto parts for Lavalette Auto Supply. Every two weeks, I drove down Route 52 to Delbarton, taking orders for auto parts from our customers. Early one morning, I was at Buster Maynard's Service Station and Garage which was located near Dunlow, West Virginia. Two young men had just left the garage and were walking up the ridge on a gravel side road. Their hair was down to their waist and they were very poorly dressed. They didn't look like locals.

"Those two guys live out on the commune, Welcome Home," said Buster, looking at the men as they continued up the gravel road. Buster rolled a new tire into the garage and put it on the tire changing machine.

"Where is Welcome Home?" I asked. "I heard it was out here somewhere."

"That road is Lykin's Ridge. Welcome Home is on it, less than a mile. There's probably twenty people out there on a hundred and eighty acres that was the old Lykin Farm," explained Buster. "They've got a pair of mules and are trying to farm. They're growing green beans, sorghum, and marijuana. They plan to sell the green beans to markets in town are going to make syrup from the sorghum cane. I'm sure they're going to smoke the dope."

"Are they local hippies?" I asked.

"No. They're from all over the country. Some from New York State, Ohio, New Jersey, and there are a few that moved here from a commune near Fayetteville, Arkansas," Buster said.

"What do the local folks think about the commune," I asked.

"Most of them don't know what to think. Since they're trying to raise crops with a pair of mules on that rough hillside, the local folks kinda admire their efforts. I've been out there to work on one of their cars and they treated me real nice. I think just a few of them do the farm work and the rest stay stoned. They have funny names. Among the women are Sky, Spring, Sunshine, and Rainbow."

"How did they get the Lykin's Farm?" I asked.

"Walter Reiter and his wife bought the property. He sold a successful dental practice somewhere in New York and bought the farm and financed the commune. The Reiters have two young boys and the family lives in the main house. There are a couple of other dwellings on the place," explained Buster.

Also at the Dogwood Festival, I met Change Parker, who lived at Welcome Home. We became friends. I had a lot of questions! Here was a group of people trying to survive by their wits and what farming skills they could learn from neighbors, Mother Earth News or a Foxfire book.

Most all of the residents were educated. Some were college graduates. Yet they were trying to live as my family did when I was a child on the farm, except for the dope. I spent the first seventeen years of my life trying to get away from the farm. Why would anyone with an education want that kind of life?

Welcome Home had electricity and running water in the main house only. I told Change that anytime he was coming into Huntington, he was welcome to stop at our house and take a luxurious shower. He could spend the night if he wished.

Change had a degree in Political Science from the University of Kuwait and his father was a Colonel in the US Army who lived in northern Virginia. Taking care of the livestock and plowing the fields were among Change's duties on the commune. He also cared for several stands of bees.

Change tried to explain how he needed to learn to survive with the bare necessities. After the 1960s, many still feared the possibility of a nuclear war. At such time they thought the survivors would have to live very primitively.

Once, Change invited me to Welcome Home to play music. I went out of curiosity. No one there could really play. Several of the people had guitars, but they just thrashed one chord and played the same musical phrase over and over. They were in a stoned stupor.

Growing up in a Puritan home in the forties and early fifties there was a taboo about using drugs, even marijuana. When I lived in Texas, in the early and mid fifties, there were harsh laws concerning possession of marijuana. As a musician, I was exposed to drug use, but I never smoked a joint.

When I lived in Houston, there was a time when I worked my regular five-day-a-week job and also played music in clubs five nights each week. For a brief period, I did take some speed.

But I think one of the most foolish things that I've ever done was to smoke cigarettes for about twenty years. All the years that I worked in night clubs, I drank only in moderation.

Later, Change Parker moved to Albany, New York, and became a lobbyist in the state legislature. When I heard from him in 1988, he was living in New Hampshire.

I think that Welcome Home lasted about three years. Walter Reiter's wife and their two sons moved to California. Once I saw Steve, who had lived at Welcome Home, in Huntington. I asked him about Walter. He told me that Walter "flipped out" and was confined to the mental hospital in Huntington. I asked him about Walter's condition. Steve said Walter was doing fine. He had met another resident in the hospital who thought he was Jesus, too.

About two weeks after my playing at the Dogwood Arts and Crafts Festival, I loaded up the family, our tent and camping gear, into our Ford van and went camping at Summersville Lake. On the one hundred mile return trip, a rear wheel bearing went out. The children complained about the roaring caused by the worn bearing. It got so hot that I was afraid the brake drum would catch on fire. Several times I stopped and took drinking water out of the cooler and poured it on the rear hub. It cooled the worn bearing enough so that we made it home.

One beautiful day, my sons, David and Dale and I took the rear axle out and pressed on a new bearing. We were in the street in front of our house installing the axle with the new bearing, when a car with several people drove up. They stopped and began getting out of the car.

I recognized the autoharp player, who said, "You sure are hard to find. I'm Dave Peyton and this is my wife, Susie."

"I've heard nothing but how smooth that fiddler played. I'm so glad we finally found you," said Susie.

The tall guitarist and singer was Charlie Bowen. I learned that both musicians were employed by the Huntington newspaper, *The Herald-Dispatch*, with Charlie the city editor and Dave Peyton a columnist. You would have never guessed this by their appearance.

That was the beginning of an exceptional friendship and mutual admiration society, which continues to this day. We didn't know it at the time but that first meeting was the birth of The 1937 Flood, our bluegrass band. The water is still rising.

# FRET'n FIDDLE

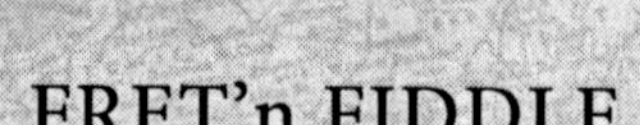

Through the years I had repaired instruments that I played or bought to sell, but in 1974 I became serious about making violins. My interest in making violins began in high school. When I had a choice on the subject of writing projects in high school and college, I would choose to write about the Old Italian violin makers. Going to arts and craft fairs and participating in folk festivals in West Virginia rekindled my desire.

There were a lot of special tools that I would need to make a quality instrument and some of them were expensive. In order to earn extra money to purchase these tools, I spread the word that I did stringed musical instrument repair.

I had done some repair work for friends. When I was in Houston, I had worked with a violin maker, Mr. Thorpe. Back East, Mr. Miller of Lexington, Kentucky, had been most helpful with his expertise.

My fellow workers brought me a few broken instruments, but in a few months the word was out that I did repair. I soon had a backlog. I had no idea there were so many instruments in attics that needed attention. Apparently, there hadn't been a repair shop in Huntington for almost twenty years. Soon they were coming from over in Kentucky and also southern Ohio.

I converted the full basement of my house into a repair shop. I even offered regular pickup and delivery service to local music stores. They were pleased to offer repair service to their customers. After about a year, I made more money working in my basement than going to my job. At this point, I went into the repair of musical instruments full time.

There is something to be said about the gratitude of a customer. Some were so pleased that I'd made grandfather's violin playable again. I forgot all about making violins. I spent my time repairing or playing instead of making.

In 1976, my youngest brother, Dennis, came to visit. He had been two years old when I left home. My family lived so far away, I saw him only when we went to Louisiana on visits. Dennis brought his wife, Barbara, their son Chris and daughter Candice, who was a baby.

Dennis worked at Dew Music, a large retail music store in Monroe, Louisiana. When he saw all the instruments I had stacked up in my basement to be repaired, he was surprised.

"Joe, you should open a music store," Dennis said. "Then you would have the traffic to sell new guitars. Selling someone a guitar is much easier that gluing one. You're passing up a lot of business."

"I know, but there are several music stores in the area and I really don't have the capital to stock a retail outlet," I answered.

Dennis went back to Louisiana. In just a few days he called and wanted to know if I would be interested in going into business with him.

"Dennis, I'd enjoy opening a business with you as a partner, but I don't want to have to open the door at nine every morning. I like my weekends to go and play at festivals," I explained.

Dennis believed he could teach me the retail business and that I could teach him the technique of repairing. He would be glad to open the store when I wanted to be out playing my fiddle.

And so it was. He moved his family to West Virginia. We rented a storefront on 14th Street West in Huntington and the Fret'N Fiddle was born. Though we opened the store with less than $200, we had a backlog of repair work. It was our only source of income in the beginning.

We worked long and hard hours repairing instruments. His

experience in merchandising and operating a retail music store was invaluable to me.

Being an excellent guitarist, Dennis created an atmosphere that attracted guitar students. Growing up in the Beatle era, he wasn't familiar with Appalachian folk music. But he had learned to accompany the old fiddle tunes our grandfather Berry had played.

There was a change to our agreement. When festival time came, Dennis didn't stay and run the store. We just put a sign on the door that read: Out to lunch. Will be back next Monday.

While we were launching the business, Amy and I divorced. I think that after all those years of struggling, she just gave up. We sure went through some hard times together; however, there were a lot of good times traveling, camping, fishing, and watching our children grow up. Through the years that followed, we remained friends and parents together.

Local musicians were very supportive of our business, but we didn't have the money to stock the store with instruments. Yet musicians just loved the atmosphere we created in the store and there were big jam sessions every Saturday.

My old fiddling friend from Kentucky, J. P. Fraley, wouldn't call it the "Fret'N Fiddle." To him it was the "Bitch and Saw".

This was so different from all the jobs where I had worked over the years. Up until then, I'd never had a day job that I enjoyed. Working at the Fret'N Fiddle must have been the way my dad felt about that poor farm in the swamps of Louisiana.

One clear summer day, I returned to the store after eating lunch. As I walked in, there was a couple playing and singing. The man looked to be in his thirties; wearing a yellow ball cap with "CAT" written in black on the front and playing a guitar. The woman looked to be in her late twenties and was playing an old fiddle tune on the banjo. I stood there and listened. They played quite well.

As they finished, Dennis said, "Where do you think these musicians are from?"

"By the style they play, I would guess North Carolina," I replied.

But I was wrong. They were from Sydney, Australia. This was the first time I met Rod and Judy Jones. They were fans of Molly O'Day. Judy explained that it was their first visit to the U.S. and they had driven to Huntington especially to see her. Molly told them to visit the Dobbs Brothers at the Fret'N Fiddle before they left town. We had repaired several instruments for Molly and her husband, Lynn Davis. This was the beginning of a great friendship with the Jones' that resulted in two visits to Australia some twenty years later.

Dennis and I never got the store's sales up to supporting two families. In 1980, Dennis moved back to Louisiana and went into a different business with his farther-in-law. The knowledge I learned from Dennis made it possible for me to move the Fret'N Fiddle to St. Albans and build a successful business.

One Saturday in 1979, I was standing behind a glass showcase showing a customer, Clarence Davis, a violin. The store was still in Huntington at the time.

"That's a good-looking fiddle. How much are you asking for it?" asked Clarence, looking at the label inside the F hole.

"Just traded for it, but I'd take $450. I'll check to see if it has any open seams," I explained. "I think it's a Lowendall."

"That's too much," said Clarence, handing the violin across the glass case to me.

"I'll see you next week," he said, going out the door.

Another customer stepped up to the showcase and asked, "May I see that violin?" He pointed to the Lowendall I had just put back in the showcase.

"Sure," I said, handing it to him. I went back to putting new strings on a customer's guitar.

The man asking about the fiddle spoke with a slow, southern drawl not common in West Virginia. He was a tall, stout man with a receding hairline and appeared to be about forty-five years old. By the way he was dressed, I determined that he could afford the fiddle. Maybe I had a much needed sale.

"That fiddle is worth a lot more than you are asking," he stated. "This is a very nice old German Lowendall," he said, while turning the violin over and looking at the well-flamed maple back. “I wouldn’t take less than $975, if I were you.”

In all of my years of trading and selling instruments, I had never had a stranger tell me that I was pricing something too low. He could’ve bought the violin and made a handsome profit.

I stopped stringing the guitar and held out my hand, “I’m Joe Dobbs.”

He took my hand and said, “Nice to meet you. I’m Tony Ellis. I’m in town to play in the fiddlers contest.”

It was the beginning of a life-long, cherished friendship. I later learned that Tony had played banjo with the Father of Bluegrass music, Bill Monroe, back in 1962. He later became famous for his innovative technique of playing the banjo. He also recorded several CDs containing selections of his original compositions for different record labels including Flying Fish and Rounder.

After Amy and I divorced, I lived with my daughter, Diane, and her son, Andy. He was in Kindergarten at the time and called me "Dad," because I was very much a father figure to him. Andy had red hair and brown eyes that were almost black. He was a joy in the family with all his energy. I’m sure he discouraged his mother from ever wanting to have another child.

Once, he climbed up on a bulldozer parked in front of our house and somehow started the machine. The engine roared to life and Diane went running out of the house. She knew it was Andy. He wasn’t even five years old.

Diane worked with me at the Fret’N Fiddle Music Store. One day, when Andy was in the store with his mom, he noticed the small-sized student violins that we had for the young Suzuki students. The next day when I came home from work, Andy was waiting for me.

"Dad, I’ve decided to learn to play the violin," he announced. "I would like for you to bring home one of those small ones so I can get started."

At the time, I occasionally played on a locally produced Public TV program. So he was very accustomed to hearing me practicing the fiddle at home.

"I think it would be good for my friends to see me playing on TV with you," he further explained.

He was a bit young for me to try to explain that it wasn't the most desirable motive for such an endeavor. I thought this was just a new idea of his and would soon go away.

"Andy, I'm so pleased that you want to play the fiddle," I said. "We could find someone to give you some lessons to get you started."

"Dad, I don't need to take lessons. I can just teach myself," he explained. "Just remember to bring my violin home when you come in from work tomorrow."

*This five year-old kid will soon forget about playing the fiddle. This is just a passing thing with him*, I thought.

For three days, he would ask, "Dad, did you bring my fiddle home today?" He was so persistent that I gave in to his demands and brought home a half-size student model violin, bow and case.

"Andy, this is a real musical instrument, not a toy," I explained. "You're not to take it outside the house. Since it is very easily broken, it must always be in the case when you're not playing it."

"I know how to take care of it, Dad," he said, excitement in his voice. I knew he expected to be playing the fiddle on TV with me.

"Would you like me to show you where to put your fingers to make the proper notes," I asked. "I've already tuned the fiddle."

"No, just let me figure this out, OK?" he replied.

He had seen me play the fiddle as far back as he could remember. When you watch someone play who has played for years and their fingers just float so easily over the strings, it looks easy.

Andy awoke early each morning. His bedroom was across the hall from mine. Several mornings, I awoke to the sound of him making screeching noises on that fiddle. He would play for about five minutes before he would stop and get ready for school.

"Would you like for me to show you some notes on the violin? I could show you where to put your fingers to play a tune like "Twinkle, Twinkle Little Star," I offered, while we were eating breakfast.

"Andy, you woke me up early this morning sawing on that thing. Why don't you let Dad show you some beginning things to practice," said his mother.

"No, I keep telling you, I can teach myself," said Andy. I didn't know until later just how much he tried to play in the evenings after school.

"Dad," Andy said. I opened my eyes to the sound of his voice. He was in his pajamas, standing by my bed, the violin in one hand and the bow in the other. It had to be about 6 a.m.

"Dad, I've decided that it's going to take longer than I thought," said Andy. With that statement he ended his hopes of having a career as a fiddler.

Prior to moving the Fret'N Fiddle to St. Albans, West Virginia, I met Linda Smith. We were studying the same religion, Eckankar. Eckankar means, 'co-worker with God' and it offers ways to explore your daily, personal connection with the Divine.

Linda was divorced and ruled four rowdy children with an iron hand. She was a short, naturally blonde lady with vivid blue eyes and an abundance of energy. After knowing each other for over a year, we were married. She worked full time for the telephone company and I was running a struggling business, but we still found time to do some traveling.

Each Saturday, musicians would gather at the shop and play acoustic music. Sometime in the late 70s, our jam session was in full swing when Jim Belcher walked in. He looked as though he had never seen such an impromptu bunch of pickers. Jim was tall and slim, with a full head of white hair and carried himself like a drill sergeant. With a sparkle in his eye and an infectious smile, Jim introduced himself.

After getting acquainted, I learned that he was retired from working as a civilian for US Army Intelligence. He lived in Honolulu and played guitar, fiddle and also sang. He was in the area because he had relatives in nearby Coal Grove, Ohio. After a couple of visits to the store, we became very good friends. I tried to help him start an instrument repairing hobby in Hawaii and he was always inviting me to come to Hawaii on vacation.

In January of 1983, Linda and I spent a wonderful vacation visiting Jim and his wife, Lois, on Oahu. We were staying in a hotel in Kono on the big island of Hawaii when the volcano Kilauea erupted. It was still erupting as of this writing.

When Jim would visit his family in Ohio, we would get together and play music. He would joke and ask me to please come back to Hawaii and turn the volcano off. Jim was a wonderful ballad singer with an exceptional sense of humor. I also learned that during the 1940s, he had sung and played guitar on WCMI, a radio station.

Linda and I had a lot of good times together, among them two vacations to Mexico. She was very instrumental in helping me survive in business. During this time, all of her children were in their teens, the most challenging years for a parent. She handled them extremely well, but it was a most difficult time for her.

I realized that our family values were opposites in many instances. Much of her youth was spent being a parent to her siblings while her mother worked and struggled to keep their family clothed and fed. It helped me to know just how fortunate I was to have grown up in a loving family.

Even though our marriage ended some ten years later, I will always be grateful for her support.

When Dennis and I opened the Fret'N Fiddle, we never anticipated the friendships we would cultivate with the customers who came in. Many lifelong friends and relationships can be directly attributed to it. Rod and Judy Jones from Sidney, Australia, and Jim Belcher of Honolulu, were just the beginning. The list is too long to mention everyone.

One Saturday morning, Sally Sublette and her friend Sue, entered the store. Sally played the autoharp and sang, while Sue played the mountain dulcimer and was a clog dancer. At the time, Sally was relocating to Huntington, and they had just been to Santa Fe, New Mexico.

Sally performed with Dennis and me for public broadcasting. Every year, when Sally came home to Charleston during the Vandalia Gathering (West Virginia's state-sponsored annual folk festival), I would have her on the program to sing. We made two trips to Australia to perform. She moved to Idaho but always kept in contact, for which I was most grateful. She remains a most cherished musician friend.

During the years that followed, the Fret'n Fiddle in St. Albans remained the focal point of musicians in the area. We were instrumental in forming two organizations of the Appalachian Fiddler's Association, one in Huntington, the other in Kanawha County. This group began in 1978, in Huntington, having monthly meetings and jam sessions. The primary goal was to introduce players looking for someone or some group to share their music. The association was also formed with the desire to preserve Appalachian folk music.

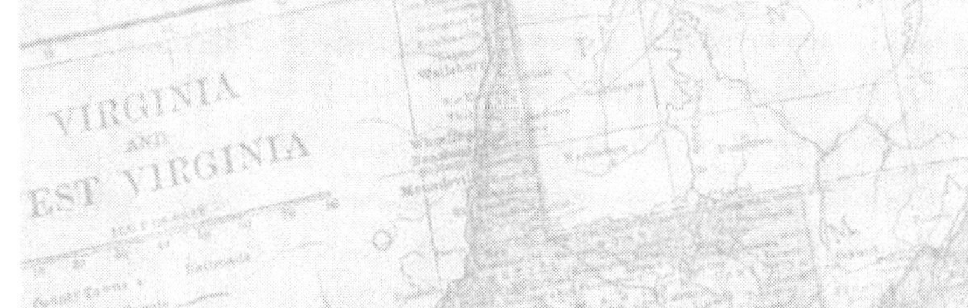


# THE SWEATER

We were returning from the 1977 National Guitar Flat Picking Festival in Winfield, Kansas, when Mary remarked, "I have to get back to Pennsylvania to get all my visas for the trip to Africa in the spring. I'll be playing Appalachian Folk Music in several countries in north and central Africa." This would be Mary's second African tour.

Since she would be performing as a solo artist, I jokingly said, "Mary, what you really need is a roadie who doubles as a fiddler."

This was said in jest, so I was very surprised when she called three weeks later and announced, "Well, I talked with the Cultural Affairs Officer in Paris and they will pay you to perform in Africa, so get your passport."

Mary Faith Rhodes lived in Pennsylvania and played the piano and several stringed instruments extremely well. She is one of the more talented musicians with whom I have worked. She also spoke fluent Parisian French. This was a great asset since most of the countries that we would visit were former French colonies. The native peoples spoke French, Arabic, and a tribal language, but no English.

This required a lot of planning, for we would be gone about two months. Mary and I planned to arrive in Inverness, Scotland, for a Folk

Music Festival on Easter weekend. From there, we would take the train to Paris and then fly to North Africa.

I thought I'd take a good sweater and wear a windbreaker jacket for the cold Easter weather in Scotland. Afterwards, it would be put in the bottom of my pack, because it would be no use to me in the Sahara region of Africa.

Our clothes and travel items were in backpacks, which would allow our hands to be free to lug our instruments on and off trains, while we were in Europe. We carried five musical instruments: hammered dulcimer, mountain dulcimer, guitar, fiddle and a mandolin.

I met Jim McHugh at the Mountain State Folk Festival in Glenville, West Virginia in 1974. He was one of those Mother Earth Hippies who moved out to a farm in Gilmer County. It was out in the hills with no electricity or running water, but the taxes were affordable. According to him, he was surviving by making sandals. He had also secured a grant to learn how to make leather harnesses for draft horses. I will not comment on the demand for harness for draft horses in the 1970s.

Two years later, my brother, Dennis, Mary and I were playing a Bluegrass Festival in Netcong, New Jersey when I heard this solo fiddler playing in the campgrounds. I followed my ears and was surprised to see Jim McHugh.

"Hey, Joe, let me show you this tune that I learned at the Fiddle Society in Inverness. It's called 'The Flowers of Edinburgh'," was his greeting. He had just returned from a six-month visit to Inverness, Scotland.

"It's so good to see you! I'd like for you to meet my wife-to-be, Barbara."

Barbara was a slender woman with curly brown hair and a very captivating smile. "We want to move to West Virginia after the wedding," she added.

This was a solution to a concern of mine about leaving my home for two months. "Jim, why don't you and Barbara just move in with me? I have a house in Lavalette, West Virginia, and you could house sit for me. I'm going to be gone to Africa for two months. That would give you time to find a place to live," I suggested. "And, by the way, we're going to be in

Inverness, Scotland for the Easter Folk Festival. How's that for a coincidence?" I added.

When it was time to leave for Europe and Africa, Jim and Barbara were settled in my home in West Virginia. At breakfast early one morning, Jim came into the dining room bringing an Icelandic Sweater. It was a pretty sweater with the typical Icelandic geometric designs across the shoulders. Three shades of brown and some white were in the design.

"You've been such a great friend to us, I have a gift for you to take on your journey," were his first words. I was sincerely surprised that he had decided to make it a gift to me. It was obviously a very special hand-woven sweater, which surely had sentimental value to him.

"Are you sure that you want me to have it?" I inquired. "This is such a great sweater, Jim."

"It's my gift to you, but there is a bit of a story that goes with it," said Jim. "In late 1974, I sold my farm in West Virginia and decided I would take a trip. One of my dreams was to visit Scotland and I had met this lovely woman who agreed to make the trip with me. We paid $120 each to fly Laker Airlines from New York to London. The plane made a stop in Iceland that was long enough for the passengers to get off and do some shopping. In one shop, there was a large selection of beautiful Icelandic sweaters and I had always wanted one."

"Since I didn't know how expensive it would be to live in Scotland, I felt that I could not afford such a pricey sweater. My lady friend suggested that I buy the yarn, and she would gladly knit me a sweater while we were visiting Scotland. From the big selection of yarn in the shop she helped choose the colors and the amount that was required to make me a sweater."

Jim continued, "We found a small apartment in Inverness and settled in, but the relationship did not last long enough for her to finish knitting the sweater. As a matter of fact, it was only about half-completed when she decided to leave."

"We lived in a tiny garage apartment behind our landlord's house. There was a high shelf in the back of the only closet, so I just stuffed the partially-knitted sweater and the remaining yarn back in a dark corner.

During the rest of my stay, I forgot about the sweater and the yarn. I came back to the States but six months later, I decided to go back to Scotland," he said.

"When I arrived back in Inverness, I visited my former landlord. I figured the apartment would not be vacant, but I had grown quite fond of the old gentleman. To my surprise, the apartment was empty, and I was able to rent the same place that I had lived in before. About a week later, I thought about the half-knitted sweater. I went to the closet and reached as far back as I could into the dark area of the shelf. Behold, it was still there with the yarn!"

"I told a friend about the partially knitted sweater and he informed me that there were ladies who knit and would finish the sweater for a fee. Well, I found such a person and look, her label is in the sweater," exclaimed Jim. He held up the sweater and inside the back of the neck was a label that said, 'Knitted in Inverness by Katherine'."

"Jim, what a great story. Are you sure you want me to have this sweater?" I asked.

"It is mine and Barbara's special gift to you. We know just how much you value the opportunity to travel," said Jim. "Believe me, the wind is cold in Inverness at Easter time and you'll enjoy the warmth."

"Thank you so much for the sweater. Looks like it will be going back to Inverness," I replied.

Inverness, Scotland is located in the north of the country. Most tourists know it because of the Loch Ness Monster, Nessie. Inverness is on an inlet of the North Sea, and Jim McHugh was correct about the cold wind that blows off the sea through the town. As I walked down the ice covered streets on that Easter weekend, it was enough to make me feel grateful for the gift of the warm Icelandic sweater.

There is always sadness when a festival ends. You've made many new friends and shared your music with audiences and other performers, and then it is back to the 'real world.' The Inverness Easter Folk Festival had come to an end, but there would be a gathering of fiddlers that evening in the lobby of the Royal Highland Hotel. The hotel was a majestic old building downtown about three blocks from the train station. This was also the hotel where we were staying. It was close to the train station where we had arrived from London.

After I left the concert area, I stopped in a local pub and ate a sandwich because I thought it could be a long night. It would depend on just how many fiddlers chose to attend the jam session. I walked along the old cobblestone street among patches of ice to the hotel.

The lobby of the Royal Highland Hotel is a picturesque place. There were old paintings on the walls and in the middle of the lobby was a winding staircase. At one end of the lobby was an ornate old bar and at the other end an elegant dining room where you could look out at the narrow, busy cobblestone streets. The floors were covered with worn Persian rugs.

I was sitting in one of the comfortable leather chairs admiring the period architecture, wondering just how old the hotel was, when I noticed a woman looking my way. When I would make eye contact with her, she would quickly look away. I couldn't remember seeing her at the concerts, but perhaps she was a fiddler.

Out of the corner of my eye, I could tell that she was still looking at me. Some minutes passed, then she walked up to where I was sitting and said, "Excuse me, but I just had to ask, is that Jim McHugh's sweater?"

After touring Africa and spending two weeks in France, I returned home to West Virginia. The McHughs had kept an eye on the home place and Jim had found a job and a place to live.

The first time Jim and I were alone and Barbara could not hear us, I said, "Jim, the most peculiar thing happened to me in Inverness. I was sitting in the lobby of The Royal Highland Hotel waiting for the fiddlers gathering to begin, when this very attractive woman who looked to be about thirty-five walked up to me."

"She was a petite woman who wore her curly black hair short and had a smooth olive complexion. When she was near my chair, she said, 'Excuse me, but I just had to ask, 'Is that Jim McHugh's sweater'?" There was a long silence.

Then Jim looked across the yard at the busy bird feeder and said, "Do you have any idea what the weather is going to be like tomorrow?"

# FOLK TRADITION

Looking out over the hills, one would think that we were in Ohio or West Virginia. Only the vegetation and trees gave it away that we were in Australia. This was my first visit to the Land Down Under, and we were camped at the Yarra Junction Folk Festival, about fifty miles northeast of Melbourne. Folk musicians and their families from Victoria, New South Wales and Queensland were camped in the wooded area. This was an old outdoor camp with a variety of buildings, cabins, and an open pavilion that proved to be excellent for a summer music festival with dancing.

"Joe, we would like for you to do at least one fiddle workshop," said Ken McMaster. "Sally, could you do a singing workshop for us today?" he asked.

Sally Sublette, a wonderful singer that I had met in West Virginia in 1977, had joined me on this trip to visit with Rod and Judy Jones. Ken was a short, pudgy man with long red hair and a full red beard. Though he looked very much like an old hippie, he was a delightful character, played the autoharp, and was very knowledgeable of American Folk Music. One would have never guessed that he was the promoter of this annual festival.

"Ken, I would enjoy doing your singing workshop," answered Sally. She was a thin, slender woman with a slight tan from Idaho sunshine, as well as one of the best singers that I had known. Her accompaniment with the guitar on my fiddle tunes was a great help and she also played the autoharp.

"Sally, since you play guitar during my fiddle workshops, I will help you with your song workshop," I offered.

"That would be just great. Maybe you could back up some of the singing with the fiddle," suggested Sally.

The morning air was rather cold and a heavy dew was on the grass when we went into the small building where the singers had gathered for Sally's song workshop. Someone built a fire in the stone fireplace at the far end of the room. There were eleven women and three men sitting around talking while waiting for Sally.

After everyone was introduced, Sally said, "There's one thing that stands out at your festival. The music and singing are wonderful. This is much like the tunes and songs you hear at folk festivals in the US. But there is one great difference. I don't see many tape recorders."

"I think that you're learning songs from books and recordings, which is OK. But I think you're missing an enormous experience of your folk traditions," Sally went on. "Over the years, I've learned most of the songs in my repertoire from individuals. This includes friends and people that I've met over the years at musical gatherings, many of whom have become lifelong friends. Each time I sing a particular song, my thoughts are of the person who taught me the lyrics. In essence, this keeps the spirit of that person alive everywhere I sing, whether it is a performance or at a musical gathering in a friend's home."

"I never sing a song but what there is a fleeting memory of the person who was so kind to take the time to help me learn it. After all, that is the definition of 'folk music.' Since the beginning of music, it has always been handed down from one person to another orally," she explained.

Holding my fiddle and bow in my lap, I sat there thinking about all the fiddlers who had helped me through the years. When Sally explained the folk tradition of learning from another person, I realized that's what I'd been doing all through the years I'd been playing. I'd just never thought about the oral tradition that way.

There were several fiddle tunes that would remind me of at least three different fiddlers from which I had stolen phrases. Not exactly stolen, but I used the versions of the tune they had taught me. The folk tradition was a new revelation for me.

The first fiddle that I bought was of very poor quality and difficult to keep in tune. I tuned it by ear, but it was not that experienced. There was a farmer, Mr. Ainsworth, whose place was about two miles from our farm. He could not play, but he would patiently tune the instrument for me. After trying and trying to tune that fiddle, I would eventually give up, go catch my pony and ride to Mr. Ainsworth's.

This presented another problem, catching the horse. Daisy was a beautiful red mare with a black mane and tail. I rode her but we also used her to plow the garden. She was difficult to catch. I would take a big handful of green alfalfa in one hand and a rope in the other and walk out to the pasture.

When Daisy saw me, she would run, and then as I got near her, she would run again. This could go on for thirty minutes to an hour. Finally, she would walk up to me, take the alfalfa hay in her mouth, and let me put the rope around her neck. I always thought it was a game she enjoyed. I tried other items like an apple or an ear of corn, but her reaction was always the same.

With the bridle on Daisy, I would put the saddle on her and ride the two miles to Mr. Ainsworth's house. He would tune the fiddle for me and sometimes, after the two-mile ride back home, it would be out of tune again. He was one of the many kind folks who helped me in my efforts to learn to play the fiddle.

Mr. Ainsworth and his wife moved away and I never saw them again. It would be nice if he could know that I finally did learn to play the violin.

When I was in high school, I would get up very early on Saturday morning and tune into the Jody Andrews Show on KTRY Radio in Bastrop, Louisiana. Jody was a wonderful fiddler and his sons accompanied him, Keith on bass and Jim on guitar.

The first time I went to his house was in the summer. He was sitting on the front porch in a big, high-back rocker drinking a glass of iced tea.

"Mr. Andrews, I'm learning to play the fiddle and I wondered if you could help me. I've listened to your radio show and I just love your fiddlin'," I said.

Jody Andrews was a big man, over six feet tall, and his hands were large. I wondered how he played that small instrument with such large hands.

"Joe, come on in, but I don't know if I can be much help." he said with kindness, opening the screen door and motioning for me to enter the living room. "This is my wife, Amy."

Mrs. Andrews was a very short woman who wore a cotton print dress and an apron. Her hair had streaks of gray and she was smiling.

"Nice to meet you, Joe, would you like a glass of tea?" she offered.

"Yes, ma'am," I answered, looking around the room.

Their home was an old wooden farmhouse. There was no paint on the wood floors and some framed pictures of family hung on the unpainted walls. The house was very clean and smelled of fresh baked bread.

"Amy, would you bring me my fiddle," said Jody, as he sat down in a rocking chair. When she left the room he said, "Joe, if you always play the fiddle smooth and pretty, the woman won't complain. I never played rough or scratchy and Amy has always liked my fiddlin'."

"Another thing, you will find that most fiddlers are nice and kind people because the fiddle is hard to play and it takes a lot of patience," he said.

Jody was an accomplished fiddler. On several occasions he declined the offer to travel and play with recording artists. He chose not to be away from his family.

The last time I saw him, he told me he had learned many of the old tunes from his mother when they lived in East Texas. His father was a fiddler and his mother had accompanied him on the piano. When Jody was about two years old, his father died.

Jody started playing the fiddle as a boy. His mother would whistle the melody until he learned his dad's versions of the old tunes.

When I asked him about fiddling contests, he mentioned that Eck Robinson had beaten him in 1939 in a fiddling contest in Ft. Worth, Texas. The winner won a twenty-four pound sack of flour.

Every time I played the tunes I learned from Jody, I always thought of him.

# FIDDLIN' IN NEW ZEALAND

In all of my travels, the South Island of New Zealand is the most interesting and beautiful place that I've ever visited. Our group consisted of three couples, Sally Sublette and Rick McCracken, Greg Shupe and Gina Schrader, and Sandy Orvis and me. Everyone played a musical instrument except Gina and Sandy. Gina was never without her camera and we thought of her as our personal photographer. Sandy was never without a small can of cat food in her purse. Every stray cat seemed to know this by instinct.

We flew into Auckland and rented a van. It was a day and a half drive to Wellington, which is on the southernmost tip of the North Island. After spending the weekend playing music at the Wellington Folk Festival, we took the ferry to the South Island. Sally and Rick were avid skiers. They rented a car and proceeded to travel through the mountainous areas of the West Coast. After several days of traveling, they flew back to Pocatello, Idaho, and we did not see them again until the next year, at a music festival in West Virginia.

Gina, Greg, Sandy and I rented a small van and drove south along the East Coast. We planned to go see the sperm whales at Kaikoura. Most of the highway runs along the coast and if you look to the west, there are snow-capped mountains reminiscent of the Colorado Rockies. This was the only place I'd ever been where you could stand on the beach and look out across the ocean, then turn around and discover you're standing at the foot of a majestic snow-capped mountain.

"We're definitely going to see the whales," said Gina. Gina was married to Greg Shupe, a wonderful singer who played guitar.

In *National Geographic*, I had read about large pods of sperm whales that gathered in that area. Kaikoura was a popular tourist attraction. Boats would take tourists out to the area so the whales could be viewed in their natural habitat. Gina looked forward to this part of our trip because she wanted to photograph the whales.

"Although the weather is not the greatest today, I hope we get to see the whales," said Sandy, who had a love for animals.

Much to everyone's disappointment, the ocean was rough. Thirty-foot seas prohibited us from viewing the whales.

"I'm not giving up," said Gina. "We'll just see them when we come back from Stewart Island."

"I sure hope so," said Sandy, "and the dolphins, too."

"There are several places to see both blue and brown penguins," said Greg, changing the subject. He and Gina were dedicated bird watchers. They were excited about visiting the islands of New Zealand and South Island is the home of many rare species of birds.

In the city of Christchurch, we visited with Rodger Lusby, a talented folk singer. We had first met him at the Wellington Folk Festival.

Just down the cliff from Rodger's home, we took a walk along the ocean. I stood with my hand outstretched, silently singing 'HU,' an ancient name for God. As I sang, a sea bird slowly lowered itself onto my hand. It stood there for several seconds, calmly looked me in the eye, then flew away.

"Now that has to be a great shot," I exclaimed. "Gina, I want a copy of that one." I'd never had a wild bird land in my hand and I was grateful she had her camera at hand. That cherished photograph hangs on my wall today.

On the evening of the third day, we arrived in the town of Dunedin, a beautiful, clean city of about 120,000 people. We checked into a motel that was within walking distance of downtown and many tourist attractions.

After spending so much time out in the bush of Australia and New Zealand, it was most refreshing to be back in a bustling city where there was a choice of restaurants.

As we ate our evening meal Greg reminded everyone, "Don't forget, tomorrow is the day we see the brown penguins. We have to be at the ocean just before dawn."

The penguins left the shore at dawn to swim out into the ocean to feed, then returned at dusk. Early in the morning or late in the evening, there was about a thirty-minute period when it was possible to view them.

I realized that I was literally wearing my cleanest dirty shirt. "Hey folks, I think that I will miss the penguins and do some laundry," I announced. I couldn't remember the last time we had done laundry.

Greg said, "This could be your only chance to see the brown penguins. Are you sure?" It was a pleasure to travel with Greg and Gina because they did all this research about the area we were visiting.

"We've seen blue penguins and at this time, clean clothes are a priority," I replied. "Sandy, you might want to go. This could be your last opportunity to see them. I simply have to do some laundry."

"I'm tired," replied Sandy. "We've been traveling for so long. We have the flight home in a few days. I think that I'll sleep in tomorrow and get some rest."

Well, I arose around nine that morning and with no remorse whatsoever of missing the penguins, I left quietly without waking Sandy.

In most of the motels and hotels where we stayed in Australia and New Zealand, there was a laundry room. Usually, it was a very small room with a coin-operated washing machine and dryer. Almost always there was also an iron and ironing board.

This hotel was no different and in the corner opposite the washer and dryer was a woman ironing a shirt. She said, "G'day."

I greeted her with a pleasant, "Good morning, my name is Joe Dobbs." She was dressed casually, with a very pleasant appearance and looked to be in her late fifties.

"I'm Andrea McGill," she said.

As I continued to load the washer, she asked, "Where are you from?"

With my American southern drawl, she knew immediately that I was not from anywhere near New Zealand.

"I'm from the U.S. I'm a member of The West Virginia String Band and we just performed at the Wellington Folk Festival. We're visiting your lovely island before we return home," I said.

"I had an uncle who was in World War II and he had fond memories of the South Pacific. He particularly enjoyed the time he spent in New Zealand."

"He used to take me fishing. I remember one time sitting in a fishing boat on Lake Washington in Mississippi. He told me if I should I ever have the opportunity, I must visit New Zealand. As a small boy, it never occurred to me that I would travel to the other side of the earth and visit your island."

As I turned from adding the laundry soap to the washer, I noticed that she was crying. At first, I wondered if something I had said made her sad.

After what seemed to be several minutes, Andrea asked, "What musical instrument do you play?" She was still ironing shirts.

"The fiddle," I answered. She seemed to gain control of her emotions and at this point, I was very puzzled as to why she was crying.

"I apologize for being so emotional, but my husband, Kevin, is not well. We live on Steward Island and this is the nearest hospital. That's why we're here in Dunedin. He's had total kidney failure and is being fitted with the necessary attachment in his arm so he can have dialysis," she said.

"The doctors are mystified as to why his kidneys failed," she continued. "Two months ago, he retired from the car dealership where he had worked for many years. We had big plans to do some traveling. He'd always enjoyed good health, so this has been a shock."

Thinking I might console her, I said, "I have a friend back in Kentucky who had kidney failure. She had a transplant five years ago. Now, she's enjoying life."

"The opportunity for Kevin to get a transplant in New Zealand is so remote," she stated. "We've wondered what we might have done in a previous life that would bring this upon us."

Changing the subject, she asked, "Would you be so kind as to come to our room and play the fiddle for him?"

"I would like that very much. What time would be convenient? I'll need your room number."

"We're in the room adjoining you," she explained. "He loves the fiddle and you could come to our room in about an hour. Thank you, it's so very kind of you to do this. Kevin just loves fiddle music."

"I would like for you to meet Sandy. Is it alright if I bring her?" I asked.

"Oh, sure, we would love to meet her," answered Andrea. "We'll be expecting you both."

I returned to our room with my clean laundry. "Sandy, we're invited to visit with the couple next door," I announced. "This is an opportunity for us to get to talk with some local folks."

She put the book she was reading on the table and said, "Do we have to bring anything?"

"No, I just have to play the fiddle," I answered and went on to explain the reason for our invitation.

Since Kevin had grown up in New Zealand, I would play as many Celtic tunes as possible. I had an hour to remember all the Irish jigs, reels, and airs that I knew. Not having a great repertoire in Irish folk tunes, I would have to do the best I could.

I placed the big mute on the fiddle which made it so quiet you couldn't hear it in the next room. And then, I practiced.

At the agreed-upon time, I knocked on the door. "Please come in," greeted Andrea. She had changed into a dress with a tropical flower design, as if this was some special occasion. "I'd like for you to meet my husband. Kevin, this is Joe who plays the fiddle."

Kevin stood up immediately and gave me a hearty handshake saying, "Nice to meet you."

"Kevin, Andrea, this is Sandy," I said.

Smiling, Sandy said, "It's a pleasure to meet you both. Thanks for inviting us."

"Thanks for coming over to play for us," said Kevin, who was looking at me.

"It's very good to meet you, Kevin, but save your gratitude. You haven't heard me play yet," I joked.

Kevin was a healthy-looking man, over six feet tall with a full head of red hair sprinkled with gray. I would have never guessed that he was ill.

"Would you like a cup of tea?" Andrea asked.

"That would be wonderful," answered Sandy. "I'll have sugar in mine."

"Yes, with a bit of cream, thank you," I said, as I took my fiddle out of the case.

The first tune I chose to play was "Miss McCloud's Reel," which I followed with the "Swallow Tail Jig." My fears that I wouldn't know the right melodies vanished as I continued to play. From Kevin's response, I thought he was going to get up and dance. With a broad smile, he clapped his hands and stomped his feet to the rhythm of those old tunes.

Between tunes, Kevin proceeded to tell me about his uncle, Sean. When Kevin was a young chap, he would go to dances where his uncle was the fiddler and played some of the same tunes. I was pleased that I could play some of those old Irish melodies that took him back to his childhood.

"Would you like a biscuit?" Andrea asked. "I baked them myself." A biscuit in New Zealand is a cookie to an American.

"What a treat," said Sandy, taking a biscuit.

"I'd love one," I said, trying to remember the last time we had eaten homemade cookies. They were so delicious, you could tell that she didn't spare the butter. I had another cup of tea with another biscuit.

The music and the sharing of experiences at dances continued for more than an hour. With some sadness, I knew I would have to end this private concert with our new friends. I chose the slow Welsh tune, "Ash Grove" to be my last piece. This is a beautiful tune but the words are about a lover who dies and is buried in the ash grove.

I was just playing the melody. The story was not cheerful at all for someone trying to survive an illness. It was possible that he would not be aware of the tragic lyrics. Since this was going to be the last song, I played as best I could.

As I finished, Kevin stood up and said, "That song has some very dirty lyrics. Would you like to hear them?"

"Kevin," scolded Andrea. "You wouldn't dare."

Before we left, Andrea and Kevin told us how beautiful it was on Steward Island. They sincerely invited us to come and visit them.

Back in our room, I reminisced about all those years of practicing. Having the ability to bring joy to someone facing an unexpected tragedy seemed to make all that practice worthwhile. *I would have practiced more if I had dreamed I would someday be playing halfway around the earth,* I thought. There is spiritual power in music. Familiar melodies can take you back to relive a time in the past.

My thoughts went to a day when I was about twelve years old. It had rained and we couldn't work in the fields. I seized the opportunity to practice on my fiddle. Words fail to describe just how bad the noises were coming out of that cheap instrument.

My dad was by far the most patient person I have ever known. After a few minutes of my screeching on that fiddle, he said, "Son, you're just going to have to take that thing to the barn to play. From the sound, I think you must be hurting the fiddle."

So, it was back to the bale of hay in the hayloft of our old barn as I tried to improve my primitive skills.

"Wouldn't it be great if we had time to visit Stewart Island?" Sandy said.

"That's a good reason to come back to New Zealand," I answered.

# IGNORANT HILLBILLY

After living in West Virginia for a while, I discovered that a large portion of West Virginians had the idea that folks outside the state thought of them as "dumb hillbillies." I'd like to know where that started. I'd never heard of it until I moved to West Virginia.

People who live just across the state line in Virginia do not share this attitude. Maybe it began after 1863, when West Virginia separated from Virginia and became a state. Maybe it was because Virginia was wealthier, had land that was more prized by farmers and was one of the original colonies.

If you cross the Ohio River, you would know that the Ohioans had self-esteem. Once you cross into Maryland or Pennsylvania, people seem to change as to how they think they are perceived by others. North Carolina, South Carolina, northern Georgia residents or folks from East Tennessee do not share the West Virginia native's image of themselves.

West Virginians with professions that took them out of state sometimes return when they reach retirement age. Many of them still carry the attitude of 'dumb hillbilly' that has been with them since childhood. In many instances, they were taught this in the home and in the classroom. I was told that when people's professions required them to move to larger cities outside the state, they wouldn't tell where they were from for fear of being ridiculed.

In 1991, I took a motorcycle trip and visited relatives. My motorcycle was a Honda Goldwing that was excellent for cross country touring. After leaving West Virginia, I stopped in Oak Grove, Louisiana, to visit with my sister, Lucille. She enjoyed riding and decided to join me. We rode west to Palestine, Texas, to visit with my brother, Dennis, and his wife, Barbara. Their daughter, Candice, was about fifteen years old and I agreed to take her for a ride.

It was a beautiful, clear summer day, just perfect for a bike ride. We rode about sixty-five miles to Tyler. On the way, we stopped at a roadside park on a hill overlooking a green valley. It had a picnic table with a shelter. As for the hill, if you were from West Virginia, it would have seemed rather small.

"Uncle Joe, isn't that a beautiful view?" Candice said, admiring the valley below. I read about this being a lookout during some war on the Historical Marker.

"Texas is the most beautiful state. I don't see why anyone would want to live anywhere else," she added. I agreed and we continued our ride.

Her words stuck in my mind. I wondered how she had come to that conclusion. I knew her parents had not taught her that attitude. They were both from Louisiana and had lived a couple of years in West Virginia.

The next day, Dennis took me to see the historical "Old Pilgrim," reputedly the oldest Protestant church in Texas, which was near Elkhart. The Church dated back to the 1830s.

I told Dennis about my conversation with his daughter. "Dennis, where did she get those ideas? Did you tell her about the great state of Texas?" I joked.

"Joe, in the school system in Texas, they start teaching the students about Texas history in Kindergarten. They're told about the Alamo. They know about Santa Ana's defeat at San Jacinto in 1836 and how Texas was once an independent Republic. It became a state with the agreement that they could secede if they wished," Dennis explained.

Listening to my brother explain the patriotism taught in the school classrooms, I finally understood why Texas folks had such a great attitude about themselves and their state. This passion for Texas by its residents is often viewed as arrogance by outsiders. Regardless of how they may have been trashed by some journalist or received any kind of bad press they were still from the "Great State of Texas."

"West Virginia sure could use some of that thinking," I said. "Students in West Virginia are taught by their parents, as well as most of their school teachers and journalists, that outsiders think of them as backward and stupid. Some West Virginians put the blame on the media outside the state."

An educated theory is that the "ignorant hillbilly" image began after *The New York Times* wrote about the Hatfield and McCoy feud. Other articles followed about the poverty in West Virginia.

I lived west of the Mississippi and traveled through the southwestern states, but I can't recall meeting anyone who was an avid reader of *The New York Times.*

The media always writes negative about everyone. I think it must be a major part of their education. After watching all the Cop Shows on television, a portion of America was afraid to visit New York City. They feared getting mugged or harmed in some way. In reality, that city is the cultural and artistic center of this hemisphere.

It seemed that anywhere I lived or traveled, there would be those who made derogatory remarks about someone from another state or country. In the Texas oil fields, the Texans would ask me if I had water marks on my legs from wading in the swamps. They wanted to know if I had web feet because I grew up in Louisiana.

We would ask the Texans if they had cow manure between their toes. After all, they were supposed to be cowboys. This happened anywhere you went. In France, they told jokes on the citizens of Belgium and in Australia there were jokes about the Irish. I was in England and the jokes were about the Scots. Maybe the only difference is that West Virginians believe the negative things said and written about them.

Some say that it could be a tradition of the Celtic culture. There are Scots-Irish folks living in East Texas and throughout the Ozarks of Arkansas and Missouri. These folks in the Ozarks have been wearing bib overalls, smoking corncob pipes and picking and grinning for the tourists for over seventy-five years. They're probably still taking the Yankee tourists' money. When I lived there I did not find the lack of self esteem that I have found in West Virginia.

What about the movies and their portrayal of mountain people? Judy Canova, Maw and Paw Kettle and Roy Acuff starred in movies about mountain folks. Many from West Virginia were upset about the television show "The Beverly Hillbillies." They believed that the show was an embarrassment to West Virginians. "The Real McCoys" was a very popular TV Show that ran from 1957-1963. It featured among others, actor Walter Brennan.

Hollywood has often presented Appalachian characters as uneducated and sometimes poorly dressed. They were also depicted as wise, cunning, honest and possessing strong family values. They always survived. As for the Beverly Hillbillies show, residents of Beverly Hills, California, could have easily been offended because they were often portrayed as kooks.

I asked a very close friend whose family had lived in West Virginia for several generations, if he thought people living in other states viewed him as a backward hillbilly. My friend said that he was not taught this at home and thought it was only the people in New York and Washington, D.C., who had these views.

When I asked how he arrived at that conclusion, he said he didn't really know. Perhaps it was related to the character of Barney Fife of the Andy Griffith show. Though Mayberry was in North Carolina, Don Knotts, the actor who played the character Barney Fife, was from Wheeling, West Virginia.

Possibly this person did not know how he actually acquired those attitudes. Could it be so strongly entrenched in the culture that one just embraces the attitude without questioning?

West Virginia is located less than five hundred miles from a majority of the population of the U.S. I was told by persons who worked in the industry, that the White Water Rafting is second to none in the country. There are excellent, affordable, and highly rated ski slopes. Several music festivals in the state attract people from outside the country. Excellent quality biking and hiking trails are found all over the state. Numerous national parks of historical significance are located in West Virginia, which include Harpers Ferry, Seneca Rocks and Blennerhasset Island. The Kanawha, Ohio, Gauley and New Rivers all contribute to the water sports. This is only a partial list of all the significant places and events that are found in this small state.

I often wonder if the "ignorant hillbilly" syndrome had any effect on the slow growth in tourism. Could this have any relation to West Virginia's economy being rated forty-ninth of the fifty states? Could this have had any effect on the school ratings compared to the other states? How long would it take to change attitudes that are still being picked up in the home and classroom?

West Virginia's lack of interest in the promotion of tourism could possibly be linked in some way to that attitude. I could not understand the lack of pride in their beautiful Appalachian region by native West Virginians.

Maybe it began when Devil Anse Hatfield was traveling with a Wild West show. I had always heard about the Hatfield and McCoy feud. But no one wanted to talk about it. I had to go to the library to find any information.

I drove to Delbarton once, but could not find the statue of Devil Anse Hatfield that was supposed to be there. Having recently lived in New Mexico, where tourism was the number one industry in their economy, I was puzzled. Busloads of tourists were taken out in that desolate high desert country to visit Billy the Kid's grave. It was in the middle of nowhere. Tourists had chipped so much of the headstone away for souvenirs, the park service had to erect a steel fence to protect the grave.

Here was West Virginia with all the beautiful lush mountains and colorful history, but no one seemed to appreciate the tourism potential. Once in Buffalo, West Virginia, which is located on the Kanawha River, I noticed this old building that looked like an ancient school house. One of the residents told me that it had been a Military Academy before the Civil War. During the war, it had been used as a hospital. I thought that would be more interesting than Billy the Kid's grave.

In 1968, when Arch Moore was running for governor of West Virginia, I was a new resident of the state. Referring to tourism in one of his campaign speeches, Arch declared "We do not want those visitors coming into our state."

# HOME

During my late teen years, I often traveled by hitch-hiking. Sometime in '54, I hitch-hiked from De Queen, Arkansas, to Houston, Texas, where I was living. It was almost dusk and I was standing beside highway 71 on the south edge of town with my thumb out. A car pulled off to the side of the road, so I grabbed my bag and walked up to the passenger's door.

"Git in," said the young man in the passenger's seat.

"Thanks," I said, and opened the back door and put my bag in the floor. I got in the car, sat down and closed the door. There were two soldiers in the front seat of the four-door '51 Buick.

As the driver pulled back on the road, he asked, "Where are you headed?"

"Houston, Texas," I answered.

"Well, you're very lucky," he said. "We just got discharged from the Army at Fort Chaffee and can't wait to get home. We've spent two years in Germany. Houston is our home." (Fort Chaffee was near Fort Smith, Arkansas.)

The soldier in the passenger's seat asked, "What address in Houston?"

"Near the end of Harrisburg," I answered.

"Wow, that's only about five blocks from where I live and we can take you by your place," he said.

The soldiers talked about what they were going to do when they arrived home. It had been a long two years away from their families. They were very excited about being out of the service and finally going home for good.

I lay down on the back seat and was soon fast asleep. About an hour later I awoke to the screeching of tires which caused me to roll off the back seat down into the floor and on top of my bag. Gravel was flying as the car slid sideways and stopped. I thought we must have wrecked.

As I sat up, I noticed it was dark outside. The front doors flew open and the soldiers jumped out of the car. In the beam of the headlights I could see the ten foot tall concrete replica of the state of Texas that is always at the state line on any main highway.

I realized that we were on highway 71 just south of Ogden, Arkansas. Here the highway ran along the Arkansas and Texas line to Texarkana. On one side of the road you were in Arkansas and on the other you were in Texas.

"Smell that Texas air," screamed the driver as he jumped high in the air.

"God, it is so good to be home. Smell that Texas cowshit," shouted the other soldier as he threw a handful of Texas soil into the air. It was another three hundred miles to Houston, but they were home.

Once, I attempted to show my children where I'd grown up in Louisiana. The one-room school at Round Hill, where I had attended and played as a child, was gone, a soybean field in its place. Two of the houses where I'd lived had been gone for years. The land where they stood had been turned into cotton or rice fields. Now the homes exist only in my memory. I was saddened by this reality and never again felt a need to return.

In the 1960s, somewhere in Arizona, I met two very good musicians from West Virginia. As far as I know it was my first encounter with people from Appalachia. I recall they were very likable and played extremely well. They thought the American West was beautiful, but most of all they wanted to go home to the green rolling mountains of West Virginia. They expressed a love for the mountains and a longing for home.

It seems to me, most of the native West Virginians that I met living out of state were literally suffering from homesickness. One of the reasons for this attachment to the land is because it has basically remained unchanged for one hundred and fifty years. Regardless of "progress" these West Virginians could take you back to the home where they had lived as a child. Many could show you the house where their grandparents and even their great-grandparents had lived.

Yes, there are more roads and the coal mining industry has left its marks on the mountains. There are strip malls and K-Marts, but the mountains haven't changed.

The late Buddy Khuns told me his doctor recommended that he move out West. Buddy was a wonderful guitar player who grew up near Charleston, but he had suffered with asthma since childhood. Sometime in the mid '50s, he moved to Amarillo, Texas, hoping the dry climate would improve Buddy's health. His condition improved; however, not even a year had passed until he became very homesick for West Virginia.

If one had grown up in the mountains of West Virginia, Amarillo on the dry, flat plains with the wind that never stopped would be very close to Hell. The sand storms and the cold winter winds became unbearable in spite of his better health and he went home to West Virginia. Buddy told me he was so homesick and afraid that something might happen on the trip that he sold his car for much less than its worth. He found it more assuring to purchase a bus ticket to West Virginia.

In the summer of 1984, I visited my brother in Palestine, Texas. Two of the tires on my van needed to be replaced and Dennis suggested that we go to K-mart.

At the cashier's window in the automotive department was an attractive young woman in her early twenties. When she saw the address on the bill of sale, she loudly exclaimed, "Oh my God you're from Huntington, West Virginia." Before I could answer she said, "I'm from Logan. It is so good to just see someone from home."

For years I had been the host of "Music from the Mountains," a weekly show that aired throughout the state. For thirty years I'd played folk festivals in West Virginia, but I had never met this young woman. I was a stranger to her.

But from her reaction, it was almost like I was related to her. I wouldn't have been surprised if she had come out from behind the counter and given me a hug.

"How did you get all the way out here to Texas?" I asked. "It is a long way from West Virginia," I said sympathetically.

"My husband is working on a construction job here. We can't wait for the job to end so we can go home. I'm counting the days," she explained. "I hope I never have to leave home again. Texas people are friendly and nice but it ain't home."

She continued to tell me all about her family and their home in the coal fields of Logan, West Virginia. I was a total stranger but I was from her state so she felt a genuine kinship.

The encounter with her reminded me of a joke. Why do the West Virginians in heaven have to be chained up? If they were free, they'd go home every weekend.

# NINETY NINE

I awoke to the noise of a squirrel munching sunflower seeds from a 'squirrel-proof' bird feeder that hung over the deck just outside the sliding glass doors. It was a bright sunny day and as I lay in bed, I tried to think of a good excuse not to go in to work. Business was slow in the middle of summer and it would be a great day to ride my motorcycle in the mountains.

The phone rang and it was my son, Scott, calling from our family business, the Fret'N Fiddle Music Store. "Dad, I just got off the phone with a man who sounded old. He has a violin for sale and I thought you might want to give him a call," he said.

Half of our business was dealing with used and vintage stringed musical instruments. It was up to me to make the decision about purchasing used violins, a very difficult line to learn. "I'll give him a call," I said, thinking that it was just another one of those 'old fiddles that had been in someone's family for decades, so it must be worth a lot of money.'

I had literally seen hundreds of those in the past forty years, but there was always the chance that someone had something of value, so you had to check out every instrument. This was just the excuse I needed to keep me from going and working in the store that day, so I dialed the number.

"Hello," answered a gentleman's voice. He did not sound that old to me.

"Good morning," I said, "my son just called me from the Fret'N Fiddle and told me you had a violin that you wished to sell." I opened the sliding glass door and startled the squirrel. It immediately jumped to the nearest limb and disappeared up the large maple tree.

"Yes, I do," he said, "but I will have to get someone to bring me over to your store so you can look at it. I live in Cross Lanes and I don't drive."

Cross Lanes was near the store, so I said, "Would it be alright if I came by your house? Would that be more convenient for you?"

"That would be much better for me," he answered, and gave me his street address with some directions.

I rang the doorbell of a large, modern, brick home and was greeted by a rather short, stooped gentleman who looked to be in his early 70s. He was very neatly dressed and had a full head of white hair.

"Come in," he invited, opening the door. "I am Lee Brill," he said, while shaking my hand.

"I am Joe Dobbs, Scott's dad," I said. All the rooms were well decorated with fancy drapes and I'm sure the paintings on the walls were of value. The furniture, obviously expensive, was arranged around thick Persian styled rugs. The house seemed very clean.

"Come on in the dining room where we can sit," he said.

The dining room was elegantly furnished with a long table and eight chairs. Against one wall was a curved glass-front hutch that was filled with what could have been rare china. An old but very cheap violin case was on the table. I was admiring the lovely tablecloth when he interrupted my thoughts.

"My wife is in a nursing home in Kanawha City, so I live alone. She is from West Virginia, so we moved here from Florida several years ago. I don't have any close living relatives," he continued. "I visit her every day. I sit for a couple of hours holding her hand and she doesn't even know who I am. We never had any children, but we've been happily married for over sixty-two years."

Tears swelled up in his eyes as he said, "She's all I have, and I miss so much her not being in this house." He took a handkerchief from his pocket and wiped the tears from his face saying, "I'm sorry, but you have no idea how much I miss her. I have a Cadillac there in the garage that I can't drive because of my knees. I could have both my knees replaced, but I couldn't bear the thought of being unable to visit her for the six weeks it would take me to recover."

My eyes went to the case and I wondered just what kind of violin he had in it.

"You know, I played that fiddle in the Armed Forces Orchestra during the war," he said, quickly changing the subject.

"World War II?" I asked.

He chuckled and said, "No, World War I. I played in the Armed Forces Orchestra in Europe."

I quickly did the math. World War I was over in 1918 and he didn't look to be that old.

"How old are you, Mr. Brill?" I asked. But he ignored my question.

"When I returned home to Chicago after the war, I had gained so much weight that I couldn't get into my tuxedo. So I called the orchestra leader at the Blackstone Hotel where we were playing. I was expected to return to my position in the orchestra that evening so I didn't have time to get the tux altered," he explained. "The orchestra leader thought a minute and told me just to wear my Army uniform."

Mr. Brill said, "I was surprised that the customers at the hotel liked me wearing my uniform. Everyone was celebrating the defeat of the Kaiser. I was relieved for I felt like I wasn't properly dressed. But the leader asked me to continue wearing it for several evenings."

I could tell he was enjoying sharing his memories but I wondered about the violin in that closed case. If he played during World War I, it had to be a least 100 years old.

"Mr. Brill, how old are you?" I asked.

But he just continued re-living his life.

"You know, I started playing in hotel orchestras a couple of years before I went in the army. There was so much work for musicians in Chicago in those days. Every hotel had an orchestra and there were orchestras in the music halls, theaters and most fine restaurants," he continued.

"I'm telling you, one had to know music to get in the Union in those days. The Union would send out a couple of musicians to give you a test to make sure that you could really play. It wasn't like it is today, just give them money." He said, "I remember when I took my test. The fellow put some sheet music on the stand that I had never seen. It was written in the key of G major. I played it because I was a good sight-reader. Then, he said, 'Now play it in B flat'."

I was captivated with the old man's stories but I wanted to see the fiddle.

"I guess it was three or four years after I came back from the war when I was playing in a ten-piece orchestra at the Drake Hotel," he went on. "I'm sure you know that many of the very rich people lived in those big hotels," he said. "Why, I can remember one night, Mr. Gary walked up to the orchestra and handed me a one hundred dollar bill attached to one of his business cards and asked for a Rachmaninov piece. You know, Mr. Gary liked Rachmaninov."

I sat there thinking just how much one hundred dollars would have purchased in 1921. It may have been about half the cost of a Model T Ford.

He could see the questioning look on my face, so he asked, "You do know who Mr. Gary was, don't you?"

Before I could tell him that I had no idea, he answered his own question, "Mr. Gary was the president of U.S. Steel. He's the man they named Gary, Indiana, after."

"Would you like to see the violin?" he finally asked. "It should be worth some money," he said, opening the old case. "I quit playing it in 1934 and I don't think that it has been played since."

I thought, *That was the year that I was born.*

"I played my way through Northwestern University with that violin," he added.

I lifted the violin out of the case and it certainly looked disappointing. It was so worn. The varnish was worn completely off in several places. It had obviously been dropped and the scroll broken off the neck, but an excellent repairman had performed a good restoration. The neck had been grafted, meaning that it had been made before or around 1800. I looked inside and the label was missing, so I could not determine the maker.

"Mr. Brill, when was the neck broken and repaired?" I asked. "And, you never did tell me how old you are."

"That neck was exactly like that when my mother purchased the violin for me when I was nine years old," he said. My question about his age, he just ignored.

"I don't have any relatives to give it to, so I've decided to sell it. I made a living with it for several years and it sure brought me a lot of joy," he explained. "I want to sell it. How much would you give me?"

After examining the violin I was not interested. I thought it was worth about $800, but it would be very difficult to sell without determining who the maker was. It had a very poor appearance because of the worn varnish.

In that condition, it would probably take us over a year to sell it. I came to the conclusion that he thought it was worth about $3,000. I didn't want to tell this nice old man that his violin was not as valuable as he thought. Our business was so slow that I really did not want it.

Changing the subject, I asked, "All those years that you played in orchestras in Chicago, did you meet any famous musicians?"

"Oh, let me think. What was the fellow's name that had such a big nose?" he asked.

"Jimmy Durante?" I suggested.

"Yes, I played with him when he was just getting started and also Jack Benny was just beginning at that time," he said. "I just cannot remember because it was so long ago."

"During your years of playing, what musician impressed you most?" I asked.

Without any hesitation, he said, "Benny Goodman. He used to come in and bring his trio and they were the best I had ever heard. You cannot imagine how Benny could improvise."

Mr. Brill became excited and told how Benny Goodman would play several choruses that were always different. "His piano player would just quit playing and start laughing while Benny kept on improvising. I never could improvise but I was a very good sight reader," he added.

"How much would you pay for my fiddle?" he asked again. "And by the way I was born in 1895. I am ninety-nine years old."

I was almost speechless. This man, sharing all these great experiences with me and so mentally aware and quick, was ninety-nine years old. I don't know how long I had been there, but I was sure we had been talking for over an hour.

"Mr. Brill, I just have to tell you I would never have guessed your age to be ninety-nine years," I said. "Do you know any secrets about how to achieve longevity? Just what is the secret of enjoying a long life?" I asked. I expected him to say something about healthy eating, lots of exercise, or maybe it would be in the genes.

He smiled and said, "Just don't quit breathing."

I'm sure that he had wanted to share his musical experiences with someone. He went on to tell me that his favorite violinist was Itzhak Pearlman. When I asked him what his occupation had been, as it was obvious he had been very successful, he would only answer, "I was in advertising."

"Mr. Brill, I don't have a market for this old violin, because most of my violin students want a bright, new instrument," I said. "But, I do want you to know that I can't remember when I've enjoyed a visit more."

"You could at least make me an offer," he said.

"I don't want to hurt your feelings, but I could only offer you $500."

"I'll take it!" he said, hurriedly.

I took out the store checkbook, my heart sinking. I didn't want the violin and I hoped we had enough money in the account to cover this check.

We said our good-byes, and I promised to come back so we could go out and eat and continue the conversation.

Carrying the violin case under my arm, I walked into the store and asked Scott, "Do we have $500 in the bank account?"

Scott said, "Maybe. Why?"

Taking the violin out of the case, I said, "I just bought this violin."

"Gosh Dad, that fiddle sure looks rough to me. You mean you paid $500 for THAT?" he exclaimed.

"I really didn't want the fiddle," I said.

"Well, why in the world did you buy it?" Scott asked.

"I made the man an offer and he took it," I explained.

"My goodness, we are so short on money, why didn't you just back out?" he said.

"I couldn't, son. He was ninety-nine years old."

# STORY OF A VIOLIN

Closely examining the old violin, I said, "Scott, get me a set of those new Zyex violin strings. I'm going to take this old fiddle home, clean it up, put on some new strings, and play it for a while."

I knew that Mr. Brill had played the fiddle for over twenty-five years. It had been old and well played when his mother bought it for him around 1902. The fiddle hadn't been played since 1934, which was the year I was born. When an instrument has been stored that length of time it does not play well. It's better to play it for several hours before displaying it for sale.

Though the varnish was worn, my new purchase did not have any cracks or open seams. To keep out moisture, I did some French polishing over the places where bare wood was exposed. Three old gut strings were still on the instrument. I put on new strings, played it for two evenings, and began to enjoy the violin.

Old instruments that have been played for many years have a wonderful response and are easier to play. This violin didn't have the volume that I preferred, but its voice was warm and mellow.

One morning, Scott asked, "Did you ever get that old fiddle that 'you didn't want,' in playing condition?"

"I kinda like the way it plays and sounds, so maybe I'll just keep it at home and play it for a while," I answered. "It's going to be hard to sell because it still looks rough even after all my polishing."

I was a dealer and not a collector, so I added, "If some customer comes in the store and is interested in a very old fiddle, I'll bring it back."

"It would be nice if we could find it a permanent home, because we could use the money," said Scott. "I still can't believe that you paid that old man $500 for that fiddle."

"He was ninety-nine years old!" I exclaimed.

The fiddle had a small neck and I had small hands so I used it when I performed. It came to be somewhat of a prop. If I felt my performance was weak, I would tell the story of my fiddle and my conversations with Mr. Brill, which the audiences loved.

In May of '94, I was scheduled to play at the Kentucky Eckankar Regional Seminar in Elizabethtown. Eckankar had been my chosen religion for over thirty years. On the way to the seminar, I planned to visit my friend, Karl, who lived in the suburbs of Lexington.

I arrived at Karl's house the evening before, which gave us time to visit and play some music. I planned to leave for Elizabethtown the next morning.

I was asleep on his couch, when I was awakened with, "My God! Your van has been burglarized!"

It was Karl, looking out the window. I got dressed and we rushed outside to the parked van. The passenger window was broken and the shattered glass was on the pavement and the passenger seat. There hadn't been enough space in his apartment to store all of my gear. Karl assured me that there had never been a burglary in his neighborhood. Convinced it would be safe, we covered the equipment and locked the van.

"I just can't believe this happened," said Karl.

"Please don't worry, I have insurance," I said while opening the side doors. "They took almost everything."

Missing was a PA mixing board, keyboard, keyboard amp, cassette tape player, speakers, speaker stands, microphones and mike stands. My briefcase lay open on the floor behind the passenger seat, its papers scattered. "The burglars were obviously looking for money," I said.

Beside the briefcase was the violin case, empty. Among bits of shattered window glass, the old fiddle lay face down on the floor. I thought this was the end of the old instrument, for the top would surely be in splinters.

All violin tops are made of spruce, which was a soft pinewood. After one hundred or more years, it was very dry and so fragile that it could be turned into splinters with a hard blow. I reached down and picked up the violin, slowly turning it over. I couldn't believe my eyes! I expected to see a totally destroyed top but there wasn't a scratch on the fiddle. The burglars had left it, thinking the old fiddle was worthless. It was truly surprising that there was no evidence of damage.

"I just have to keep this fiddle," I said. "It hadn't been played since I was born. Maybe there is a message here."

Once, after I told this story, a lady in the audience suggested it was that perhaps the old violin made its self "invisible" in order to survive the robbery. I did not reply, but thought, *"I just have to keep this fiddle."*

In February of '95, I took the violin to Australia where my musician friend of many years, Sally Sublette, and I visited Rod and Judy Jones. We played the Music Festival at Yarra Junction, which is just northeast of Melbourne.

While I played the fiddle with friends in Sydney, I thought of Mr. Brill playing that same instrument in the WW I Armed Forces Orchestra in Europe. I had talked with Mr. Brill, who was then one hundred years old, just before my flight to Sydney. "I just have to keep this fiddle," I thought.

My daughter, Diane, and Harold, were married in June of 1995 in Gallatin, Tennessee. The reception was in her backyard and she invited several musicians to play. Lester Baldwin, one of my dear friends and a good five string banjo player, brought Frazier Moss. I had first heard Frazier play on the Grand Ole Opry. At this time, Frazier was eighty-six years old and one of Tennessee's most famous old-time fiddlers. Through the years, he had won numerous fiddle contests. He had even won Weiser, Idaho.

We played for a couple of hours in the shade of the maple trees on that beautiful June day. I let Frazier play the old violin and he liked it.

"It's not for sale," I said, before he could ask.

"I just have to keep that fiddle," I added.

After the reception, I spent the night at my daughter's home in Gallatin. The next morning, I got up early and drove to Clarksburg, West Virginia for a regional Eckankar meeting.

Two days later, on my return trip from Clarksburg, in the early hours of the morning, I lost control of my Dodge mini van in a construction area of I-79 near the Clendenin exit. The van hit some loose gravel and rolled several times down the median between the northbound and southbound lanes. When the van stopped rolling, it landed on its wheels in the grass of the medium.

First, I checked to see if all my limbs worked. Having no broken bones or pain, I got out of the van and noticed that the violin case was lying in the southbound lane. I picked up the violin case and placed it on the top of the wrecked van just as a traveler stopped,

"Are you OK," asked the man as he got out of his car. "I reported the accident on my cell phone."

"I'm fine," I said, "And thanks for stopping."

"After looking at your car, I don't see how you walked away from that wreck. It appears to be totaled," he added.

The Dodge mini van was certainly smashed. The side doors and the back doors were open. "Just lucky, I guess," I answered.

After answering questions for the State Police, I saw my son Scott drive up. "Are you OK?" he asked, as he got out of his Bronco, "Look at the van, Dad, you could have been killed!" he said, extremely agitated.

He had been so frightened when he got the call, he left before getting dressed. He stood there beside the Interstate in his pajamas.

I sat in his truck and asked, "Why don't you get my stuff out of the van. I know that it's totaled. Don't forget the violin that I placed on the top. When I finally stopped, it was lying in the road."

On the way home, suddenly I was in so much pain that Scott took me to the Charleston Hospital where I spent the night. Later in the day he came to the hospital to check on my condition. "You know, Dad, when I got home I opened the fiddle case. I knew it had been thrown out on the road by the force of the wreck. But I can't find a scratch on it. As a matter of fact, it is still in tune."

"I just have to keep that fiddle," I said.

During a performance in Pittsburgh I told this story. Afterwards, an older woman walked up to me and said, "I guess you know, you owned that violin in a previous life."

In the fall of '96, I returned to Australia with some of my dearest friends. Sallie Sublette, and her husband, Rick McCracken, Greg Shupe and I called our group The West Virginia String Band. We played the Bluegrass Festival in Harrietville, Victoria.

After leaving Australia, we went on to play at the Wellington Folk Festival in New Zealand. There were many jam sessions everywhere we played, and many times other fiddlers would ask to play my fiddle. If they expressed any interest, my reply was always, "It's not for sale. I just have to keep that fiddle."

In '98, Fiddler Bobby Taylor, and I did a Fiddle Workshop at the String Band Festival at Cliff Top, West Virginia. Participating in the workshops was an array of wonderful fiddlers: J. P. Fraley and Art Stamper from Kentucky, Charlie Walden from Chicago, Franklin George from West Virginia, Jody Stecker from California, Bruce Green from North Carolina, Speedy Toliver from Washington, D. C. and several others I can't remember.

As Bobby and I finished the workshop, which was held on the stage in the lodge, I picked up my fiddle case and swung the strap across my shoulder. The unlatched case opened and the fiddle bounced across the hardwood floor like a bowling pin.

Bobby, who loves violins, said, "Oh, my God. I hope that it's alright!"

My heart was broken. For the first time in my life I had broken a fiddle. Sadly, I picked up the pieces of the scroll that had broken off the neck. I was careful to collect all of the pieces of broken wood.

"Bobby, it can be repaired. The repair done on the peg box sometime back in the 1800s gave way," I said. "In all my years of playing and repairing violins, this is my first time to damage a fiddle."

The next week, I took the violin to Harold Hayslett, a very famous West Virginia violin and cello-maker. He repaired it so it looked better than it did before it was dropped.

Now, I was sure that I would never part with the violin. "Thank you, Harold. That's a superb bit of craftsmanship," I said. "I just have to keep that fiddle."

I took a motorcycle trip to the West Coast with the fiddle tied on the seat of my Gold Wing. While visiting Sallie and Rick in Idaho, we went to the Fiddle Contest at Weiser. After leaving Idaho, I rode to the town of Duncan, which is on Vancouver Island, and visited with some of my dearest friends, Peter and Barbara Sussman. That violin was my companion the entire trip.

Eventually, I became curious about the origin of the old instrument and took it to an appraiser. They check all of the dimensions, varnish, and quality of craftsmanship, in order to determine the maker, even if the label inside is missing.

Bruce, the violin expert, came to the conclusion that Johann Georg Leeb the 2nd (1779-1817), made my violin in Pressburg, Hungary. He had also lived in Posoni, Hungary, and had made a large number of violins. His father was a violinmaker and lived to be over seventy years old, but the son made a better instrument. Because of the grafted neck, I had always thought it was made around 1800.

"Why do you suppose that the son, Johann, died at the early age of thirty-eight?" I asked.

"We really don't know, but at that time, there were no antibiotics so he could have developed an infection from something as simple as a cut finger and died," answered Bruce.

"I just have to keep that fiddle," I said.

When I go back to Europe, I plan to make a trip to Pressburg and Posoni. These were towns in Hungary where Johann Georg Leeb II, the violinmaker lived. I'd like to learn more about the craftsman who made the fiddle.

# SOLO

It was July and the sky was clear and beautiful, so I rode my Honda Goldwing Touring Motorcycle to an Eckankar Retreat in Boiling Springs, Pennsylvania. This was an historic, beautiful place south of Harrisburg. Eckankar was my chosen religion and I was attending an annual event, a gathering of about fifty people whose spiritual growth was their first priority.

"Joe, you play so well that I think you should send a tape to the Activities Director," suggested Henry, my roommate.

This came as a surprise to me. In my fifty years of playing the fiddle, I had never considered performing solo.

Henry Gross was a very dear friend and since he was the Regional Eckankar Spiritual Aide for Pennsylvania and West Virginia, I valued his opinion. He was of average height, dark curly hair, and looked like an athlete. Eating the right foods, taking the proper vitamins and working out regularly was important to him. For many years, he had worked with Special Education students in the public school system in Philadelphia.

"Well, thank you, Henry, but I don't think I play that well," I said. "I've always played with some kind of accompaniment, such as the guitar or piano."

"I'm not a musician, but I think you play well. Here is the name and address where you can send the tape," he said, handing me a piece of paper. "They're always searching for someone to play at major seminars."

"Thanks, Henry, I'm flattered that you feel so positive about my playing," I replied, as I put the piece of paper in my pocket. "It's frightening to think about playing without any accompaniment, but I'll give it some thought."

During the past twenty years, I had played music festivals in the U.S. and Canada. It would be a great experience to play in front of an audience of over 3,000 people who came from all over the world. When I attended Eckankar events, I was always on the lookout for some musician I might know. Perhaps, I could find someone with whom to form a duet.

Back home in West Virginia, I went to the Public Radio Station to record a weekly program, "Music from the Mountains," that I had been producing for over fifteen years. While in the studio, I remembered Henry giving me the address for the audition tape.

I placed a new cassette in the recording machine, opened the microphone and said, "My friend, Henry Gross, asked me to send you this tape. I play the fiddle."

I played several tunes into the recording machine. As I mailed the cassette to the designated address, I thought that chances were slim that I would get a reply. Well, at least I could tell Henry that I had sent an audition tape to the Spiritual Center.

One morning about three months later, the phone rang. I answered and the voice said, "Joe, I'm Beverly Foster. I'm calling to see if you're planning to attend the International Eckankar Summer Festival in Philadelphia this summer. I'm coordinating the entertainment and we would like for you to play violin in the orchestra."

For a couple of seconds, I was speechless. I couldn't believe what I was hearing. I guess they did listen to that tape. If I had known this was going to happen, I would've taken more time and made the effort to play better on that recording.

"Beverly, thank you for calling and inviting me to play. I must tell you, I'm very surprised," I answered. "About playing in the orchestra, there's one big problem. I don't read music so I can't read the written arrangements. I'm just an ear musician," I explained.

"What if we sent you a recording of the part we want you to play? Could you participate then?" she insisted.

"That is so kind of you, but I don't think it would be fair to the other members of the orchestra," I said.

"Are you sure?" she asked. There was a sincere gentleness in her voice.

"Thanks for asking me to participate, but I don't feel comfortable trying to play in the orchestra," I said. This was one of the many times that I wished I'd disciplined myself and learned to read music.

It was only a few days until Beverly called again. "Joe, we would like for you to do the 'warm up' on Friday night on the main program," she said. "You'll play about ten minutes."

Being asked to play on the main program was very exciting.

"Will I be playing with someone?" I asked.

"Oh, you can just play solo. That will work just fine," explained Beverly.

The opportunity of performing for such a large international audience with similar spiritual goals was most inspiring. But fearful thoughts came into my mind about playing alone.

"Thanks, I'll see you in Philadelphia," I said. After hanging up the phone I thought, *Surely I can find a guitarist who will accompany me on several simple melodies.*

With the advance notice, I had about two months to prepare. I tried to remember solo acts I'd seen who were entertaining. My dear friend, Bobby Taylor, who was an exceptional traditional Appalachian fiddler, loaned me a video of a performance by Isaac Perlman. Bobby and I had been friends for over thirty years.

In the video, Perlman was performing solo at some music hall in London. The only thing on the stage was a chair. I felt sure that he would much rather have performed with an orchestra or at least

a piano. He walked out, sat down in the chair, and announced the pieces he was going to perform. Then he played for about an hour.

The camera would show shots of the audience and they were taken by the solo performance. The audience was in awe of his playing and so was I. The video helped me to realize that a performer should think from his audience's point of view, rather than from that of his accompanist. This gave me more confidence to do solo playing. It was a change of attitude that encouraged me to strive to be a better player.

The 1998 Eckankar International Summer Festival was held in the Convention Center in downtown Philadelphia. I arrived on Thursday to make sure that I had time to practice and be prepared for the main program on Friday evening. After selecting just what pieces I would play and spending ample time rehearsing, I was anxious to meet the person who would be my accompanist.

Hurriedly, I went to the designated meeting of musicians and other creative artists. I kept looking at nametags until I found Beverly Foster. We had never met except on the phone, so I introduced myself.

"Thanks for coming, Joe, and agreeing to do our Friday evening warm up," she said, flashing her big smile. Beverly was a petite woman, casually dressed. One could tell by the sparkle in her eye and her enthusiasm that she loved her job. Before I could ask if I could find a guitarist, she said, "You'll be playing alone. There's no need for you to come to the sound check."

I went back to my hotel room to practice and think. To make my part of the program easier, I could take time to introduce the pieces and give a bit of history on each selection. This would hold the attention of the audience and my explanation could be as interesting as my playing.

Thirty minutes before my performance I went backstage as instructed. The first backstage person I met was a lovely lady wearing a bright blue suit. She had blonde hair and a pretty smile. "Hi, I'm Amy Sailer," she said. "I'm from Nashville and I play the violin, too."

"You should be on the program," I said nervously. I was surprised that I was experiencing such stage fright. I'd been playing the fiddle most of my life, so why all the fear? Performing on my fiddle, I'd literally been all over the world and had never experienced such uncontrollable shaking.

*Maybe it's because this is my church and I am playing for God,* I thought. *God, if You are listening, You might take away some of this nervous shaking, at least in my hands, so I don't embarrass myself and the audience.*

"We need to get you in 'make up'," said a voice behind me. I turned around and it was Beverly.

I wondered if my nervousness was obvious, because she added, "You're just what we need to start the weekend."

While powder was being applied to my face and bald head, she continued, "When the time comes for you to begin, walk up those steps and look for the big X on the floor. Just stand on that spot and the soundman will lower a microphone and you can begin to play. Don't say a word."

When she told me not to speak, my heart went to my throat. There went half of my planned and rehearsed performance.

"Can you play for fifteen minutes," she asked, without pausing. I suppose she saw the concerned look on my face, and before I could answer, she asked, "How about ten minutes?"

"Sure, I can do ten minutes?" I said, trying to speak with some authority.

Looking to the other side of the stage area, I saw an old friend, Ken Klug, who lived in Cleveland, Ohio and had been the Stage Manager at the International Seminars for many years. He smiled and waved to me and I temporarily forgot about my stage fright.

"You have about five minutes before you go on," said Amy. "Stand at the foot of the steps and a sound man will tell you when you are to go on stage," she instructed in her kind Tennessee drawl.

While waiting to go on stage I remembered a conversation that I'd had with a musician some ten years earlier.

I had a booth at the Nashville Guitar Show. A husky, casually-dressed man asked, "Is it OK if I play one of your acoustic guitars?" He looked to be in his forties. "How about this one?" he pointed to an older D-28 Martin.

"Sure, please feel free to play on any instrument you like," I said.

He took the guitar off of the display rack, sat down on a stool by the display table and began to play. I looked at the crowd of people on the floor of the show, hoping to find Mike Tepe, a dealer from St Louis. I had a guitar that might interest him. Suddenly, I realized, *This guy is an excellent player.*

"Are you someone famous?" I asked, jokingly.

"Nope, just a picker," he said, without interrupting his playing.

"You sure play well. You must be one of those slick Nashville session players," I said.

He switched to another guitar. "No, I just love playing the guitar. I appreciate you letting me play on these expensive instruments. If I find one I like, I'll buy it," he said, continuing to play as he talked.

I sat down and became his audience. I was captivated with his playing technique. After about fifteen minutes, he paused.

"You're so accomplished on the guitar. You've done a lot of playing," I said.

"For about three years, I opened the show for The Grateful Dead," he said. "That was several years ago and I'd like to get back into playing with some friends."

"Let me see if I understand this," I said. "You walked out on stage with just your acoustic guitar to face several thousand "deadheads" waiting for Jerry Garcia."

"You got it," he said. "Each time it was the same big challenge. I reached a point where I would have that audience in the palm of my hand after one verse."

"In the beginning, did they throw anything?" I joked.

"Not that I remember. I got a big rush facing that challenge each time I opened a show," he explained. "I finally gave up the job. The Grateful Dead loved me and Jerry Garcia was especially nice to me."

"Why did you quit? Just tired of the road?" I asked. Someone in the next booth started playing a loud Rock and Roll guitar and I had to stand close to hear his answer.

"No, not at all. I decided to go back to school, get an Engineering degree and get a real job," he explained. He put the guitar back on the display rack. "I'm going to look around the show. If I don't find something better, I'll buy that last guitar I played."

We shook hands and he walked out of my booth. I never got his name or saw him again.

I was brought back to the present by the stage manager motioning for me to go out on stage. I dried my sweaty palms, walked to the X, and the microphone was lowered to a point just above my violin. My legs were shaking with fear and I wondered if the audience could see them.

Beginning to play, I closed my eyes. I concentrated hard, thinking maybe folks would be inspired to get up and dance in the aisles.

Two large screens on each side of the stage showed me playing so folks in the cheap seats could see my performance. Having always had the accompaniment of another instrument, to me, the solo performance sounded naked. At the end of my ten minutes of fame, I opened my eyes to see no one dancing in the aisles. But they must have enjoyed my tunes for there was thunderous applause.

As I walked down the steps of the stage, there was Larry Siegel, a wonderful musician from New York who was the MC for the evening.

He greeted me with, "Thanks, Joe, that was great. It was just what we wanted to get the program started."

Relieved that my performance was over, I thanked him. I put my violin in its case and made my way up to the cheap seats to relax.

During the weekend, there were many people I'd never met before greeting me with complimentary remarks about my fiddle playing.

On the elevator, an older woman, who spoke English with a very strong accent, said, "I loved your violin playing Friday evening."

Looking at her name tag, I saw that she was from Hamburg, Germany.

"Thank you. You're very kind," I replied.

Maybe the people in the audience heard a different sound than I did. As the elevator door opened on my floor, I thought, *Do you suppose that God could have made it more pleasant and melodic before the sound reached the listener's ear?*

This experience took me in a new direction with my playing. I accepted opportunities to play at weddings, memorial services, and civic organization meetings. I began to volunteer to play regularly at a hospital and a nursing home, just me and my violin. I'm thankful to Henry Gross for his encouragement and steering me in that new direction.

It got to the point that I preferred doing many performances alone. This way, I didn't have to explain the arrangement to my accompanist or find out if he knew the song or the proper tempo. My only concern was just to play. I could have been doing that for the past fifty years, but perhaps beforehand, it wasn't time.

# SAINT FRANCIS

It was Christmas morning of 1999, and I was living in my 'leaning house' on a hillside in rural Putnam County. The hillside had slipped and my house was leaning toward Lake Washington. My dear friend, Buddy Griffin, referred to it as 'The Leaning House of Dobbs.'

Phantom, my cat, was sitting patiently, looking up at the doorknob which was her way of saying, *Please open the door and let me out.* She was a great cat, and had a dark, multi-colored coat. Someone had given her to me when she was very young.

It seemed like she was wearing gloves because she had six toes on every foot. I read somewhere that six toes were a result of inbreeding. In Key West, there are a large number of six-toed cats. Some refer to these animals as 'Key cats.'

There was about three inches of snow on the ground, so when I opened the door, she looked out and paused. Turning around, she went back to her spot on the couch.

Back in November, sometime before Thanksgiving, Robin Kessinger, a champion guitar player, and I had just finished playing the monthly Footmad Square Dance. After the dance ended, several of us stopped by Shoney's and got a big table to enjoy dessert, coffee, and friends before going home.

I happened to sit beside Kathy Willoughby, the organizer for the monthly dances. She was a Chaplain at St. Francis Hospital in Charleston, West Virginia.

Back in the '70s, I had played in a hospital for the patients, so I turned to Kathy and said, "Do you think it would be possible for me to play for the patients at St. Francis on Christmas Day?" I recalled how gratifying it had been to perform for them with a trio of singers. An old friend, Bill Hoke, had played guitar.

Christmastime is probably the worst time one can be hospitalized. Everyone well enough is discharged so they can spend Christmas with their families. There's only a minimum staff on duty.

"Oh, that would be wonderful, Joe. I'd be more than pleased to contact the Nursing Supervisor and make all the arrangements," Kathy replied. Kathy was a warm, delightful person with chestnut brown hair, and a wonderful smile that activated her deep dimples. She was also learning to be a caller at the folk dances.

"It will just be me playing. I've been unable to find anyone who wants to be away from their family on Christmas morning," I explained.

"That's just great," Kathy had said, "you don't know what something like that means to a person having to spend Christmas in the hospital."

It was time to leave for the hospital. I dressed warmly, for the ground was frozen and the wind was brisk. Looking out across the white hillside, I began to have doubts about playing solo. This would be a new experience. If I had not promised, I would not have done it.

Kathy had emailed me the contact person's name at the hospital. Everything was all set for my visit. I placed the fiddle case on the back seat and drove down the icy hill. Wearing my natural, full, white beard and a Santa's hat, I was thinking, *This is going to be an unpleasant experience.*

I'm sure if I were ill enough to be in the hospital, I wouldn't want anyone coming in my room and sawing on a fiddle. Wasn't this just a bad decision on my part?

The road crews had removed the snow off Route 60. Since it was Christmas morning, there was no traffic. I drove east toward St. Albans.

Just before I approached Coal Mountain, I saw a man walking in the snow along the shoulder of the road.

"Merry Christmas," I greeted, as he opened the van door. "Get in. What are you doing walking in the snow on Christmas morning?"

He quickly sat down in the passenger seat and closed the door. Pushing the hood of her coat off her head, she said, "I'm freezing! Thank you so much for giving me a ride."

Walking stooped in the cold morning air, this woman had looked like a man. Her shoulder-length dark red hair was uncombed and she appeared to be in her thirties. Her face was a map of hard times.

"I'm going to my sister's house in St. Albans," she explained. Her breath brought the strong odor of stale beer.

"Where in St. Albans?" I asked, turning the heater to high.

"Her house is on West Main. I'll show you. You can't imagine just how much I appreciate you giving me a ride." She began to sob and said, "I just got out of prison. I went to my brother's house out in the country and we got into this terrible fight. I left, walking."

She raised her head to look at me and I could see tears flowing down her cheeks. Holding out her hand, she asked, "May I hold your hand? I just need to hold someone's hand."

I reached toward her with my gloved right hand while driving with my left. She took my hand and held on tightly. "It's Christmas morning. Do you have any children?"

"My sister and my mom have been keeping my kids while I've been in prison. That's why I'm going to her house. This is the first Christmas we've all been together in two years."

She let go of my hand and pointed to a brown house. "That's my sister's house. The one on the left with the swing on the porch."

I let her out and wished her a Merry Christmas. Switching the heater control to "low," I continued toward Charleston. *With my full white beard and wearing this Santa hat, she probably thought I was Santa. When she sobers up, she'll have a story to tell her children. "'I know you won't believe it, but Santa Claus gave me a ride on a cold Christmas Morning.'"*

Walking up to the entrance of the hospital, I was even more skeptical. *If Joan is the least bit reluctant, I'll just thank her and say maybe I should come back another time. Then I'll go back home,* I thought.

Joan was the Nursing Supervisor on duty and the blue-haired lady volunteering at the Information Desk paged her. After a brief wait, a woman with short red hair and a beautiful smile, who looked to be in her mid thirties, walked up. There was a gleam in her light blue eyes that was fitting for a Christmas morning.

She shook my hand and said, "You must be Joe. We've been expecting you."

Her attractive red hair must have been natural, because it matched her freckles. She had on a blue hospital scrub uniform. As we walked down the hall to the elevator, I said, "It must be difficult for you to have to work on Christmas day. I'm sure you would prefer to be home with your family."

"Not really. Actually, I volunteer to work so other staff members can be home with their families for Christmas. My husband works in broadcasting and we don't have any children. He's working at the TV station today so someone can be with his or her family," she explained. "We feel like it is our gift to our co-workers. We do this every year."

The elevator door opened at the fifth floor. "We'll start here," said Joan. As we walked past the Nurse's station, she announced, "This is Joe and he'll be playing the violin for some of our patients today."

Joan took me down the hall to a recreation area. There was a TV in one corner and a small kitchen at the other end with two round tables. Through the large windows you could look out over the city.

"This is where you'll be playing for a group of patients. We'll bring in the patients and when you are finished here, we will take you to different rooms on other floors," she told me as she left to wheel in patients.

After removing my coat and hat, I took my fiddle out of the case. I still wasn't sure this was going to work. I placed the mute on the violin so the music would not be loud enough to interrupt patients in other rooms down the hall. When it is cold, it takes a couple of tunes to get my fingers working properly. I began practicing while my audience was being brought into the room. As I finished the melody, ‘Stardust,’ I noticed a male patient in a wheelchair. He wore a faint smile and looked to be in his golden years.

"Hoagie Carmichael," he said, softly.

"You must like Hoagie Carmichael songs," I said.

He nodded. So while waiting for the other patients, I played several Hoagie Carmichael compositions: ‘Georgia On My Mind,’ ‘Up A Lazy River,’ and ‘Back Home Again In Indiana.’

I probably played for about a half an hour in that room. Then I was taken to rooms where I played melodies the patient requested. Being so focused on the new experience of playing solo, I failed to observe my audience. My concentration was on playing as best I could and finishing the job.

When we were finished, Joan walked with me to the elevator saying, "Joe, I’m sure you don’t realize how much these patients enjoyed your playing. They were listening to the music instead of wishing to be home for Christmas."

"I didn't think it went so well," I said. "This is the first time I’ve ever tried to do something like this alone."

Looking me in the eye, she asked, "Joe, do you remember the man who enjoyed the Hoagie Carmichael melodies? That's Mr. Hawkins. He was brought here over a week ago after having a stroke. We knew he had played the piano, but he had not spoken a word until he heard you play ‘Stardust.’"

While driving home, I was grateful that my playing had lifted someone's spirit. After playing the fiddle with all kinds of bands doing so many different types of music for over fifty years, I had unknowingly accumulated a vast repertoire of tunes. This experience made me realize that I knew several hundred melodies. Only one patient had asked for a song that I couldn’t remember how to play, ‘The Sidewalks of New York.’

With this experience came the realization that I could have been playing solo violin for the sick over the past twenty years.

# BIRTH OF A SHOW

In the early fall of 1974, Patty Frazier of the Wayne County Arts Council, in Kenova, West Virginia, contacted me about conducting music workshops that were being offered to the public. The Arts Council had classes in pottery, sculpture, and woodcarving that were supported and well-attended by the community.

There were no specific guidelines, but I was expected to create and begin these music classes. The Arts Council advertised this as an opportunity to learn to play music. No particular instrument was mentioned except they were to be of the string type, such as fiddle, guitar, banjo and mandolin. Any person interested in participating was expected to bring his or her own instrument.

Classes were held at the Arts Council, which was in an old, empty storefront on Main Street in Kenova. On the evening of the first class, I parked across the street of the building. Through the large, glass windows I saw several groups of people standing about laughing and talking.

"Hello," greeted Bill Adkins as I walked through the door. "It's about time you got here."

"Hello, Bill. Are all these people wanting to be in the music class," I asked. "Am I late? Why, there must be over thirty people in here."

"No, you aren't late. Everyone is just anxious to get started," said Mike Hawkins, who was carrying a guitar case.

Mike and Bill were the only people in the room that I knew. They wanted to learn how to accompany their singing by playing the guitar. Mike was tall, probably in his late thirties and drove a truck. Bill was short and stocky and what little hair he had left was blond. He worked as a plumber.

"I never imagined that this many folks would want to learn to play music," I said. Looking around the room, I saw several women and three teenagers. There were fiddles, banjos, guitars, mandolins and one autoharp.

"My name is Helen," said a voice behind me.

I turned and there was a neatly dressed older woman, smiling and holding out her hand. Before I could shake her hand, she said, "My grandmother gave me this Zither and I have always wanted to learn to play it. My grandfather brought it over from Germany." She held a very old, rather ornate Zither I was sure had not been tuned in at least thirty years. The strings were old and it certainly wasn't in playing condition.

*What had I gotten myself into?* I thought. *How can I possibly teach all these beginners on different instruments in one class?* My mind kept telling me that this was a big mistake.

In preparing for the workshop I thought there would probably be less than ten people with guitars and maybe one fiddle. I certainly did not have a method of conducting a workshop with this many players.

"I'm so pleased to finally find someone who can teach me to play the Zither. I'm so excited," said Helen.

"Helen, I dislike having to disappoint you, but I cannot teach you how to play the Zither. I've never seen anyone play the instrument and you are the only 'Zither Picker' I've ever met," I said, with a big smile on my face.

Turning to the class, I said, "OK everybody, let's see if we can get all these instruments tuned together."

"Well, next week, I'll bring my guitar," said Helen, somewhat disappointed.

The class met on Tuesday evenings for six weeks. There were several students in the class who played exceptionally well and were kind enough to help me conduct the workshop. Everyone had a good time and several of the students met others who played, so they formed groups that continued to get together to play and sing long after the classes were finished. But I don't think it was that successful.

One of the things that I learned from that first class was the interest in folk music in the mountains of West Virginia. Two years later, when my brother, Dennis, and I opened the Fret'N Fiddle Music Store in Huntington, I met a significant number of musicians who played on a professional level. However, they had no ambition to perform outside their homes or churches. This high percentage of people who play music of some kind exists throughout the Appalachian Region from Southern Pennsylvania to Northern Georgia.

When I left Albuquerque, New Mexico, where I had been Station Manager at a local Radio Station, I vowed to *never* work in radio again. I was tired of producing screaming commercials. Now, nine years later I was trying to get a program on Public Radio (no screaming commercials) that would be about local musicians and singers who were as talented as many professional recording artists. I thought to myself, *Never say never.*

"I don't think it will work," explained Larry. Larry Hall worked for West Virginia Public Television. He was an enthusiastic producer who grew up in West Virginia and loved Appalachian Folk Music. We had worked together on a series of programs he produced for Public Television called 'Sugar in the Gourd.'

"I think it's a good idea to have people record something while they are in your store. But there's a question about the broadcast quality of the recordings. All the machines used at the Public Radio Station are two channel full-track tape machines," he explained.

"Larry, I just don't think that these amateur musicians and singers would feel comfortable going into a studio and doing a recording. They'll play better if I can record them in a setting that's familiar and they find comfortable," I said.

"I'm sure that's true, but it's going to be difficult to get a program director to regularly air field-recordings," warned Larry.

Larry had a lot of experience and he was probably right. But I purchased some broadcast quality recording equipment and taped several of my customers who came into the store. With these recordings, I produced a number of good quality programs that I presented to West Virginia Public Radio. For one reason or another, all of the sample programs were rejected. (Several of these programs were later aired on 'Music from the Mountains.')

Realizing this to be an unsuccessful way to launch a program, I sold all the recording equipment and temporarily forgot about the possibility of doing radio again. Two years later, the phone rang.

The voice on the phone said, "Hello, this is Paul Epstein." Paul was hosting a two-hour program on West Virginia Public Radio each Saturday night entitled 'Saturday Night Breakdown,' where he played folk music recordings.

"Hi, Paul," I said, "how are you doing?" I had known Paul for several years. We met in the early 70s at a Fraley Family Festival in Greenup, Kentucky. He was a good fiddler and a member of the ole time string band, Booger Hole Revival.

"Joe, I've decided to go back to college. I'll have to give up my radio show and I wondered if you would be interested in hosting 'Saturday Night Breakdown'."

I was working long hours in my business, so I said, "Paul, thanks for asking, but how much time would I have to spend doing the show?"

"It only takes two hours each week and you can record the programs in advance, if you need time off. This way you can play the festivals on the weekends," he explained.

"Thanks, Paul. I'll do it. But I'll need someone to teach me how to operate the board in the studio," I said.

"I'll teach you how to run the board and record your shows," said Paul. He was very kind and taught me how to operate the equipment in the broadcast studio and introduced me to the Station Manager, Rich Eiswerth.

Standing up from behind his desk and extending his hand, Rich said, "Welcome aboard and thanks for agreeing to do 'Saturday Night Breakdown.'"

Shaking his hand, I asked, "Rich, would it be possible for me to have live performances on the show?"

"Sure, that would be great. Do you need an engineer?" he asked. I didn't tell him that I had previous radio experience. I also thought that since I was beginning, I shouldn't ask for an engineer.

"I don't think that I will need one. These will be simple acoustic acts whose performances will be easy to broadcast," I replied.

"If you need anything or have any questions just let me know," Rich kindly offered. Rich had an abundance of energy. He was of average height with brown hair and there was a sparkle in his eye. Rich had a great sense of humor and I found him to be a delightful person with whom to work.

One Sunday, I was in the studio recording a show with a Bluegrass band from Kentucky, when Rich came in the building with his young son. He rearranged some furniture and portable equipment. As we finished the last song, Rich, dressed as casual as a gardener, walked into the room watering the various potted plants.

"Rich, I would like for you to meet these performers who drove up from Kentucky to do the show," I said. "We've just finished recording a very good bluegrass performance."

He warmly greeted the band members and thanked them for coming and recording the show and shook hands with each performer.

To add a bit of humor, I said, "Rich, when you come in the studio on Sunday, you shouldn't dress so casual. I would like the Station Manager to make a good impression on my guests."

He stood with the pail of water in his hand and joked, "Please don't tell them the plants are all plastic." Then, he quickly turned and left the room. That was an example of his quick wit and wonderful sense of humor.

When I could coax someone to play or sing, the program had live music. I made it a point to tell everyone I met at festivals about the live music on West Virginia Public Radio. We made a special effort to tell the customers who came in the Fret'N Fiddle.

"Ger, I think that I'll be able to get some of our customers to perform on this radio show I am doing, 'Saturday Night Breakdown,'" I said looking down the repair bench where he was gluing a bridge on a D-28 Martin.

Gerry Collyard had moved from Minnesota to West Virginia to become the luthier at the Fret'N Fiddle Music Store. Having studied at a special school in Red Wing, Minnesota, he was more than qualified to repair musical instruments. Ger managed the repair department for more than twenty years.

Even though he grew up in St. Paul, he never cared for skiing or ice fishing and loved the warm sun of the South. One winter morning, we were looking out of the front windows of the store and it had been spitting snow, which left a thin, white coating on the pavement. Everyone who came in the store was making comments about the first snow of the year. Being used to Minnesota winters, I heard Ger on the phone with his mom in St. Paul saying, "Mom, people think it is snowing here."

"There are some very talented performers that come in the store," said Ger. "The next thing is convincing them that they are good enough to play on the radio."

"I've been thinking about changing the name of the program," I said. "I'd like a title that would give me the freedom to air any type of acoustic music I wanted, such as a folk group or a string quartet. What do you think about the name, 'Music from the Mountains?' I asked.

There was a long pause. While putting the last clamp on the guitar bridge, Ger said, "That has a nice ring to it. I think it's a good idea."

After I had been doing the show for about three months, I came into the studio one evening to find a note from Rich Eiswerth asking me to come to his office. Public Radio had just finished a major fund drive. My first thought was that there were complaints from our listeners about the live music during the fundraising, and management had decided to cancel the show.

Live music was not as perfect as music recorded in the professional studios of Nashville, Los Angles or New York. All of the human errors had not been edited out like on a commercial record. This had been one of my concerns. *Well, if the show was to be cancelled, I didn't care, because I wasn't interested in hosting a disc jockey show.*

The door was open, so I walked into the Station Manager's Office.

"Please sit down," invited Rich. "Thanks for coming. I'm very busy today, but I wanted to know if there is anything you need for your show? Is there any way we can assist you with your broadcast?"

This was the opposite of what I thought he would say and I was pleasantly surprised. "I can't think of a thing that I need," I answered, somewhat relieved.

"Oh yes, there is one thing. I'd like the program to be called 'Music from the Mountains,' which I like better than 'Saturday Night Breakdown,'" I added. "Then I could have any type of live music on the show. 'Saturday Night Breakdown' sounds like a hillbilly music program to me."

"I agree, 'Music from the Mountains' it is," said Rich. As I walked out of his office, I was sure that the response by the listeners during the fund-raising had left a positive impression on the station manager.

"Music from the Mountains" went through many changes during the next fifteen years. When a program director reduced the program to one hour, I was relieved. Several times, the show was rescheduled at new time. For years it was heard on Saturday night, then moved to Friday evenings.

We used many methods of promoting the show because there was no mention of it during other broadcasts on the West Virginia network of stations. There were several occasions when persons in management wished to discontinue 'Music from the Mountains.' but somehow, it survived.

It would have been an asset to have saved copies of those programs. I wish that I had kept a list of the hundreds of guests who performed on the show, some of whom have gone on. It was a great experience just getting to meet and visit with the many performers.

There were numerous performers from far outside the U.S. Some of the ones that I remember was the bluegrass band from Finland, who played American Bluegrass Music so well. All of the members except one were named Pederson, but they were not related, and only one spoke English.

There was the ole time group ‘Fried Chicken.’ from Lincoln County, who were playing live when Bill Ragette's violin came apart. All during the show he was out in the hall trying to get the fiddle into playing condition. Paul Gartner played guitar and Warren Owings was on the banjo.

On the air between songs we can be heard asking Bill if he had the fiddle fixed, yet. Finally, during the last tune, Bill got the instrument back together, but it was so badly out of tune that the performance was hilarious. Paul and Warren played the remainder of the show as a duet. (I still have a copy of that show.)

Once, we tried to sell someone's milk goat, and another time, secure a ride for a musician to California. We failed with both attempts.

‘Music from the Mountains’ was well into its nineteenth year when James Mohammed joined West Virginia Public Radio as the new program director. I was recording a music performance in Studio B when he entered.

"I just wanted to meet you. I’m James Mohammed, the new program director," he said, extending his hand. He was so tall, I had to look up. He was an elegant man who looked more like a pro basketball player than a program director. "I really enjoy your show," he added. He was from Tuscaloosa, Alabama, but there was no southern drawl in his speech. The years in broadcasting had taken that away.

"Thank you, James. It’s good to meet you," I said. "There’s no need to try to make points with me, because I have no clout around here."

"No, no. I’m a fan of ‘Music from the Mountains.’ I listen to your show," he said, with a big smile and chuckling. "I really like your program."

Several months later, James asked me to come to his office and talk about the show. When you were called into the Program Director’s Office, you always prepared for the worst. I thought if they wanted to make a lot of changes in the format or move me to another time slot, I would just suggest they get someone new to host the show. Twenty years is enough and I was tired.

"Joe, we want to give you a producer and promote your show," said James. "I think that 'Music from the Mountains' warrants promoting."

"James, I've always thought that folks living in the Appalachian States would enjoy the show. I'm not so sure that it would be accepted in Denver or Seattle," I said.

"I think it would," said James.

I was wondering just how much more work these changes would mean for me when James said the magic words, "It will mean a lot less work for you. Now you can concentrate on what you do best, your interviews, and never be concerned with the technical aspects of the production. George will do all of that for you," he added.

I was sixty-eight years old and I could not think of anyone that I would rather have as a producer than George Walker. The gentleness of this man flowed through his wonderful voice, the envy of many announcers. I always referred to him as the 'voice of the valley' because he could be heard on so many commercials on radio and TV. I later learned that George had been a fan of "Music from the Mountains" long before he came to work for West Virginia Public Radio.

"Thank you, James," I said. "This is a good day for Folk Music in West Virginia and I appreciate your faith in the possibilities of the show."

"Glenna Racer will be the assistant producer and you'll find that she is very efficient with all the technical matters concerning production and distribution," said James.

Leaving the office, I was walking on air. I just could not believe that after twenty years, someone had finally heard the show and understood what we had been trying to do all those years. After George Walker began producing the show, the quality of the production became much more professional. His editing and ideas were a positive influence, which resulted in a new popularity the show enjoyed.

In 2004, we were authorized to record live performances at many festivals in West Virginia. Mr. and Mrs. Edgar Kitchens who promoted the Summersville Bluegrass Festival, invited 'Music from the Mountains' to record their festival. We recorded the String Band Festival at Cliff Top, West Virginia. Kenny Parker at the Stonewall Jackson Jubilee gave us permission to record there on Labor Day weekend.

Bringing live performances into the living rooms of our listeners was a boost for the popularity of the program. George included interviews and special performances that gave the listener a front row seat at many of these festivals.

We continued to produce our usual variety of shows from the studio. When I asked listeners what they enjoyed most about 'Music from the Mountains,' my most frequent answer was, "You have such a variety. We never know what you will have on next week."

In 2005, we began recording shows in the Fret'N Fiddle Studios, which were located in the back of the store building. With the state of the art recoding equipment and the engineering of George Walker, the quality of the show continued to improve.

# A GOOD NEIGHBOR

The first time I met James Strong was the January morning he rode up to our house on his dark red horse named Dick. On the saddle in front of him was his six-year-old son, Jimmy.

"Mr. Dobbs, Joe can ride behind me and I'll take him to the schoolhouse," offered Mr. Strong. "It looks like it might rain and that's too far for these boys to walk on a cold morning like this." It was less than a mile to Round Hill School, a three-grade one-room school Jimmy and I attended.

Lifting me up on the horse, my dad said, "Mr. Strong, it sure is neighborly of you to take Joe to school. Now his mother won't worry." No one in the community owned an automobile, so riding a horse was not unusual.

The Strong farm joined our place on the back. James and his wife, Sybil, raised eleven children — eight boys and three girls. He was the most likable man I can remember from my childhood. It must have been his love for children that led him to assign nicknames to all of his kids and some of the neighbor children. I would wager that some of his boys didn't know their real names until they enrolled in school. The nicknames I remember are Slim, Red, Coon, Cat (a daughter), Tobe, Stormy (he was born during a thunderstorm), and Paw.

Once, he found out that I was looking for a cypress board large enough to make a boat paddle. He found it amusing that I wanted to make a paddle when we lived over a half mile from the Beouf River and did not own a boat. From that day on, he referred to me as "Boatpaddle."

The Strongs were pleasant people and always wore big smiles, regardless of the occasion. James was a stocky man of medium height and the strenuous work of the farm showed in his hands and arms. He had dark reddish brown hair that eventually showed some gray but never receded. It seemed like he had an endless number of funny stories to tell you.

Sybil was about the same height as James and was a stout woman. Her black hair and sparkling brown eyes indicated her American Indian heritage. She possessed the uncanny ability of answering and controlling a half dozen kids at one time, while cooking and continuing to smile.

When I was at the Strongs' house playing with the children, Sybil fed me like I was one of her own. Like any of the poor families, there were hard times but I thought their family seemed to have more fun. On rare occasions we all worked in the fields together. I can remember picking cotton with them but the most memorable was making sugar cane syrup.

Mr. Morgan was Sybil's father and lived with his wife in the old house across the road on a sandy ridge at the edge of their peach orchard. . It was typical of the rural houses built all through the South and Southwest in the early 1900s. It had a big porch across the front and a large open hall down through the middle that separated two or three rooms on each side. The hall was often referred to as a dog trot hall, and there was a pitcher water pump at the end near the kitchen.

Though he was an old man when I was a kid, probably in his mid-70s, it seemed effortless for him to walk the twenty-three miles to Oak Grove and back in one day. Everyone said he was an American Indian. He and Mrs. Morgan were always good to us kids.

Mr. Morgan had one of the few cane mills in the area, powered by a mule at the end of a long pole walking around in a circle. The neighbors in the area cut their sugar cane when it was mature and hauled it to Mr. Morgan's syrup mill in a wagon. It would be processed into that wonderful tasting ribbon-cane syrup that was so good poured over a hot buttered biscuit.

The mill had two ten-inch vertical rollers that squeezed the stalks of sugar cane, forcing the juice to run down into a large container. The sweet smelling juice was then poured into the big metal pan that was about three feet wide and eight feet long and lay on a brick furnace, which was similar to a huge barbecue pit. A roaring fire was kept burning under the pan and it took someone very skilled to know just when the syrup was cooked enough to be poured into a shiny new bucket.

All the young ones took a turn at feeding the stalks into the mill. It was tempting to drink the sweet fresh-squeezed juice. But if you happened to drink too much, you would be making several trips to the outhouse. Though it was extremely hard work for everyone, it was also a very festive time with all of the families working together.

It wasn't just playing with the kids that had me visiting the Strong household as often as I did. When Jimmy Strong, the oldest, and I were about ten, he took up the guitar and I started trying to play the fiddle.

I had never gotten over seeing that fiddle on our wall when I was a little one. A neighbor of ours, Keith Fowler, had a fiddle that I told my parents that I borrowed. They never knew I paid $10.00 for it, from money I earned by picking cotton for another neighbor.

My parents were not pleased, thinking you went to hell if you played the fiddle. Once, my dad suggested that instead of rosin, I use the bee's wax Mom used on her iron. The wax made the fiddle silent. It was somewhat of a joke, but I was angry because the wax was very difficult to remove from the horsehair strings. Since I didn't have lessons, I think they thought I would give up playing. Instead, I wanted to play all the more and I slipped over to the Strongs' whenever I could.

"Jim, if you can make the guitar chords, I think that I can play 'Goodnight Irene'," I said. We were sitting in the shade of the chinaberry tree behind the Strong family's house.

Jimmy was a tall skinny boy with black hair and very shy. At school, he always sat at his desk in the back of the room drawing cartoons and hoping that the teacher would not call on him. Out on the playground, he was quiet and didn't play with the other children very much, but he was an excellent student.

"This guitar looks good, but the neck is so big that I can hardly hold down the strings to make a chord, but I'll try," said Jimmy. "My fingers are sore." His dad, James, had recently purchased the guitar from the Western Auto Store in Oak Grove.

Jimmy and I had been practicing for several weeks, convinced we were going to learn to play. All we had was a chord book and determination since there was no one that we knew in the community who played.

As we were attempting to play "Goodnight Irene," Mr. Strong came by the chinaberry tree on his way back from the barn.

"Now you boys have really got it!" he exclaimed. "You sound so good. I just can't believe how well you're playing. Why one of these days y'all are gonna be on the radio. I can just hear it now," he said, in encouragement.

"Sybil, come out in the backyard and hear these boys play," he said, looking toward the house.

Through the kitchen window, Sybil answered, "That's all right — I can here them from here."

It was years later that I realized that Jimmy had been playing the guitar chords in the key of C while I played the melody on the fiddle, in the key of G. Since we were playing in different keys, I'm certain we sounded just horrible, but James was making his best effort to encourage two ten-year-old boys learning to play.

Jimmy and I played our instruments all through high school. After we graduated, Jim went into the Navy and I went to Texas. Regretfully, I never saw him again.

There were years that I was far away from the region where I grew up and seldom made the trip back to Louisiana. When I did, I always visited James Strong. I'm sure he never knew how much his great sense of humor and funny stories left an impression on me. I always took my fiddle and would sit and play the songs he requested.

"Joe, would you play the 'San Antonio Rose'?" he asked. We were sitting on his porch and Sybil was in the kitchen cooking what smelled like a roast. Mom told me that Mr. Strong had survived a heart attack, but I thought he looked like the same James I knew as a kid.

"Sure," I said, taking my violin out of the case. Mr. Strong always liked Bob Wells' songs. As I played, I remembered when he would plow his cotton patch next to our farm, shirt wet with sweat, covered with dust, walking briskly behind a team of mules.

As I finished the tune, he said, "Joe, I want to apologize to you for not going to the hospital and visiting your dad when he was so sick." My dad had been diagnosed with stomach cancer and had recently gone through surgery. "I just couldn't bear the thought of seeing your dad lying sick in a hospital bed. I wanted to remember him like I used to see him, plowing in his cotton field next to our farm."

I thought I saw a tear in the corner of his eye. Quickly changing the subject, he said, "Would you play 'Faded Love'?" That was another Bob Wells song and his favorite. I played the tune, making a special effort to play my very best.

"Joe, would you like some coffee?" asked Sybil, handing me a cup and holding a pot of fresh coffee.

"I sure would and maybe a little cream," I answered. I lay my fiddle and bow in the open violin case and took a drink.

"Joe, one time when all my boys were still at home," began James, smiling, "I counted either eight or nine dogs at the back door." I knew then that I was going to hear another of his wonderful stories.

Taking a sip of his coffee, James continued, "I thought to myself that we have to get rid of some of these dogs. So at the breakfast table that morning, I told the boys that we just had too many dogs, and we were going to take several of them to the animal shelter so they could find new homes. All the boys agreed that was a good idea."

"Yes, Dad, we do have too many dogs," one of the boys said. "Now these dogs were just pets that the boys had accumulated, not thoroughbred anything. Just dogs," explained James.

"One Saturday morning, I pulled the pickup truck in front of the house and told the boys that this was the day we would decide which dogs we would take to town," continued James. "I'd been hauling some cows, so the high wooden bed was still on the truck which would keep the dogs from jumping out. The boys were standing there and dogs were everywhere so I picked up one mutt and said, 'Here's one we don't need,' but before I could put him in the truck, one of the boys said, 'Now, Dad, you can't get rid of him – he's the only one that will chase rabbits.'

'I set him down and picked up another ugly little dog but before I lifted him off the ground, one of the boys said, 'Dad, you can't get rid of him – he's the only dog we got that will herd the cows into the barn."

"Well, how many dogs did you take to town?" I asked.

Sybil came out on the porch and refilled our coffee cups. "I can answer that question, Joe," she said. "Not a one! Not a single dog!"

"Joe, every time I would pick up a dog, somebody would say, 'Now, Dad, you can't get rid of that dog — he's my favorite. So I went on to town and we still had all them dogs," said James, chuckling. "Each one of them dogs was special to one or more of the boys and I just couldn't bring myself to get rid of any of them."

James looked at me and asked, "Joe, would you like a piece of cake with your coffee?" He put his cup down on the small table.

"Yes, I would, that would be just great," I answered, trying to remember just how long it had been since I had eaten a piece of Mrs. Strong's cake.

James looked toward the kitchen and called out, "Sybil!"

"Yes," she answered.

"Sybil, bake me and Joe a cake," said James, turning to me and asking, "Can you still play 'The Tennessee Waltz'?"

I often wondered if that was a normal request for the cook or if he was using me as an excuse to get Sybil to bake a cake. She never replied, but before long, I could smell a cake baking. I played more tunes. We ate warm cake and James told more of his delightful stories. His stories were amusing and entertaining, but underneath the humor was always a subtle spiritual message.

After that wonderful visit, I never saw James Strong again. Sometime later I learned that he had died of a heart attack. Through the years when

I would play one of those Bob Wells songs, I would think of a special person who had encouraged me to play when I was so very young.

Often we are so busy living we just assume that everyone will live forever. Even today when I return to Louisiana to visit relatives, I miss sitting on that front porch and playing the fiddle for James Strong.

# THE NATCHEZ TRACE

In 1999, the 47th Berry Reunion was going to be held at the Holmes County State Park near Jackson, Mississippi. I felt it important to go because some of Mom's brothers and sisters were entering their eighties.

I called to tell my plans to Diane, my oldest daughter, who lived near Nashville in Gallatin, Tennessee.

"These folks aren't going to be around forever. This could be my last opportunity to visit with some of Mom's brothers and sisters," I explained to Diane. "Uncle Arthur and Aunt Lillian died a few years ago."

Instantly, she replied, "Dad, I'd like to go with you. On your way down from West Virginia, just pick me up. Harold (her husband) will be working. He can't take off."

"I'm planning to go down the Natchez Trace."

"That's a beautiful drive. We'll sure have a good time sightseeing and visiting with relatives," she said.

I hung up the phone.

The reunion was a joyous occasion for the Berry family, their relatives and friends. Diane and I arrived at the Holmes County Park on Friday afternoon, the 18th of June. Families were checking in at the lodge. Relatives came from Arkansas, West Virginia, Missouri, Florida, Indiana,

Kansas and Texas.

"The Berry family had their first reunion in Greenville in 1952," I explained to Diane. "All of my family was there. Then, I didn't go back until 1978." That was the year Dennis, my brother, and his son, Chris, drove down from West Virginia. I took Scottie, my youngest son. "Dennis and I played music for about an hour in the big room of the lodge. I remember Uncle Leon and his sister, Vera, dancing to some of the same old swing tunes they had danced to during WWII."

"The place had a fenced-in marsh area with a wooden walkway going out over a pond. The pond was the home of several alligators there to entertain the park visitors. These reptiles were not huge, just about four feet long. A high fence around it prevented anyone from becoming alligator bait.

"Uncle Leon had brought two five-gallon buckets of fish from his catch. He took a group of kids out on the walk, then began throwing the fish into the water. There was a feeding frenzy with alligators lunging into the air. Some of the older boys enjoyed throwing fish into the swirling waters. The small kids screamed with excitement and fear as they witnessed the feeding reptiles just a few feet below," I explained to Diane.

"That was also the year that I met Laurene Berry Elkins. She was Mom's first cousin, born in 1918. Mom and Laurene began a correspondence when they were young girls. Mom lived in the Mississippi Delta and later in the swamps of northeast Louisiana. Laurene lived on a ranch near Tulia, Texas, which was located in the Dust Bowl of the panhandle, about halfway between Lubbock and Amarillo. The women regularly wrote letters to one another throughout the great Depression, WWII and continued until Mom's death in 1985," I said to Diane.

"As far back as I can remember, there were letters periodically from Laurene. Even though the parents of both were from the hill country of eastern Mississippi, one raised a family on a dusty ranch out on the West Texas plains. The other raised a family in the swamps of north Louisiana. I often wondered what they wrote about all those years. None of the letters were kept," I said.

My brother, Dwayne, served in the U.S. Air Force from 1966 to 1970. He and his wife, Martha, lived in Lubbock, Texas, and their son, Dee, was born there in 1969. In 1970, Mom went out to visit them. She went up to Tulia to meet Laurene for the first time. Mom was sixty years old. No one knew for sure, but we thought they exchanged letters for about fifty-five years. Laurene died in 1991.

"That's interesting. Did I ever meet Laurene?" asked Diane, with the curiosity of a child wondering what they'd seen and done before they could remember.

"No, that was the only time I ever saw her. There were over one hundred and fifty relatives and friends of the family at the reunion that year. It was held at Leroy Percy Park, over near Hollandale. On the way home, Scottie talked about not knowing he had so many relatives. He just couldn't believe he was kin to all those people," I said. "It was then I realized the stability a child develops by having personal contact with their relatives while they're growing up. I wish I had taken you kids to visit relatives more often."

I had attended the reunion only three times since its beginning in 1952. Much of my time was spent asking my sister, Lucille, "Who is that person?"

Diane and I had a great time visiting with my mother's family. I talked at length with Uncle Lloyd about his service in the Army during WWII. He drove a truck hauling supplies behind the lines all across North Africa at the time of Rommel's defeat. He was also in the invasion of Sicily. In Europe, he was attached to General Patton's army during the latter part of the war. After the war, he returned home without an injury.

Uncle Leon told me about how good his garden was that year. I listened as he told me about trapping two of the largest beaver he had ever seen the previous winter. Leon was eighty-four years old. I was surprised that he was still trapping and commercial fishing.

In 1997, I had attended the reunion alone. That was the year I rode my touring bike, a Honda Goldwing.

I gave rides to several of my cousins when Aunt Juanita walked up and said, "Joe, that is sure a pretty motorcycle."

She was a small lady dressed in slacks and blouse with a flower design. Her hair looked as though she had just stepped out of the beauty shop.

"Aunt Juanita, would you like to take a ride?" I asked. I was sitting on the bike, wearing my helmet.

"I'd love to," she replied with smiling eyes. I remembered that she and her husband, Uncle Dewey, had ridden an old Indian motorcycle to visit us in Louisiana about 1948. Uncle Dewey owned several motorcycles during the late 40s and early 50s.

"You'll have to wear a helmet. I'm afraid it'll mess up your hair," I said.

"I don't care. I want to ride," she said, with the excitement of a young girl. Her daughter, Ellen, helped her carefully put on the helmet.

"Mother, just put your left foot on that footrest and swing your right leg over the seat like you were getting on a horse," instructed Ellen.

Aunt Juanita did as told and settled on the seat behind me.

"Are you ready?" I asked.

"This is so comfortable. I'm ready. Let's go," she said. The face shield muffled her voice.

We rode down the long curved road out of the park to the local highway. As I turned right on the highway, Aunt Juanita said, "Joe, this is such a smooth ride. Does this motorcycle have an automatic transmission? It's so quiet."

She was remembering riding the Indian motorcycle some fifty years earlier. Those bikes had a foot clutch and shift lever on the side of the gas tank. Modern bikes have a clutch operated with the left hand while you shift with your foot. The changing of gears was so instant and smooth that to her, it seemed automatic. The Goldwing's six-cylinder engine was very quiet compared to the loud exhaust pipes of the Indian she had ridden.

We went about a mile and came to the Interstate. Turning north on I-55, we began cruising at seventy-five mph. At this speed I thought she might be frightened, but I heard the muffled voice say, "This is wonderful. You sure have a nice motorcycle."

At that time, Aunt Juanita was seventy-six years old. A couple of years later, I visited her and we rode over two hundred miles through the western Louisiana countryside near Texas. As we left her house, I could see her waving at friends she knew as we passed. Since she was wearing the full face helmet, they had no idea who she was. She just kept waving.

My mother's brother, Uncle Nathan and his wife, Aunt Jenny, had both served in the Navy during WWII. After the war, they settled in Marion, Indiana, which was her home state. Every year, they came to the reunion.

One time in the early 70s I drove a large U-Haul truck to Michigan. I was making a delivery for a company that I worked for in Huntington, West Virginia. As I drove north from Indianapolis, I decided to go by Marion and see Uncle Nathan.

Everyone outside his family knew him as "Bill Berry" and he operated a Standard Oil service station. I found his address in the phone directory and drove to the station unannounced. As I pulled in, I noticed there were two bays where mechanics were servicing vehicles. When I stopped at the gas pumps, he came out of the station. He was a short, fat man wearing the Standard Oil uniform and a smile.

"Fill er up," I said. Since my truck had saddle tanks, I added, "Both tanks."

He put the nozzle in the tank and set it on automatic. Then, he cleaned my windshield.

As he put gas in the second saddle tank, I looked him in the eye and said, "I'll bet you could never guess who I am."

Grinning and studying my face, he confessed, "I have no idea."

Without looking away, I said, "I'm Lillie's oldest son, Joe." I hadn't seen him since 1952, some twenty years earlier.

I really did not know he would be emotional. Tears filled his eyes and he began to cry. "I'm so glad to see you," he said. "It's been a long time."

We talked for a while, but then I told him I had gone out of my way to see him and I was running late. As I drove toward Ft. Wayne I thought, *I probably should have called Nathan first, instead of just driving to his station.*

On Sunday of the reunion, folks took pictures of one another and said their goodbyes. Diane and I wanted to make it to Nashville that day, so we left the reunion a little early.

It was quiet driving up the Natchez Trace. The well-groomed two- lane paved road lay like a dark ribbon on a green carpet as it wound through the Mississippi pine lowlands. Occasionally, we could see a farm house off to the west.

As I drove, we talked about the reunion and the importance of family. I again expressed the regret that I hadn't taken the kids to meet their relatives at the reunions. There were so many with stories like the ones I'd been telling her.

"Well, we never lived near any of our relatives," Diane said. "Did you notice those two young kids that looked to be part black?"

"I saw them playing with all the other kids down near the Lake. Several of the children were having a good time fishing. Sometimes I think the young enjoy reunions more than the adults," I told her.

"They were adopted kids of some of your distant cousins. They drove up from Tampa, Florida," Diane continued. "I heard some of the women in the family talking. Before the cousins came up, they asked someone in the Berry family if it would be OK for them to attend. I never heard of such a thing."

"Welcome to Mississippi," I said. "You sure wouldn't want to drive all the way from Florida and then be turned back."

"One lady said that they were told if the black kids were adopted, it was all right. Just so they were not blood kin."

We drove by a large lake on our right. Along the shore were groves of sleepy cypress trees. Among the cypress knees, two white egrets stood fishing in the shallow water.

"This is the Ross Bennett Reservoir," I said. "I rode by here a couple of years ago on the bike. I saw two large alligators lying on the bank enjoying the warm sun."

Traveling on the Natchez Trace always reminded me of the Blue Ridge Parkway. They were very similar, but the Blue Ridge was always up high, on the very top of the mountain range.

"What are these signs marked 'Old Trace,' that I keep seeing along the road?" asked Diane.

"This beautiful, paved road doesn't run precisely over the original trail. The old, original trail winds back and forth on each side all the way up to Nashville. We'll stop at one of those signs and walk out to the edge of the forest where you can see the remains of the original trail.

"In most places, it's about four feet wide. That was the width of a wagon in the early 1800s. The trail was so well traveled that it's about ten inches deep. It is just amazing that the old trail has survived all the years of wet weather. Each time I walk down the old trail, I imagine the flood of travelers passing through," I explained.

Historians believe that the Natchez Trace began as a trail used by animals. Then it became a major trail for the Native Americans, running from present day Natchez, Mississippi to Nashville, Tennessee. Around 1800, it became a major route for boatmen, traders and trappers. Those who drifted down the Ohio and the Mississippi to New Orleans on flat boats would use the Natchez Trace to return north.

"Early in the 1800s, it became wide enough that wagons traveled on the Trace. General Jackson and his troops went to New Orleans using this trail. About 1820, with the introduction of the steamboats on the Mississippi, traffic on the Trace began to diminish. Travelers and traders could take a steamboat up the river rather that traveling overland. Steamboats added luxury to traveling upstream.

"When I was a small boy, Dad talked a lot about the Natchez Trace. His family had lived near the old trail when he was a kid," I said. "At that time, I wasn't aware that it was so much a part of southern history. He would tell me stories about Uncle Jesse and him squirrel hunting in the woods along the Trace. Uncle Jesse was Dad's brother who died in 1962. They lived near Mathiston. We'll go through there in another hour or so."

Tall pine forests were on each side of the road. Time prevented us from reading all the historical markers. As we neared the sign indicating the exit for Kosciusko, Diane asked, "Isn't this Oprah Winfrey's home town?"

"Yeah. Do you want to stop?"

"No, let's keep going," she answered. It's a long way to Tennessee."

# SOUTHERN MAN

As Diane and I headed north on the Natchez Trace, I spoke of my childhood, and told her of the way things had been when I was younger. "Out in the western part of the Parish where we lived, there were no black people. But in Oak Grove, there were several black families. You could drive all the way across West Carroll Parish and there was not a public eating establishment that served African-Americans.

"Pippin's Café, the only restaurant, had been in Oak Grove for thirty or forty years. It was located near the railroad on the west end of Main Street. If you were black, you weren't allowed to enter. They would hand your food to you out the back door."

"Is it still that way?" asked Diane.

"No, that ended in the 60s during the movement for equal rights," I answered.

"I was young, maybe eight years old, when a black family moved into the Benton place down on Beouf River. It was sometime during the summer and we were working in the fields," I said.

"One day, when I went fishing, I met one of the boys, who was about my age. I don't recall their names," I told her. "Back at the house, I asked

Dad where the black children went to school. I knew that they wouldn't be permitted to go to Goodwill Grade School, where I attended. He told me that they would move before school began. I asked Dad why he thought they would move. He told me that someone would tell them they could not live in the community. Sure enough, before school began in September, the black family had moved."

As I drove, I continued to talk about the South of my young life. "I think that it was about 1959 that a writer from Texas named Griffin wrote a book entitled, *Black Like Me.* With the help of a dermatologist, he had taken some injections that caused his skin to turn dark. After spending time under a sun lamp and using coloring, he could pass for a black man. He lived in New Orleans for a short time as a Negro," I explained.

"What happened to him?' asked Diane. She was interested.

"He wrote the book describing how difficult it was to live in the South as a black person. Later, they made a movie from the book, but I never saw it. Griffin became active in the civil rights movement," I told her.

"Having wondered just what it must be like to be black, I read the book. I thoroughly enjoyed it. But I don't remember it answering my many questions."

"What other questions did you have, Dad?" she asked

"As a child, I didn't understand how southern folks like my dad, who was so religious, wouldn't accept a black person as an equal human being. Dad was an elder in his church and made a supreme effort to live a good Christian life. He never used foul language, drank alcoholic beverages or used tobacco. But he was a segregationist. I suppose that my questions may have been annoying."

"What questions?"

We had just driven out of a forest and on our left was a field where a farmer was cutting hay. On the right was a pasture with scattered black cows grazing. The fragrance of fresh mown hay filled the car.

"I'm sure you remember me going to Calhoun, Louisiana, to visit him for a few days. That was in the summer of 1974, about a year before he died. Dad and Mom lived across the road from Aunt Juanita and Uncle Dewey. Dad was being treated for stomach cancer at the time and the family knew he didn't have long to live.

"I'm so glad that I went and spent that quality time with Dad before he died. We sat in the shade of one of the large pine trees with this pleasant smell of pine needles in the air. We talked at length about the farm and the good times our family enjoyed. At some point, we got around to religion, and I told him he was held in high esteem by his neighbors and fellow church members."

"Was he physically able to get out and go places?" asked Diane.

"His health was very poor. He was still recovering from surgery, but he could walk around some," I continued. "They had been in Calhoun less than a year. I asked him where they went to church and he said the Calhoun Church of Christ."

"I knew there was a large black community there, so I asked him if there were any African-Americans who attended their church. He told me they had their own church," I said.

"Why did you ask him about black people going to their church?" asked Diane.

"Oh, I was just curious to see if the churches in that area had become integrated. Then I asked him if there wasn't a black church in the area, could the African-Americans attend his church? I was surprised when he reluctantly said, 'I suppose so'."

"I asked him if there would be any colored people in heaven. If not, would there be a heaven for 'whites only' and one for 'coloreds only'?"

"What was his answer?" Diane asked. She was opening a bag of potato chips and looking out the window at an historical sign about the Cherokee Indians. On the opposite side there were two park workers driving small tractors mowing grass.

"He never answered those types of questions. Most of the time, he would cleverly change the subject. I had no intention of making my dad uncomfortable. I was more interested in seeing how his views had changed over the years," I said.

"Here was a man who lived over sixty years in a changing time. Not just changes in technology, but think of the community in which he was born. The Civil War had ended just forty-two years earlier and there were numerous Civil War Veterans still living. Many former slaves lived throughout the South. There also remained the bitter taste left by Reconstruction after the Civil War." I wanted to explain to her where Dad was coming from.

"Near the end of his life, he worked in a local all-white grade school that employed a black teacher, whom he liked and admired. Schools in the heart of the Mississippi Delta had been integrated. These had to be difficult changes for him to accept. With the help of his faith in God, I think, he handled the changing times quite well." I said.

"There's the exit for U.S. 82," I said. "Now we are near Mathiston, Maben, and Eupora, Diane. This area is where my parents and their families lived before 1920. We have a lot of distant relatives in these hills of Mississippi."

"I like this area a lot better than the flat land of the Delta," she said. "It is so green and beautiful."

I continued, "After reading Steinbeck's book, *My Travels with Charlie*, I had a much better understanding concerning the southern attitude. In that book, Steinbeck went back to the time of slavery to explain the reason for the bigotry still in the country one hundred years and better after the slaves were freed."

"In order for a man to enslave another human being and keep his sanity, he must convince himself the person he's enslaving is inferior. He went on to write that it would take many generations for this attitude of superiority to vanish," I explained.

"There's the exit for Mantee, Mississippi. One of Dad's brothers lives there. Uncle Elmer was the postmaster until he retired some years ago," I said. "This is a great way to travel through these hills."

"It sure beats traveling on the Interstate," said Diane. "There are no trucks and you can't be in a hurry."

"Did I ever tell you about the time your mom and I went fishing on Lake Lee with Uncle Leon?" I asked, as a patrol car passed.

"I don't think so," answered Diane.

"We may have been living in Houston at the time. I don't remember, but we brought all you kids to Louisiana to visit your grandparents. Amy and I left you kids with them and went fishing in Louisiana with Parnell, Lucille's husband. Several days later, we crossed the Mississippi River to Greenville to visit kinfolks in the Berry family," I said.

"I'd told Amy that Uncle Leon would take us fishing. He said they were catching fish on Lake Lee, which was a lake near the Mississippi River in Washington County."

"Since we were living in Texas, we had to get an out of state fishing license. Early that morning, Amy and I left Grandma Berry's house with Uncle Leon. We rode in his pickup down to Gene Underhill's Store to get our license and some fish bait. Gene was an old man then, but I could remember going in that store when I was five years old," I said.

"When we walked into the store, there were two men buying some minnows for bait. I didn't pay that much attention to them, but I did notice that they were both big, husky men. And they wore Army fatigues."

"We visited with Gene. After buying our fishing license and bait, we got back in the pickup. As we drove down the road toward Lake Lee, Uncle Leon asked me if I knew who those men were. I told him that I didn't. He said that those were the two men who killed the black boy in Money, Mississippi. They shot him and threw his body into the Tallahatchie River."

"I remembered reading the story in Life Magazine in 1955. The fourteen year-old boy was Emmett Till and he lived in Chicago. He had been visiting his grandfather in Mississippi when some kid dared him and he whistled at a white woman in a country store. I asked Uncle Leon if they had served prison time. He said that they were arrested, charged with murder and then acquitted."

"Look at all those pretty motorcycles," said Diane. We were approaching a large group of bike riders with camping gear tied on the back of each bike. "I wish we were riding, this is such a beautiful day."

"I admit it's a lot of fun to ride among these trees and through the cool shady spots. The Trace is very popular with bikers from all across the country. I remember riding up I-55 to Memphis the last time I was at the Reunion. It must have been close to one hundred degrees. I was so hot, I stopped somewhere around Grenada at a Shoney's just to enjoy the air conditioning," I said.

As we drove north on the Natchez Trace, I continued talking with Diane. "In the late summer of 1964, I worked as a roughneck on an oil rig near Venice, Louisiana. Venice is south of New Orleans at the very end of the Mississippi River. I only worked there for a couple of months. As soon as the radio station reopened, I went home to New Mexico. Junior Meeks, my boss on the rig, was from Aztec, New Mexico, and he had gotten me the job. I'd been out of work and couldn't find local employment," I explained.

"We lived in a rooming house behind Sheffield's Café in Buras, which is the first little town north of Venice. Every morning, the café was noisy and busy with oil field workers. Junior and I were sitting at a table when he called my attention to a man that was sitting across the room having breakfast with three other workers.

"The man looked to be about thirty years old and tall enough to be a receiver on a football team. Junior explained that he was one of just a few people who had the expertise of assembling the platforms for the off-shore drilling rigs. The man got up and walked over to the cashier to pay his bill. I thought he had the looks of a movie star.

"Then, Junior asked me if I remembered when someone threw a bomb in a church in Clarksdale, Mississippi at the time the comedian, Dick Gregory, was making a speech. This man was the person that threw the bomb. He was never caught."

We traveled along in silence for a bit. The bright, beautiful day contrasted with the dark history I was telling her.

"I'd like to stop somewhere and get something to eat," said Diane. "Look, there are three turkeys up near those two large trees. It looks like an old hen and her two young ones."

"I've never been down the Trace without seeing turkeys. I think there are more on the upper part in Tennessee. Notice you will seldom see a gobbler," I said.

"If you could wait, I know where there is an excellent Mexican

Restaurant in Tupelo," I said. We were following a car pulling an Airstream camper trailer with Wisconsin license plates.

"I can wait," she said. "Especially for Mexican food."

While driving and watching for the Tupelo exit, I continued talking about my childhood. "Just growing up in the south and having your friends, relatives and so many people that you loved and respected all living in that racially charged environment was somewhat confusing for me.

"Looking back with another view, it was a good time to be living and witnessing the struggles of our society slowly, and sometimes dangerously, improving these issues. I was always wishing I could find a black person to tell me how it was to grow up in the South. This was so difficult. There was an invisible barrier between the black and white individuals that prevented sincere discussions.

"In 1956, your mom and I were living in Little Rock, Arkansas. Dale was just a baby. I worked as a book keeper for a construction company that had a contract with the US Corp of Engineers to build dikes on the Arkansas River. These dikes were made of quarry-run granite that we mined just south of town. We, the R. C. Cudd Company, had a fleet of large dump trucks that moved the granite from the quarry to the construction site on the river.

"A large service center and garage serviced all these trucks. One of my duties was to audit invoices and see that the service center was paid. I remember it was a Texaco Station on Highway 365, near the southern city limits of Little Rock. They were a vital part of our operation. I became very good friends with the boss, Herman." I put on my sunglasses and continued.

"I don't recall his last name. Herman was a tall, thin black man. He had suffered a birth defect that caused his left arm and hand to be much smaller than the right. By our conversations, I could tell he was well educated.

"I asked him if he was from Arkansas. He told me that he grew up in the Rio Grande Valley of Texas and studied physics at the University of Mexico in Mexico City. During some of our conversations, I asked him what it was like to grow up as a black man. He told me that growing up black in south Texas where the majority of the population was Mexican was not that bad.

"But the first time he came to Arkansas to visit relatives, he had a memorable experience. Being unaware of the racial conditions in Arkansas, he made the mistake of going into a white café. He was physically attacked and thrown out. Herman feared for his life. This would not have happened where he grew up," I said.

"Why do you suppose he would talk to a white man about these racial problems he had?" Diane asked.

"Well, he was an educated man. I'd known him for about a month. And, through our business dealings, we had a lot of respect or each other," I explained.

"Herman was the first African-American with whom I had personal conversations about race. I also remember talking with him about atomic energy.

"That was during the time when there were nuclear tests being conducted by the US and Russia. There were fears of nuclear wars and the possible destruction of the earth.

"Since he had a degree in physics, I asked Herman if he agreed with the theory of the possibility of an atomic chain reaction which would burn the atmosphere around the planet. He answered my question by saying, 'it might be possible, but not probable. No need to worry about it. Just keep hauling the granite and I'll keep fixing the trucks.'"

After driving into Tupelo, Mississippi where we ate at a Mexican restaurant, we continued driving north on the Natchez Trace to Colbert's Ferry.

"This is where we cross the Tennessee River. It wasn't this wide when Colbert's Ferry and Stand was here. In the early 1800s, there were many inns all along the trail. Locally, they were called 'stands.'

"The Pickwick Dam that forms Pickwick Lake is north of here. The dam is near the Shiloh Battle ground," I explained.

"I wish we had time to visit Shiloh," said Diane. "But we're still a long way from Gallatin. Let's keep driving."

"When General Jackson brought his Army down the Trace, on the way to New Orleans, it was reported that Colbert charged him $75,000 to ferry the troops across the river. I wonder how much money that would be today?"

We continued on the Natchez Trace, crossing the corner of the state of Alabama into the state of Tennessee. The two-lane highway was well groomed the entire way. Most of the drive was through forests of hardwoods and some pines.

As we went further north into Tennessee, the road wound around and over the hills along the original trail. There were a few short distances where a farm was on each side of the road.

One of the more famous stands is Grinder's Inn near Hohenwald, Tennessee. It was our last stop. Meriwether Lewis died there in 1809 and we visited his grave, where a monument stands. I had thoroughly enjoyed this trip with my daughter.

# AFTERWORD

Thank you for joining me for this trip back in time.

As of this writing, I am seventy-seven years old and I feel fortunate that I can still work at the Fret'N Fiddle music store, play with the band "The 1937 Flood," and the Ritchie Collins Three-O. I still travel and play the fiddle at a variety of festivals and I enjoy playing for Civil War and colonial reenactments.

I have some very special friends who are wonderful musicians like Jesse Smith from Ohio and Jack Abeel, who lives in Virginia. We get together and play as often as possible. They are my heroes, but that is another story.

I don't think that I will live long enough to play the violin as well as I would like. I am so lucky to be living my dream and still learning to play my fiddle.

CPSIA information can be obtained at www.ICGtesting.com
Printed in the USA
BVOW042258260412

288814BV00003B/3/P